# THE
# TEMPLE
*in the*
## GOSPEL OF MARK

# THE TEMPLE

# TEMPLE

*in the*

# GOSPEL OF MARK

A Study in Its Narrative Role

# TIMOTHY C. GRAY

**B**

**Baker Academic**

*a division of Baker Publishing Group*
Grand Rapids, Michigan

© 2008 by Mohr Siebeck, Tübingen, Germany

Published in 2010 by Baker Academic
a division of Baker Publishing Group
P.O. Box 6287, Grand Rapids, MI 49516-6287
www.bakeracademic.com

Originally published in 2008 in Tübingen, Germany, by Mohr Siebeck GmbH & Co. KG Tübingen.

Printed in the United States of America

Library of Congress Cataloging-in-Publication Data is on file at the Library of Congress, Washington, DC

ISBN 978-0-8010-3892-1

10  11  12  13  14  15  16      7  6  5  4  3  2  1

This work is dedicated
to my wife Kris

# Preface

In a seminar on the Gospel of Mark, led by Fr. Frank Moloney, the narrative artistry of Mark's story captured my imagination. One section particularly struck me, the eschatological discourse in Mark 13. Mark 13 is one of the rare departures from narrative in Mark and certainly contains the longest discourse in the story. Attempting to tackle this complex and controversial discourse in a simple seminar paper was rather like trying to take a sip of water from a fire hydrant. My inititial work for that seminar sparked a desire to better understand Mark's purpose in such a dramatic departure from his more typical narrative style, and led me to the focus my dissertation on this topic. Given this starting point, it was natural to have Fr. Moloney direct the project. I am deeply grateful for all he has taught me about narrative and scholarship, and I count myself blessed to have had such a wise and learned guide.

Years before, while studying for my Th.M. at Duke University, I had the opportunity to study under Richard Hays. In his New Testament Intertextuality seminar I had the chance to read through many important texts in Mark. I will always remain deeply grateful for the generous time and assistance he gave me. Looking back now, it is clear to me that studying intertextuality with Richard Hays and narrative analysis (intratextuality) with Frank Moloney provided key methodological tools for my reading of Mark, to which this work and I am greatly indebted.

Besides the fortune of having Fr. Moloney, I profited tremendously from Frs. Frank Matera and Frank Gignac. I doubt if anyone could have had three readers more committed and meticulous. Their diligent reading and feedback was a model of professionalism from which I benefited more than words can say. Of course I am responsible for the flaws that remain, but this study is far better thanks to their invaluable assistance. To Frank Gignac in particular, I owe a deep debt for going above and beyond the call of editing and giving me critical feedback that has saved me from many errors and clarified my thought throughout the work. His love for the Greek text and accuracy is a great inspiration and model.

At the start of my writing I had the daunting challenge of having just moved to Denver to start a new job teaching at St. John Vianney Seminary. I am grateful to the rector, Fr. Michael Glenn, and the entire Scripture department, Sr. Timothea Elliot and Frs. Andreas Hock and Federico

Colautti, for giving me a lighter teaching load while working on the dissertation. I am especially grateful to Sr. Timothea Elliot, a wise and learned Scripture scholar, for giving me constant encouragement and hope along the way.

Above all I want to thank my beloved wife, Kris. Without her incalculable patience, sacrifices, and assistance I could never have persevered. I find marriage a shared adventure, and she has been a partner in this project with me in many ways. I hope I am a better man from this process and that it will enable me to better serve and love her and our son Joseph.

Timothy C. Gray

# Table of Contents

Chapter 1

# Demonstration in the Temple

The drama of Mark's narrative is generated by the conflict between the Jewish leaders and Jesus, which reaches a climax with Jesus' arrival in the temple (Mark 11). From this point forward the temple plays a prominent role in the narrative. Scholars have recognized for some time the salient place held by the temple in Mark's story. The temple plays a vital role in the temple cleansing, trial, and crucifixion scenes, each time in a way that is unique to Mark's gospel. The importance of the temple for Mark is not in question, but what remains to be examined is why Mark gives the temple such a conspicuous place in his narrative. In order to explore this question, a careful analysis of how Mark shapes his narrative needs to be given. This chapter will begin such an analysis by sketching the temple's place in Mark 11–15, illustrating how Mark structures the latter part of his narrative on Jesus' relationship to the temple.

After giving a broad sketch of the literary role of the temple in Mark, I shall examine how Mark begins the climax of his story with Jesus' entry into the temple. Jesus' entry is a watershed moment, one that illustrates the temple's pivotal role. Jesus' entry into the temple leads to a dramatic conflict between the authorities and Jesus when Jesus enacts his demonstration. The importance of this demonstration for Mark is evident by the rhetorical framing of this episode with the cursed fig tree, an account unique to Mark. Thus, the three parts of this chapter are: (1) an overview of the narrative role of the temple in Mark 11–15; (2) an examination of how the entry narrative is a watershed moment in Mark; and (3) a careful exegesis of Jesus' temple demonstration, the understanding of which is vital for understanding the role of the temple in Mark's narrative.

## 1.1 Narrative and Intertextual Approach

In order to explore the reasons why Mark gives the temple such prominence in his Gospel, this study will present a narrative analysis of Mark 11–15 as its narrative relates to the temple. Narrative analysis seeks to discern the plot of a given story by examining the parts of the story in relation to the entire narrative world depicted in the story. Since the temple motif is interwoven throughout Mark's narrative, its meaning for Mark's Gospel is embedded in the overall plot of the story. Therefore, the study of the temple theme in Mark requires that we examine the role of the temple within Mark's larger plot.

Although many insights into Mark's narrative and overall theology have been gleaned through redaction criticism since the 1950s, this method has largely neglected the temple motif in Mark.[1] To explain further why redaction criticism has not given much attention to the temple motif in Mark, a brief sketch of the methodological nature of redaction criticism, in comparison to narrative criticism, shall be given.

By noting editorial emendations, redaction criticism seeks to understand the aims of an author.[2] The theology of the author is reconstructed based on how he adopts and modifies the traditions inherited through his sources. Redaction criticism has sought to understand more fully the contributions that the authors of the gospels have made, whereas earlier form critics focused on discovering the traditions and sources behind the gospel narratives. Redaction critics, such as G. Bornkamm and H. Conzelmann, emphasized that the authors of the gospels were more than mere collectors of traditions and that their shaping of their sources was done with the care and ingenuity of an author. Thus, redaction criticism built upon the form critic's focus on sources and concentrated on how the gospel authors used those sources as well as what that said about their theology and outlook.

---

[1] Both William R. Telford (*The Theology of the Gospel of Mark* [New York: Cambridge, 1999] 28) and Francis J. Moloney (*The Gospel of Mark* [Peabody, MA: Hendrickson, 2002] 9) list the major themes of Mark that have been the focus of Markan redaction criticism, such as the "messianic secret," Son of Man, Kingdom of God, Jewish leadership, geography (such as Galilee vs. Jerusalem), Gentile mission, persecution, discipleship, Son of God, cross, suffering, eschatology, gospel, identity of Jesus, passion of Jesus. In neither list is the temple motif found, because this theme has not come into the purview of redaction critics. Two redaction studies that give significant attention to the temple theme in Mark are John R. Donahue (*Are You the Christ?* [SBLDS 10; New York, 1973]) and Donald Juel (*Messiah and Temple: The Trial of Jesus in the Gospel of Mark* [SBLDS 31: Missoula, MT: Scholars Press, 1977). However, in the introduction to his recent commentary on Mark (*The Gospel of Mark*, written with Daniel J. Harrington [SacPag; Collegeville, MN: Liturgical Press, 2002] 8–47), Donahue makes no mention of the temple motif in his discussion of the gospel's major themes.

[2] For a further discussion of redaction criticism, see Norman Perrin, *What is Redaction Criticism?* [London: SPCK, 1970]; C. M. Tuckett, "Redaction Criticism," in *A Dictionary of Biblical Interpretation* (ed. R. J. Coggins and J. L. Houlden; London: SCM, 1990) 580–82. For a review and critique of redaction criticism of the Gospel of Mark, see Christopher D. Marshall, *Faith as a Theme in Mark's Narrative* (SNTSMS 64; Cambridge: Cambridge University Press, 1989) 8–14.

To uncover the agenda and theology of the author, one needed to analyse precisely how he used his sources. The method of redaction criticism required that one be able to isolate the contribution of the evangelist from the material inherited from earlier sources. Thus, redaction criticism, not unlike form criticism, focuses on the seams in the narrative and the sources they may bespeak.[3] Redaction critics do not aim to understand the unity of the narrative as a story. Coherence is found by deconstructing the sources behind the text to discover the unity of perspective or apologetic concern of the author.

This stands in contrast to narrative criticism, which sees coherence as deriving from the plot and ideological point of view displayed in the story as a whole. For narrative criticism, the theology emerges from the story, not vice versa.[4] On the one hand, redaction critics tend to view the text as an effect, the cause of which must be understood as extrinsic to the text itself – hence the energy to uncover what lay outside the text. On the other hand, narrative criticism sees that cause and effect as enmeshed into the narrative logic of the text itself and a careful analysis of the plot as the best means to uncovering the causation that moves the story and gives it meaning.[5] Thus, redaction criticism ultimately aims beyond the text and is characteristically extrinsic, whereas narrative criticism looks within the text and is intrinsic in regard to the text. This is why redaction criticism is more interested in the intention of the redactor (author) than in the intention of the text as it stands, which is the interest of narrative criticism.

This background may help explain why the temple as a dimension of Mark's story has not been within the purview of redaction critics. Given the inclination of redaction criticism to look for extrinsic causes of the text, the focus on the temple inevitably turned to the historical events surrounding the destruction of the temple in A.D. 70. It was believed that the events surrounding the temple's demise generated much of the eschatological emphasis in Mark (particularly Mark 13) as well as the significant attention to the temple in Mark's story. Thus, redaction critics felt that the effect (the temple's prominent focus in Mark) was to be understood by the cause (the destruction of the temple in A.D. 70). Whether this historical analysis of the Gospel of Mark and the end of the temple is correct (and it may well be), this approach leaves aside the question of Mark's theological understanding of the temple's demise. It is precisely Mark's theological concerns regarding the temple that will be

---

[3] Marshall, *Faith as a Theme*, 9.

[4] Thomas R. Hatina, *In Search of a Context: The Function of Scripture in Mark's Narrative* (JSNTS 232; New York: Sheffield, 2002) 88.

[5] Hatina, *In Search of a Context*, 87.

pursued in this present study by examining how Mark carefully teaches about the temple and its relationship to Jesus throughout. What the author of Mark conveys to his readers through the inner dynamics of his story is a theological message that cannot be reduced to historical analysis of the temple's destruction and its relation to Mark's story. However, the historical events surrounding the destruction of the temple influenced Mark and his audience, since Mark's text was generated within that particular historical context. In this case, redaction and narrative criticism need not be in opposition. Redaction criticism on Mark has illustrated the importance of the destruction of the temple as a context for reading Mark's narrative. Narrative criticism, as this study hopes to show, can show another dimension to Mark's story: a theological account that gives meaning to the temple's demise for the Markan community. Redaction criticism in Markan studies has so often focused on the historical events behind Mark's text that it has neglected Mark's theological reflection on these events.[6] The aim of this study is to explore the role of the temple within Mark's narrative world while at the same time recognizing that that world was generated by the events surrounding the demise of the temple.

Throughout Mark's narrative world, the Scriptures of Israel have a prominent place.[7] Howard Kee observed, "The Scriptures are indeed an indispensable presupposition of all that Mark wrote."[8] Thus, the narrative approach of this study will be accompanied by an investigation into Mark's intertextuality in the sections that pertain to the temple theme.

---

[6] Raymond E. Brown (*An Introduction to the New Testament* [New York: Doubleday, 1997] 26) asserts that one of the strengths of narrative criticism is that it moves beyond the historical context to speak to the theological interpretation that is given in narratives to that history: "Narrative Criticism counters the excesses of historical investigation and helps to highlight the author's main interest."

[7] Many works have noted the vital role played by the OT in Mark, e.g., Willard M. Swartley, *Israel's Scripture Traditions and the Synoptic Gospels: Story Shaping Story* (Peabody, MA: Hendrickson, 1994); Howard Clark Kee, "The Function of Scriptural Quotations and Allusions in Mark 11–16," in *Jesus und Paulus* (ed. E. Earle Ellis and E. Grasser; Göttingen: Vandenhoeck and Ruprecht, 1975) 165–88; idem, *Community of the New Age: Studies in Mark's Gospel* (Philadelphia: Westminster, 1977) 46–49; Rikki Watts, *Isaiah's New Exodus in Mark* (Grand Rapids: Baker, 1997); Joel Marcus, *The Way of the Lord: Christological Exegesis of the Old Testament in the Gospel of Mark* (Louisville, KY: Westminster John Knox, 1992); Thomas Hatina, *In Search of a Context*; W. S. Vorster, "The Function of the Use of the Old Testament in Mark," *Neot* 14 (1981) 62–72; H. Anderson, "The Old Testament in Mark's Gospel," in *The Use of the Old Testament in the New and Other Essays: Studies in Honor of William Franklin Stinespring* (ed., J. M. Efird; Durham: Duke University Press, 1972) 280–306; R. Schneck, *Isaiah in the Gospel of Mark 1–8* (BIBALDS 1: Vallejo, CA: BIBAL, 1994).

[8] Kee, "The Function of Scriptural Quotations,"165–88.

An important methodological presupposition of this study holds that Mark's use of Scripture is often more than atomistic, and so the wider context of the OT citation or allusion will be examined.[9] The literary method of evoking a particular context and meaning of one text through an allusion or brief citation of that text in another is called metalepsis. The rhetorical function of this literary trope is the echoing of an earlier text by a later one in a way that evokes resonances of the earlier text beyond what was explicitly cited or alluded to directly.[10] Richard Hays, building on the work of John Hollander who illustrated that this was a common trope among ancient and modern literature in the West, demonstrated how often the technique of metalepsis was used by Paul.[11] Other scholars have noted that this method was used by ancient Jewish sources, and therefore it is not surprising to find it employed similarly in Mark.[12] Of course, there is danger of this method being abused, and so the methodological controls suggested by Hays for discerning metalepsis shall be referred to and presumed in this study.[13]

Just as Markan scholarship has advanced beyond the notion that Mark was a simple collector of traditions to the point that he is a very capable storyteller and author of significant ability, so too this study hopes to advance the view that Mark is not simply proof-texting Scripture but rather is a sophisticated author who often employs the contextual richness of the OT texts he uses, which he interweaves into his wider narrative. It is vital that the careful narrative reading of Mark be combined with an attentive intertextual reading that examines how the OT citation or allusion affects

---

[9] Marcus (*The Way of the Lord*) has argued against seeing Mark's use of the OT as atomistic, and throughout his work he demonstrates that the wider context of the OT citation often sheds light on Mark's narrative and use of Scripture. More recently, Thomas Hatina (*In Search of a Context*) and Rikki Watts (*Isaiah's New Exodus*) follow up the work of Marcus in illustrating the importance of noting the contextual background of OT citations and allusions in Mark.

[10] Richard Hays, *The Conversion of the Imagination: Paul as Interpreter of Israel's Scripture* (Grand Rapids: Eerdmans, 2005) 2–3, and *Echoes of Scripture in the Letters of Paul* (New Haven: Yale University Press, 1989) 14–21.

[11] Hays, *Echoes of Scripture*, 18–21.

[12] Rikki Watts (*Isaiah's New Exodus*, 111) observed that "in the absence of chapter and verse divisions, partitions were apparently used as shorthand references to larger contexts, and the same could reasonably be expected of allusions." See also C. E. B. Cranfield, "A Study of St. Mark 1:9–11" *JST* (1955) 53–63; C. H. Dodd, *According to the Scriptures* (London: Nisbet, 1952) 126; Joachim Jeremias, *TDNT* 5. 701.

[13] Hays (*Echoes of Scripture*, 29–33) gives seven tests for discerning intertextual echoes in Scripture. More recently, he has given an updated description of these seven tests in *The Conversion of the Imagination*, 34–45.

the larger narrative context in Mark.[14] Thus, not only is there an intelligent intratextuality in Mark's narrative, but there is a sophisticated intertextuality as well.[15] Moreover, as this study hopes to illustrate, the intratextuality and intertextuality are deeply linked in Mark to significant effect. Often, the OT motifs quoted or alluded to by Mark are planted in his narrative and spring up throughout the story as the common themes of the Gospel. Thus, Mark weaves the key points of his OT texts into the tapestry of his narrative: thus to understand fully Mark's narrative logic one must unearth the role of the Scripture passages embedded in his story.

## 1.2 Narrative Overview: Mark 11–15

The tension between Jesus and the temple dominates the landscape of Mark 11–15 and propels the narrative to its climax.[16] Much of the narrative

---

[14] Thomas Hatina (*In Search of a Context*, 49) captures the importance of reading Mark's narrative with a view to its use of intertextuality: "A reciprocal dynamic is necessarily effected: the narrative serves as the context for reading the quotations; and yet the quotations play an important role in contributing to the understanding of that narrative."

[15] Elizabeth Struthers Malbon (*In the Company of Jesus: Characters in Mark's Gospel* [Louisville: Westminster John Knox, 2000]) as well as Donahue and Harrington (*Mark*, esp. 1–3) note the importance of intertextuality and intratextuality for reading Mark. However, neither book shows how intimately these two methods are related in Mark, with his taking OT themes (intertextuality) and weaving them into his narrative motifs (intratextuality).

[16] Although the salient role of the temple in the latter part of Mark's narrative is widely recognized by scholars, there is no single monograph on the temple in Mark's narrative. Juel's work, *Messiah and Temple*, focuses on the role of the temple in the Markan trial narrative. Lloyd Gaston, *No Stone on Another: Studies in the Significance of the Fall of Jerusalem in the Synoptic Gospels* (NovTSup 23; Leiden: Brill, 1970), is focused on historical questions regarding Jesus and the temple, and although he draws heavily upon Mark, Gaston never draws any conclusions or synthetic analysis of the role of the temple for Mark's story. Sam P. Matthew, *Temple-Criticism in Mark's Gospel: The Economic Role of the Jerusalem Temple during the First Century CE* (Delhi: ISPCK, 1999), focuses, with a historical aim, on the socio-economic issues in Mark's gospel. He does not focus on the role of the temple in Mark's narrative or theology. The importance of the temple for Mark's gospel has also attracted much attention in scholarly articles, e.g., John Paul Heil, "The Narrative Strategy and Pragmatics of the Temple Theme in Mark," *CBQ* 59 (1997) 76–100; Ernst L. Schnellbächer, "The Temple as Focus of Mark's Theology," *HBT* 5 no. 2 (1983) 95–112; David Seeley, "Jesus' Temple Act," *CBQ* 55 (1993) 263–83; Paula Fredriksen, "Jesus and the Temple, Mark and the War," *SBL 1990 Seminar Papers* (SBLSP 29; ed. David J. Lull; Atlanta: Scholars Press, 1990) 293–310; Morna Hooker, "Traditions about the Temple in the Sayings of Jesus," *BJRL* 70 (1988) 7–19.

in these chapters focuses on this tension or is colored by Jesus' controversial actions in the temple.[17] Jesus' entrance into Jerusalem (11:1–11) raises questions about Jesus' identity and authority, questions that come to the fore after his demonstration in the temple (11:27–33). Jesus answers questions about his authority with the parable of the wicked tenants (12:1–12), which vindicates his authority while also criticizing the temple establishment. Jesus' parable provokes questions aimed at entrapping him (12:13–34), after which Jesus responds with further criticisms (12:35–44). Finally, Jesus leaves the temple – never to return – (13:1) and gives an apocalyptic-style discourse ostensibly about the end of the temple (13). Mark 14–15 is the story of Jesus' passion, but even here, the temple occupies a presence in the narrative. When Jesus is arrested, he questions why they did not arrest him when he taught every day in the temple (14:49). At Jesus' trial, he is accused of threatening the temple (14:58). Jesus is mocked, with this same charge, during the crucifixion (15:29). Finally, as Jesus dies the curtain in the temple is torn from top to bottom (15:38), and Jesus' death is mysteriously linked to the end of the temple.

There is little doubt that the temple dominates Mark's brief narrative about Jesus, particularly Mark 11–15. Indeed, Mark not only positions the temple at the center of the narrative, he also draws parallels between Jesus and the temple. This can be seen at the macro level with Mark's subtle division of 11–15 into two halves, one about the end of the temple (11–12), and the other about the end of Jesus (14–15). Mark enhances this division as he carefully juxtaposes the preparation of Jesus' entry into Jerusalem and the temple with the preparation of Jesus' Last Supper. Mark's focus on Jesus' obtaining the colt is unique to his gospel; the detailed account of Jesus' ride on the colt into Jerusalem is also found in Mark's description of the Passover preparations (Mark 14:12–16). Mark has deliberately and subtly crafted the two units to create the striking parallel. This parallelism creates two narrative units, Mark 11–12 and 14–15. The two narratives of preparation – obtaining the colt for entering Jerusalem (Mark 11:1–6) and obtaining the room for Passover (Mark 14:12–16) – each mark the beginning of a new and significant narrative section. The two episodes have strong verbal parallels, illustrated in the following chart:

---

[17] John R. Donahue ("Temple, Trial, and Royal Christology," in *The Passion in Mark: Studies on Mark 14–16* [ed. W.H. Kelber; Philadelphia: Fortress, 1976] 61–79) highlights how the motif of the temple is threaded throughout Mark 11–16. For Donahue, the Temple is at the heart of the dramatic conflict in the latter half of Mark: "From Mk 11 onward the opposition is directed clearly at the Temple" (ibid., 69).

|         | Mark 11 |          | Mark 14 |
|---------|---------|----------|---------|
| vs. 1c–2a | ἀποστέλλει δύο τῶν μαθητῶν αὐτοῦ καὶ λέγει αὐτοῖς | vs. 13a | ἀποστέλλει δύο τῶν μαθητῶν αὐτοῦ καὶ λέγει αὐτοῖς |
| vs. 2a | ὑπάγετε εἰς τὴν κώμην | vs. 13a | ὑπάγετε εἰς τὴν πόλιν |
| vs. 3b | εἴπατε· ὁ κύριος | vs. 14b | εἴπατε τῷ οἰκοδεσπότῃ ὅτι ὁ διδάσκαλος |
| vs. 4a | καὶ εὗρον | vs. 16b | καὶ εὗρον |
| vs. 11b | ὀψίας ἤδη οὔσης τῆς ὥρας, ἐξῆλθεν εἰς Βηθανίαν μετὰ τῶν δώδεκα. | vs. 17 | καὶ ὀψίας γενομένης ἔρχεται μετὰ τῶν δώδεκα. |

These two narratives of preparation serve as introductions to the two halves of Mark 11–15 and thus suggest that each part, on the temple and Jesus respectively, is related to the other. More specifically, the preparation for Jesus' entry into Jerusalem serves as a prologue for Mark 11–13, which focuses on the temple; this first narrative unit, Mark 11:11–13:1, recounts Jesus' words and actions in the temple and the subsequent conflict between Jesus and the Jewish leaders. Jesus' entry (εἰσῆλθεν ... εἰς τὸ ἱερόν, 11:11) and Jesus' exit (ἐκπορευομένου αὐτοῦ ἐκ τοῦ ἱεροῦ, 13:1), frame this tight narrative.

Mark 14 begins a new focus in the narrative, marked by the notice that Passover will occur in two days (v. 1). If in Mark 11–13 the temple provides the spatial context of the narrative, the Passover sets the temporal context for Mark 14–15. At the beginning of the chapter Mark presents a story of a woman who anoints Jesus, which is interpreted by Jesus as an anointing "for burial" – this story clearly foreshadows Jesus' impending passion and death. This story is also positioned in parallel to the last incident of Jesus in the temple, wherein he sees the widow at the treasury (12:41–11). The parallel of the widow who gives ὅλον τὸν βίον αὐτῆς to the temple (12:44) with the woman who pours out the costly ointment upon Jesus (14:3) fits the classic pattern of Markan intercalation. The intercalation of the generous women serves to frame the almost free-standing discourse of Mark 13, a subject I shall examine in Chapter Three. The parallel between the two women mirrors the deeper parallel between Jesus and the temple: the object of the widow's gift is the temple, whereas Jesus is the object of the gift of ointment. It is just such a parallel that is suggested in the narrative account of the disciple's preparation for both Jesus' entry into the temple and the Passover meal. With these preparations, Mark underscores the importance of the temple incident and Jesus' Passover meal and suggests, at a narrative level, that there is an important relationship between Jesus and the temple. The temple demonstration augurs the temple's end, and Jesus' silencing of the Jewish leaders also portends to the reader that the Jewish leadership that opposes Jesus is coming to an end. The end of both the temple and the entire Jerusalem establishment comes into sharp focus in the ominous discourse of Mark 13, an apocalyptic discourse that takes up the end of the temple, Jerusalem, and even the world. In the same way, the end of Jesus shadows all the events of the Passover meal, the garden of Gethsemane, and the rest of the passion narrative. Therefore, the end of the temple (11–12) and the end of Jesus (14–15) are juxtaposed, with Mark 13 standing in between these narratives as the vital link.

Mark 13 stands apart from its surrounding narrative for several reasons. First, Jesus exits the temple (ἐκπορευομένου αὐτοῦ ἐκ τοῦ ἱεροῦ), which sets the stage for 11:11–12:44. Next, the context of Mark 13, the Mount of Olives (τὸ ὄρος τῶν ἐλαιῶν, 13:3), allows the teaching here to have a geographical marker that sets it apart from the surrounding locations of Bethany, temple, and Jerusalem. Finally, from a narrative perspective, Mark 13 is unique in that it is the only long discourse, besides Mark 4, delivered by Jesus in the entire story. Another distinctive feature of this discourse is its apocalyptic style. Despite the unique features of Mark 13, the content of Jesus' discourse serves as a bridge for the narrative units that precede and follow it.

Although Mark 13 in many ways stands apart from its surrounding narrative, it does have an important relation to the temple-dominated narrative of Mark 11–12, for three reasons. First, the discourse of Mark 13 begins with a discussion of the wonderful (ποταπός) stones and buildings (ποταποὶ λίθοι καὶ ποταπαὶ οἰκοδομαί) of the temple (13:1–2). Second, Mark describes Jesus as sitting opposite the temple, κατέναντι τοῦ ἱεροῦ, thus employing imagery that suggests, particularly after the events of Mark 11–12, a hostile relationship. Finally, Jesus foretells the end of the temple (13:2, 14–23). Thus, the established conflict between Jesus and the temple in Mark 11–12 is addressed in the apocalyptic discourse of Mark 13, where the temple prophetically comes to an end.

Mark 13 does not merely focus on the end of the temple, however; it also takes up the apocalyptic imagery of the son of man's triumphant return at the end. This complex eschatological discourse concludes with an enigmatic parable that has strong narrative links to the passion narrative and the death of Jesus. No one knows the time the master will come, but the servants must watch (γρηγορεῖτε, Mark 13:33,34,35,37) lest he find them sleeping (καθεύδοντας, v. 36). The focus on temporality is made explicit in four instances in verse 35: evening (ὀψέ), midnight (μεσονύκτιον), cockcrow (ἀλεκτοροφωνίας), and morning (πρωΐ). Three out of the four are named, with the other being alluded to, in exactly that order in the passion narrative that begins with the Last Supper (14:17, 41, 72, 15:1). Thus Mark 13 continues the motif of the temple found in Mark 11–12, while at the same time it looks forward to the story of Jesus that follows in Mark 14–15. Mark 13 plays a pivotal role in Mark's narrative by bridging the story of the temple's end with that of the end of Jesus. By highlighting the similarities and differences between the ends of each, Mark intends to lead his reader into a deeper understanding of the relationship between Jesus and the temple, an understanding that is – from Mark's perspective – the key to eschatology.

## 1.3 Jesus' Way to the Temple

Mark's account of Jesus' entry into Jerusalem (Mark 11:1–11) functions in many ways as a prologue for the remainder of his gospel, particularly for Mark 11–12. While this entry pericope anticipates many of the themes and issues that will soon unfold in the rest of Mark's story, the entry narrative also looks back to several themes that have run through Mark's preceding narrative. This oscillation illustrates how imperative Jesus' entry into Jerusalem is; indeed, I argue that it is a watershed moment in Mark's drama.[18]

To appreciate this narrative significance fully, I will trace the elements of the entry narrative that relate to the temple, as well as details that anticipate the subsequent story of Jesus' teaching and actions in the temple. There are four items in the entry narrative that have special relevance to the subsequent story of Jesus in the temple: (1) the details and pace of the narrative; (2) the motif of royalty (ὁ κύριος); (3) the motif of "the way" (ἡ ὁδός); and (4) the motif of "the coming one" (ὁ ἐρχόμενος) from Psalm 118. Finally, I shall conclude with a brief summary of how these details and themes from the entry narrative prepare the reader in important ways for the story of Jesus that unfolds in the temple.

---

[18] Narrative forecasts and echoes are a common feature of Mark's narrative. Joanna Dewey ("Mark as Interwoven Tapestry: Forecasts and Echoes for a Listening Audience," *CBQ* 53 [1991], 224) observes that the "Gospel of Mark does not have a single structure made up of discrete units but rather is an interwoven tapestry or fugue made up of multiple overlapping structures and sequences, forecasts of what is to come and echoes of what has already been said." This nature of Mark's narratives will often be a focus of our study. See also Elizabeth Struthers Malbon, "Echoes and Foreshadowings in Mark 4–8: Reading and Rereading," *JBL* 112 (1993) 211–30.

## 1.3.1 Narrative Pace

One of the most striking features of Mark's account of Jesus' entry (Mark 11:1–11) is the narrative pace, punctuated by intense detail. The reader, accustomed to the typically breathless pace of the Markan narrative, would note this significant change in narrative pace.[19] By slowing the pace, Mark intensifies the reader's sense of drama, thereby sharpening the narrative focus on Jesus' entry into the city where, as the reader well knows, he will be killed.[20] This change in narrative tempo is not meant to depict Jesus' journey as leisurely; rather, the narrative tempo gives a deliberative, even solemn, tone to the pace, serving to highlight the importance of Jesus' entry and presence in Jerusalem and its temple.

## 1.3.2 Which Lord? (κύριος)

Commentators have been divided as to precisely whom κύριος refers to in Mark 11:3, and recent commentators tend to be against seeing Jesus as the referent. Craig Evans is representative of many when he says, "To whom ὁ κύριος, 'the Lord,' refers is not easy to decide: Jesus, God, and the owner of the colt seem to be the options."[21] Evans ultimately posits that κύριος refers to the colt's owner or God. He excludes Jesus as a possibility, concluding: "The Markan evangelist (in contrast to Luke) never calls Jesus ὁ κύριος, so it is probably not prudent to see it as a reference to Jesus."[22] John Donahue and Daniel Harrington agree with Evans.[23] But R. T. France argues that the referent is God, as Jesus boldly enlists God as the κύριος, thereby giving legitimacy to Jesus' claim on the colt.[24]

Although the title "lord" (κύριος) is not a prominent christological title in Mark as it is in Luke, Mark nevertheless offers narrative clues that point to this possibility; indeed, the particular context of 11:3 even allows for this alternative reading. Mark begins his story of Jesus with the authoritative word from Scripture (Isa 40:3) commanding the voice in the wilderness (John the Baptist), ἑτοιμάσατε τὴν ὁδὸν κυρίου (1:3). Thus, from the very beginning of Mark's gospel, the reader is prepared to see

---

[19] "This narrative style creates a sense of urgency in the narrative. The Markan Jesus appears as a person in a hurry, moving somewhat breathlessly from place to place, taking the lead and determining the direction of the narrative. Yet the pace of the narrative slows as the Passion approaches" (Donahue and Harrington, *Mark*, 17).

[20] Mark forecasted Jesus' death in the three passion predictions, Mark 8:31, 9:31, 10:33–34, which lead up to Mark 11.

[21] Craig Evans, *Mark 8:27–16:20* (WBC 34B; Nashville: Thomas Nelson, 2001) 143.

[22] Ibid.

[23] Donahue and Harrington, *Mark*, 321–22.

[24] R. T. France, *The Gospel of Mark* (NIGTC; Grand Rapids: Eerdmans, 2002) 432.

Jesus as the κύριος. The terminology of ὁδός and κύριος are repeated when Jesus makes his 'way,' ὁδός, to Jerusalem (10:52; 11:8) and preparations are made for the last portion of the journey by procuring a colt, likely leading the reader to see Jesus' way to Jerusalem as the way of the Lord.[25] Indeed, that the κύριος had need of the colt (v. 3), and that the colt was then given to Jesus to ride (v. 7), makes it clear that Mark intends the reader to see Jesus as the κύριος. Thus, the Markan reader, equipped with Mark's prologue, should read the reference to κύριος in 11:3 as a reference to Jesus. The Markan reader would then see what could only be ambiguous at best for the characters in the Markan narrative, that the Isaianic κύριος is Jesus.

What is more, this passage includes Mal 3:1, a crucial text for the subsequent temple incident.[26] Moreover, the motif of κύριος not only serves as the backdrop to Mark's larger story; it is precisely as Jesus makes his last ascent up to the temple that he assumes the title κύριος.[27] Mark has reserved the title until this climactic point, thereby deepening the reader's sense of the solemnity and importance of what is about to unfold in the temple.[28] Thus, Mark's constraint is narratively significant. The use of κύριος in 11:3 looks back to the prophetic oracles of Isaiah 40 and Malachi 3 cited in the prologue, while at the same time it anticipates the authority

---

[25] Frank J. Matera (*The Kingship of Jesus: Composition and Theology in Mark 15* [SBLDS 66; Chico: Scholars Press, 1982] 74) observes, "As Mark's community reads this story, it understands what the historical actors could not. The *Kyrios* of 11:3 is the one Isaiah prophesied at the beginning of the gospel (1:3), and the one that David must call Lord (12:37), i.e., the Messiah King." Matera also notes how Mark intentionally strikes an ambiguous portrait of Jesus' kingship until the cross. "Thus, in this pericope, *Kyrios* and *ho erchomenos* serve as surrogates for the royal title which cannot be publicly revealed until the passion has begun" (ibid., 74).

[26] Marcus, *The Way of the Lord*, 12–17.

[27] Morna Hooker (*The Gospel according to Saint Mark* [Peabody, MA: Hendrickson, 1991] 258) sees this possibility, "Nowhere else (except perhaps in 5.19) does Mark allow the title to slip into his narrative in this anachronistic way, but it is possible that Mark felt that at this point in his narrative the identity of Jesus is being made sufficiently plain by events for him to use the title: it is 'the Lord' who is entering Jerusalem and coming to the temple (cf. Mal 3.1)." I hope to show that Mark's employment of the term here is precisely part of his narrative strategy, underscoring the climactic importance of the entry into the temple for his story.

[28] Once the narrative reasons for Mark withholding the title κύριος until this turning point in the narrative are seen, the rare use of the term in Mark can be better understood. This narrative explanation solves the problem of seeing the use of κύριος here as "uncharacteristic" for Mark, as D. E. Nineham (*The Gospel of St Mark* [Baltimore: Penguin Books, 1963] 295) observed, "The fact that the word is not used as a title for him elsewhere in Mark (or Matthew) only points to the late and exceptional character of the story; it does not justify taking the word here = 'God' or as = 'the owner of the ass.'"

Jesus presumes for his actions and teaching in the temple and the question regarding his authority that follows (Mark 11:28). In other words, Mark informs his readers, by way of the prologue and several clues along the way – most notably in the entry pericope – of the true nature of Jesus' authority as Lord of the temple.

### 1.3.3   The Motif of "the Way" (ὁδός)

As Jesus makes his triumphant entry into Jerusalem, Mark describes how the πολλοί spread their garments out before him on the ὁδός (Mark 11:8). Here ὁδός connotes more than a mere road, but rather the ὁδός of the Lord (1:2–3), which Mark suggests is now the ὁδός of Jesus.[29] Mark employs the term "the way," ἡ ὁδός, seventeen times in his gospel.[30] In Mark, this term can often be fraught with meaning, as its programmatic position at the start of Mark's prologue suggests. Moreover, immediately preceding the occurrence of the word in 11:8, ὁδός occurs seven times in the central section of the gospel (Mark 8:27–10:52), where it also serves as the literary frame for this unit in the phrase ἐν τῇ ὁδῷ (8:27 and 10:52). The Markan reader, after becoming sensitized to the importance of "the way" in Mark 8:27–10:52 and in the prologue, would see the use of ὁδός in Mark's account of Jesus' procession into Jerusalem as charged with meaning. At the very least, the narrative repetition of ὁδός puts emphasis on Jesus' journey, thereby deepening the reader's anticipation of what will happen when Jesus arrives in Jerusalem. What Mark intends the reader to see in the ὁδός of Jesus can be ascertained only after drawing a brief sketch of its various roles in the narrative.

### 1.3.3.1   "The Way" in Mark's Gospel

Mark's narrative opens with the motif of "the way," and he weaves this theme through the narrative tapestry of 1:2–11:8. The gospel is marked by a constant sense of motion, often characterized by urgency.[31] Indeed, it is the image of ἡ ὁδός that is central among all the Markan words evoking motion because Mark has placed the motif of ἡ ὁδός at a most prominent position – the opening of his prologue.[32] Mark opens the narrative with a

---

[29] See Marcus, *The Way of the Lord*, 37–41.

[30] Mark 1:2,3; 2:23; 4:4,15; 6:8; 8:3,27; 9:33,34; 10:17,32,46,52; 11:8 (2x); 12:14.

[31] "There is a continual sense of motion; indeed this is true of the whole Gospel of Mark; he uses verbs of motion more frequently than any of the other evangelists" (Ernest Best, "Discipleship in Mark: Mark 8:22–10:52," *SJT* 23 [1970] 326).

[32] Watts (*Isaiah's New Exodus,* 90) notes the significance of Mark's positioning of the motif of ἡ ὁδός by its placement in the opening sentence as well as in the only explicit editorial citation of Scripture: "In keeping with the role of the opening sentence

citation from the book of Isaiah, which is really a conflation of three OT texts; Exod 23:20, Mal 3:1, and Isa 40:3.[33] All three texts share a common hook word that ties them together and brings this key term, ἡ ὁδός, into sharp focus.[34] Many scholars have observed that this opening citation, focused on ἡ ὁδός, is intended to invoke the significant theme found throughout the book of Isaiah of the "way" of Yhwh's new exodus, which characterizes Isaiah's conception of the restoration of the Lord's kingdom as the eschatological renewal of Israel.[35]

"The way" motif is particularly evident in the literary unit that is often considered the central section of the gospel, 8:27–10:52. In addition to beginning and ending with the healing of a blind man, this section is framed by the phrase "on the way" (ἐν τῇ ὁδῷ, in 8:27 and 10:52), and is woven together by "the way" motif.[36] Three times in this section (8:31–38; 9:31–50; 10:32–45) "the way" is followed by Jesus' prediction and teaching about his coming sufferings in Jerusalem. The theme of "the way" in the central section is intensified in Mark 10. In chapter 10 alone, the word ὁδός is repeated four times (10:17,32,46,52), which is significant since Mark 10 immediately precedes the royal entry pericope. In addition to the frequent ὁδός terminology, the goal of the way is brought into sharp focus here for the first time. In v. 32 Mark sets the way, ἐν τῇ ὁδῷ, in apposition to ἀναβαίνοντες εἰς Ἱεροσόλυμα, "going up to Jerusalem," thus identifying Jerusalem as the destination of the way.[37] The word ἀναβαίνω is particularly significant because it can signify a cultic pilgrimage to

---

in literary antiquity, Mark's sole explicit editorial citation of the OT should be expected to convey the main concerns of his prologue and, therefore, his Gospel."

[33] Marcus (*The Way of the Lord*, 15–17) argues that this conflation comes from Mark himself. Whether or not Mark took this over from tradition or created this OT conflation does not impact our argument, as either way it has a prominent place in the final form of Mark's narrative.

[34] "Finally, the elimination of 'before you' accents the parallelism between 'your way' (1:2) and 'the way of the Lord' (1:3), and the resultant emphasis on the theme of 'the way' coheres with the stress laid on this theme throughout Mark's Gospel" (Marcus, *The Way of the Lord*, 16).

[35] See Willard M. Swartley, "The Structural Function of the Term 'Way' (ὁδός) in Mark's Gospel," in *The New Way of Jesus* (ed. W. Klassen; Newton, KS: Faith and Life, 1980) 68–80. See also his book *Israel's Scripture Traditions*, 99–115; Marcus, *The Way of the Lord*, 12–47; and the exhaustive study of Watts, *Isaiah's New Exodus*, especially 53–90 and 124–36.

[36] "Thematically, this mid-section is structured by the motif of the way" (Werner H. Kelber, *The Kingdom in Mark* [Philadelphia: Fortress, 1974] 67).

[37] The narrative importance of the identification of Jerusalem as the *telos* of the way is reemphasized in the very next verse as Jesus himself declares to his disciples, "Behold, we are going up to Jerusalem" (Mark 10:33).

Jerusalem.[38] Going up to Jerusalem did not refer to a simple topographical ascent; rather, it signified a pilgrimage to the temple in Jerusalem, usually made during one of the three great pilgrimage festivals. This gives greater perspective to the image of the disciples, the crowds, and Bartimaeus following Jesus, for they are not just following Jesus on an abstract "way," but rather, they are pilgrims being led by Jesus to the holy city and particularly to the temple. Joel Marcus observes how the reader has been prepared to perceive the deeper meaning of this "way" to Jerusalem:

"He has, moreover, prefaced this reference to the Lord's way with the conflated citation that speaks of the way of Jesus. When, therefore, those readers encounter in 8:22–10:52 the picture of Jesus and his disciples *on the way* up to Jerusalem, they will probably be led to surmise that this way of Jesus is the Deutero-Isaian 'way of the Lord.'"[39]

Thus the "way" is identified in chapter 10 as a holy pilgrimage that prepares for the cultic significance of the subsequent procession narrative.

It must be acknowledged, however, that there are instances in Mark where ὁδός refers simply to a road, with no theological or narrative connotations (e.g. 2:23; 4:4,15; 6:8; 8:3). Robert Gundry takes such mundane examples of ὁδός as evidence that Mark does not invest this term with any wider narrative significance than simply a way of travel.[40] He concludes, "These earlier uses do not encourage a sudden switch to the way of the Cross."[41] On the surface, Gundry's point is well taken, in that there certainly is a shift in Mark's use of ὁδός. However, he ignores the programmatic and certainly theological sense given to ἡ ὁδός in the prologue (Mark 1:2–3).[42] Second, Gundry does not acknowledge, although many other scholars do, that the use of ὁδός in 8:27–10:52 is undoubtedly redactional, and thus it plays a uniquely Markan literary role.[43] Third, Gundry misses an important precedent to Mark's "sudden switch" from the mundane to theological sense of "the way," for this is typical of LXX Isaiah, which can move from ὁδός as a simple road (Isa 7:3, 33:8,21; 36:2;

---

[38] See Schneider, "ἀναβαίνω," *TDNT* 1. 519.

[39] Marcus, *The Way of the Lord*, 35.

[40] Robert H. Gundry, *Mark: A Commentary on His Apology for the Cross* (Grand Rapids: Eerdmans, 1993) 442. He claims that "'the way' is simply the road on which an event takes place as Jesus and others travel between localities, whatever the direction or destination of their travel."

[41] Ibid., 442.

[42] Marcus, *The Way of the Lord*, 12–29.

[43] See, e.g., Ernest Best, *Following Jesus: Discipleship in the Gospel of Mark* (JSNTSup 4; Sheffield: JSOT, 1981) 15: "The journey Mark presents is consequently his own creation and the 'way' which Jesus goes is not just a literal journey to Jerusalem but is intended also to be understood spiritually." See also Watts, *Isaiah's New Exodus*, 129; Marcus, *The Way of the Lord*, 32.

37:29,34; 41:3; 59:14) to ὁδός as an ethical way (Isa 8:11; 26:7,8; 30:21) to "the way of the Lord" (Isa 2:3; 35:8; 40:3,14,27; 42:16,24; 59:8). The book of Isaiah displays a strikingly wide semantic range for ὁδός, even within a few verses (e.g. 59:8 vs. 59:14). The most simple explanation, missed by Gundry, is that Mark follows his source; thus, ὁδός can shift in meaning and carry different nuances according to its context.

### *1.3.3.2  Cultic Contexts and Connotations of "the Way"*

The end of "the way" in Mark is Jerusalem, and here Mark may again be taking his script from OT sources. The original context of "the way" in the opening Scripture citations from Exodus, Malachi, and Isaiah is the festal pilgrimage to Jerusalem's temple. Joel Marcus, building on the work of F. M. Cross, shows how "the way" in Deutero-Isaiah is transfigured into the Lord's eschatological pilgrimage to Zion.[44] The exodus connotations of "the way" in Isaiah are assumed into the motif of a festal pilgrimage to Zion. The new exodus motif used by prophets in describing Israel's restoration is not only accompanied by pilgrimage procession imagery, but the Exodus imagery actually culminates in a depiction of a holy pilgrimage to Zion. As one OT scholar observes: "...the return itself is not merely a wandering through wilderness toward a land flowing with milk and honey. It is a pilgrimage, a solemn and yet joyous procession of YHWH's redeemed to the high and holy precincts of Zion."[45] The prophets, therefore, reconfigured the New Exodus imagery into an eschatological pilgrimage to the temple. This is well illustrated by Eugene Merrill:

The language of the prophets in describing this procession becomes transmuted from that of exodus and redemption to that of pilgrimage and worship. ... For the prophets to appropriate the imagery of processional and pilgrimage literature in describing Israel's historical and eschatological return to Zion suggests, therefore, that modern interpreters of those prophets must look not only to exodus contexts for their meaning but to pilgrimage and procession as motifs of Israel's return.[46]

---

[44] Marcus gives this citation from F. M. Cross (*Canaanite Myth and Hebrew Epic: Essays in the History of the Religion of Israel* [Cambridge: Harvard University Press, 1973] 108): "The Old Exodus-Conquest route, the way through the wilderness, becomes at the same time the pilgrimage way to Zion. The march of the Conquest abruptly shifts into the festal, ritual procession to Zion. The procession to Zion and the feast on the holy mountain (compare Isaiah 25:6–8; 55:1–5) have recast, so to speak, or redirected the route of the Exodus and Conquest to lead to Zion" (cited in Marcus, *The Way of the Lord*, 33).

[45] Eugene H. Merrill, "Pilgrimage and Procession: Motifs of Israel's Return," in *Israel's Apostasy and Restoration* (ed. Avraham Gileadi; Grand Rapids: Baker, 1988) 270.

[46] Merrill, "Pilgrimage and Procession," 270.

Thus LXX Isaiah employs both ἡ ὁδός and ἀναβαίνω (a combination found in the central section of Mark) in the context of Israel's festal pilgrimage tradition. "In Deutero-Isaiah ἀναβαίνει (go up) and ὁδός link the theological traditions of festal procession to the holy city..."[47] What is the point of this eschatological pilgrimage? The climax of the way of the new exodus in Deutero-Isaiah is reached when the Lord returns to Zion and once again takes up his reign, thereby redeeming Jerusalem (52:8–10), which is the subject of the proclamation (εὐαγγελίζω) of the gospel in LXX Isaiah (Isa 52:7).[48] Isaiah 52 is closely tied to the programmatic opening of Deutero-Isaiah, where the key imagery of the Lord leading his people and taking up his reign is clustered.[49] Rather than being a generic motif, pilgrimage in Deutero-Isaiah belongs to the autumn festival of Tabernacles, which celebrates the enthronement of Yahweh. This is evident in Isa 52:6–7 where in "that day" it is declared to Zion, "your God reigns." The refrain is taken from the enthronement psalms and evokes the enthronement liturgy of the Feast of Tabernacles.[50] Thus, the pilgrimage way ends in the place of Jerusalem's temple, with the Lord's enthronement.

Like Deutero-Isaiah, Malachi 3 speaks of the Lord's return to his temple. "The scenario envisioned by Deutero-Isaiah and the enthronement psalm is complemented strikingly by Mal 3:1 and other verses within the prophecy," states Beth Glazier-McDonald in her commentary on Malachi.[51] She places Malachi 3 in the context of the autumn festival of Yhwh's enthronement, noting its liturgical kinship with Deutero-Isaiah. In

---

[47] Swartley, *Israel's Scripture Traditions,* 110.

[48] "To a large extent, the message of Deutero-Isaiah has been couched in the language of the enthronement festival. Yahweh is about to appear in triumph, like a king, his 'glory' revealed, 40:3,5. He is coming to Jerusalem, his temple, 40:9" (Beth Glazier-McDonald, *Malachi: The Divine Messenger* [Atlanta: Scholars Press, 1987] 138). She sees a similar pattern in Malachi.

[49] "The striking feature of this oracle is its close relation to the prologue of Second Isaiah (40:1–21). Again we hear of the herald of good tidings announcing the return of God to Zion in might, and the leading of his flock before him. In a very real sense, vv. 7–10 form a suitable conclusion to the eschatological drama first announced in chapter 40 and then unfolded in chapters 40–55" (Brevard Childs, *Isaiah* [OTL: Louisville, KY: Westminster John Knox, 2001] 406).

[50] See John Gray (*The Biblical Doctrine of the Reign of God* [Dulles, VA: T&T Clark, 2000]) for a defense of Mowinckel's classification of enthronement psalms and their relation to Sukkot. Gray also correlates the feast imagery of Deutero-Isaiah with the autumn festival of Sukkot. He claims that Isa 52:7 is a "citation from the liturgy of the autumn festival, to be recognized as such in the light of the parallel in Nah 2:1 (1:15)..." (ibid., 164).

[51] Glazier-McDonald, *Malachi,* 138.

addition to Deutero-Isaiah, Mal 3:1 is closely related to Exod 23:20, according to Glazier-McDonald. She claims that "the relationship between Mal 3:1 and Exod 23:20 is too striking to be accidental. In fact, the passage in Malachi appears to be a reworking of the מַלְאָךְ text in the Book of the Covenant."[52] The messenger in Exod 23:20 must guard Israel on its way to "the place" that the Lord has prepared. The "place," although undoubtedly the Promised Land in the Book of the Covenant, is clearly associated with the temple in the Deuteronomic tradition. Thus all three OT texts (Isaiah, Malachi, and Exodus) are concerned about the way that leads to Jerusalem and the temple, a "way" fraught with connotations of cultic pilgrimage. Since "the way" in Mark's story shares the same temple orientation found in the very OT texts Mark cites in his programmatic prologue, it seems evident that the prophetic eschatological image of "the way of the Lord" shapes the Markan Jesus' way to the temple.

Kelber notes that Mark's journey language evokes the imagery of a cultic pilgrimage. He put forward the notion, first observed by H. Windisch, that "entering" (εἰσέρχομαι) in Mark, particularly in connection with the kingdom, is taken from the scriptural traditions of Israel. The entry motif has two sources: the Deuteronomic traditions regarding entry into the promised land and the cultic tradition of entering the temple found in the psalms.[53] Kelber has advanced Windisch's insight by arguing that the entrance language in Mark, linked with ἡ ὁδός, models Israel's journey and entrance into the promised land.[54] Kelber observes how "the way" is punctuated with "entering" and "exiting":

This way of Jesus is made up of a continuous sequence of entries and exits. Both *eiserchesthai* and *exerchesthai* appear to be part of a Markan scheme which is in

---

[52] Ibid., 130. See also Klyne R. Snodgrass, "Streams of Tradition Emerging from Isaiah 40:1–5 and Their Adaptation in the New Testament," *JSNT* 8 (1980) 24–45.

[53] Werner H. Kelber, "Kingdom and Parousia in the Gospel of Mark" (Ph.D. diss., University of Chicago, 1970) 108–9. See also Marcus, *The Way of the Lord,* 33.

[54] "... the Markan entrance formula is ultimately derived from a translation of Deuteronomy's entrance tradition into an eschatological key. Modeled after Israel's first entrance, the present journey into the Kingdom constitutes a second entry into the promised land" (from Kelber's dissertation, "Kingdom and Parousia in the Gospel of Mark," 108, as cited by Swartley, "The Structural Function of the Term 'Way' (*Hodos*) in Mark's Gospel," 79). Kelber (*Kingdom*, 68) observes that εἰσέρχομαι (entrance) and ἐξέρχομαι (exit) in conjunction with ὁδός, are an important part of Mark's rhetorical strategy. These terms create a "rhythmic pattern of involvement and breakup [that] impose a mark of urgency and restlessness upon the ministry of Jesus. He journeys from place to place as if drawn by some distant goal... The way ties experiences into a comprehensive sequence and thereby suggests the purposefulness of Jesus' life." I would argue that, just as with ὁδός, the use of εἰσέρχομαι climaxes with Jesus' entrance into the temple (Mark 11:11,15). It is also significant that this is the last place that Jesus enters.

evidence throughout the gospel. The entry motif is used in almost stereotyped fashion to depict Jesus' entrance into a house, a boat, a synagogue, a town, the temple, and the Kingdom. The following occurrences may be said to be redactional: 1:21,45; 2:1; 3:1,20; 5:39; 7:17,24; 9:28,43,45,47; 10:15,23,24,25; 11:11,15.

Just as with ὁδός, εἰσέρχομαι is especially clustered in Mark 9–10 and, like ὁδός, the last occurrences of Jesus "entering" occur at the end of Jesus' procession to the temple and his return to the temple the following day (11:11,15). Swartley follows Kelber and Windisch in seeing a correlation between the "entrance" and "way" motifs.[55] The procession narrative, particularly Mark 11:8, brings to a final climax "the way" and "entering" of Jesus; the ultimate destination of both is Jerusalem's temple.

### 1.3.3.3 The Goal of "the Way"

Various interpreters tend to moralize the significance of "the way" without giving attention to its narrative function. Gundry has argued vigorously against seeing any connection between ἡ ὁδός and the Cross. For Gundry "the way" in Mark is no *via dolorosa*: "to interpret 'the way' in 8:27 and following passages as the way of the Cross runs into a ditch."[56] Gundry gives examples of narrative uses of "the way" that do not correlate with the cross, while also pointing out the complete absence of ὁδός from the passion narratives:

At the Triumphal Procession, crowds spread their garments and straw on "the way" into Jerusalem (11:8). Here we have the way of honor and acclamation, not of crucifixion. And "the way of God" that Jesus teaches according to 12:14 does not include his crucifixion, for the expression refers to his public teaching, from which his crucifixion is absent.[57]

My previous criticisms of Gundry's position make it clear that his absolute denial of any theological connotation for "the way" is wrong; however, Gundry's point that "the way" ends in Jerusalem and not Golgotha is well taken. "The way" cannot simply be identified with the Cross, since "the way" is not mentioned in the entire passion narrative. In fact, the last narrative occurrence of "the way" is in the description of Jesus' procession into Jerusalem (Mark 11:8).[58] For Mark, the theology of the way has its primary locus in Jerusalem's temple. This by no means suggests we must

---

[55] Swartley, "The Structural Function of the 'Way,'" 81.

[56] Gundry, *Mark*, 442.

[57] Ibid.

[58] Mark 11:8 is the last time that ἡ ὁδός is used in the sense of road or movement. The only other time it is used afterward is in Mark 12:14 in typical Markan irony as the Pharisees and Herodians say to Jesus, "Teacher, we know that you are true, and care for no man; for you do not regard the position of men; but truly teach the way of God."

follow Gundry in rejecting any association between "the way" and the cross. As Jesus led his disciples "on the way," he singled out Jerusalem as the place where the Son of Man would be rejected, slain, and resurrected (Mark 10:33–34). At the same time, however, it is important to recognize that in the foreground of Mark's narrative, "the way" leads to Jerusalem and, more accurately, the temple, while the cross looms in the narrative background.

The ὁδός motif gives purpose and direction to the story; it is intensified in the central section, as Jesus gets closer to Jerusalem and the end of the way. Moreover, the sharper focus that Mark gives to Jesus' ὁδός as a pilgrimage to Jerusalem not only prepares the reader for the importance of Jesus' entry, actions, and teaching in the temple, but it also gives the reader a sense that, among other things, the eschatological fulfillment of God's plan awaits Jesus in Jerusalem.

### 1.3.4   Psalm 118: He Who Comes (ὁ ἐρχόμενος)

Jesus processes up to Jerusalem amid a kind of cortege, as those who go before him (οἱ προάγοντες) and those who follow him (οἱ ἀκολουθοῦντες) cry out (ἔκραζον), singing the famous Jewish pilgrimage hymn, Psalm 118. The crowd's crying out celebrates the coming of the Davidic kingdom (ἡ ἐρχομένη βασιλεία τοῦ πατρὸς ἡμῶν Δαυίδ) and echoes Bartimaeus's cries of υἱὲ Δαυίδ heard in the previous pericope (κράζειν, ἔκραζεν 10:47,48). This singing is later greeted with stony silence at the temple (11:11), highlighting the ambiguity that pervades Jesus' so-called triumphal entry. Indeed, the triumphal cries fit into the pattern of Markan irony, as it is only a matter of days before the crowd will be crying out for Jesus' death (ἔκραξαν· σταύρωσον αὐτόν (2x) 15:13,14).[59]

In verses 9–10, Mark gives the reader a sampling of the crowd's rendition of Psalm 118; the psalm's parallel puts the motif of "coming" in sharp focus. Lane recognizes the chiastic structure of this couplet:[60]

---

[59] "...here is more irony for Mark's story: the cry here is that God might 'preserve' Jesus, who himself seems determined to go the way of the cross. The narrative interplay of the various cries (*ekrazon*) of the crowd in the story underscores this irony... Consequently, after Jesus is arrested, a different cry will come from the crowd. They will clamor for the release of a 'genuine' revolutionary – Barabbas – and demand the execution of the imposter, Jesus (15:13)" (Ched Myers, *Binding the Strong Man: A Political Reading of Mark's Story of Jesus* [New York: Orbis, 1988] 296).

[60] William L. Lane, *The Gospel of Mark* (NICNT; Grand Rapids: Eerdmans, 1974) 397; more recently France, *Mark*, 433.

(a) ὡσαννά

(b) εὐλογημένος ὁ ἐρχόμενος ἐν ὀνόματι κυρίου·

(b´) εὐλογημένη ἡ ἐρχομένη βασιλεία τοῦ πατρὸς ἡμῶν Δαυίδ

(a´) ὡσαννὰ ἐν τοῖς ὑψίστοις

The first half of the couplet is an accurate citation of Psalm 118, celebrating "he who comes." The crowd interprets this line, along with Jesus' ascent to Jerusalem, as signifying the advent of the kingdom of David.

There is a dissonant note sounded in the crowd's song, as R.T. France observes: "The concept of a kingdom 'coming' is familiar from 1:15 and 9:1, but that was the kingdom of God announced by Jesus. The kingdom of David has an altogether more political and nationalistic ring."[61] Indeed, the crowd's notion of the kingdom of David stands in sharp contrast to Jesus' notion of the kingdom of God. Francis Moloney notes the problem behind the crowd's expectations:

The disciples and the crowd develop what is meant by one who comes in the name of the Lord (v. 9) with a description of their expectation: he is bringing in the kingdom of David (v. 10; see Amos 9:11; Isa 9:6–7). Nothing could be further from the truth. Jesus is bringing in the kingdom of God, and he has made it clear that this kingdom will be established by means of rejection, death, and resurrection in the city of David.[62]

Mark and his readers know well that the crowd's nationalistic hopes for Jesus' "coming" to usher a restored Davidic kingdom are deeply mistaken.

Mark has spoken of Jesus as the one "coming" earlier in his narrative, thus preparing the reader to see the relevance of Jesus' being designated as the "coming one" of Ps 118:25. Just before Jesus is introduced into Mark's story, John tells of a stronger one who "is coming," ἔρχεται ὁ ἰσχυρότερός μου ὀπίσω μου (Mark 1:7). Jesus himself gives cryptic hints that he is the one who "is coming" (ἔρχομαι) to sow the seeds of the kingdom of God (Mark 1:38; 4:3,21). So in what sense does Mark want us to understand Jesus' "coming" in the entry narrative?

The prophecy of Malachi, to which Mark has previously alluded, provides the key clues. Mark intends the motif of the "coming one" to evoke prophetic, rather than royal, associations. Thus Timothy Geddert observes, "However little the crowds themselves understand, Mark wants their celebration of the coming one (11:9) to serve as an announcement that Malachi's prophecy is being fulfilled. The messenger (John) has prepared the way, now the Lord is coming to his temple, 'but who can

---

[61] France, *Mark*, 434.
[62] Moloney, *Mark*, 219–20.

endure the day of his coming?' (Mal. 3:1–2; Mark 1:2, 11:11,15–16)."[63]
The ambiguity surrounding the "coming one" (ὁ ἐρχόμενος) matches the
ambiguity surrounding Mark's use of ὁ κύριος as previously noted. This is
not to deny either the sense of Jesus' royalty or kingship but rather to
redefine the meaning of Jesus' messianic royalty in distinction from the
crowd's nationalistic fervor, as the politics of the kingdom of God are of a
different order.[64]

Once the motif of Jesus' "coming" is understood before the backdrop of
Malachi, the narrative strategy of Mark becomes clear. The crowds see
Jesus' coming as the advent of the politics of national restoration, in the
tradition of David and probably of the more recent restoration stories of the
Maccabees. However, Jesus is "coming" not as the political liberator of the
temple, as was Judas Maccabeus, whose violent revolution threw off
Gentile oppression, but rather as the "Lord" described by Malachi, ἰδοὺ
ἔρχεται (Mal 3:1), who comes as judge of the temple, a "coming" wholly
different from the one the disciples and crowds expect.

### 1.3.5  Summary of Entry Narrative

We have seen how the entry narrative anticipates many of the key themes
that are developed in the latter part of Mark's gospel. Mark takes much
care in preparing the reader for seeing Jesus' coming to the temple as the
climax of "the way." The density of details, and thereby slower narrative
pace, all point to the momentous importance of Jesus' coming to
Jerusalem's temple. The absence of any mention of the temple, or more
importantly, any previous visit of Jesus to the temple in Mark's story,
shows how Mark reserves the temple as the place where Jesus' story will
reach its climax. The messianic and royal imagery evoked by Jesus' entry
illustrate the disciples' and crowd's misunderstanding of the nature of
Jesus' coming to the temple. The earlier allusions to Malachi's "Lord"
suddenly appearing in the temple to judge the sons of Levi serve as an
ominous anticipation of what will soon unfold in the temple. However, the
ambiguity surrounding the royal trappings of Jesus' entry will be carried

---

[63] Timothy J. Geddert, *Mark* (Scottdale, PA: Herald, 2001) 262.

[64] Matera explains well the narrative tension created by the ambiguity in Mark
surrounding Jesus' kingship: "The tension between such a blatantly royal tradition and its
anticlimactic, redactional setting is purposeful. Through it, Mark did not deny the
Davidic promises; rather he showed that they cannot yet be publicly proclaimed. It is no
accident that in this pericope Mark has not announced Jesus as the King of Israel and that
so much is done by allusion as if to create a sense of ambiguity. The reason is that the
redactor has carefully reserved the title 'King' for Chapter 15 when it will be impossible
to misunderstand the character of Jesus' kingship" (Matera, *Kingship*, 73).

forward in the story, as further questions are raised about the nature of Jesus' authority (Mark 11:28). The reader will move forward in the narrative with these questions in mind, the solution of which will not arrive fully until the trial and passion narrative. The last narrative use of "the way" (Mark 11:8) serves to highlight further how Jesus' journey reaches its final destination at the temple. Drawing on the Deutero-Isaianic imagery of the Lord's coming back to Zion along "the way," Mark shows that Jesus' journey to Jerusalem is the fulfillment of the Isaianic "way of the Lord." This "way" has taken an Isaianic path, but its destination follows the script of Malachi's "way," with the Lord coming to the temple in judgment. Thus, the reader is given important clues with the combination of the ὁ κύριος and ἡ ὁδός imagery, which together echo the eschatological warnings of Malachi 3. The eschatological importance of Jesus' encounter with the temple is also anticipated by the crowd's singing of Psalm 118 at Jesus' entry. This psalm is a pilgrim song about the temple. The crowd sings the song with clear messianic hopes, as they see Jesus as the "coming one" (ὁ ἐρχόμενος), a description that the reader well knows has already been ascribed to Jesus by one of the story's most authoritative characters, John the Baptist (Mark 1:7). This will not be the last time the reader hears of Psalm 118, as this temple psalm will play a key role in Jesus' self-identification during the encounter with Jerusalem's authorities in the temple. The nature of Jesus' "coming" and the relation of Jesus to the temple will be the focus of the following narrative, to which I now turn.

## 1.4 Demonstration in the Temple (11:15–19)

After briefly describing Jesus' initial arrival at the temple (11:11), I shall focus on Jesus' actions in the temple (vv. 15–16) and his teaching following the demonstration, based on Isaiah 56 and Jeremiah 7 (v. 17). Finally, I shall argue how Mark contextualizes, and thereby interprets, Jesus' demonstration by framing it with the two episodes of the barren fig tree (vv. 12–14 and 20–21).

### 1.4.1 Looking upon the Temple (11:11)

Those who accompany Jesus into Jerusalem hail his entry as the return of the kingdom of David (Mark 11:10). After the careful preparations for obtaining the colt and the exuberant procession that accompanies Jesus' entry into the temple, the subsequent scene certainly seems anticlimactic as Jesus, seemingly alone, looks around the temple and then leaves for Bethany. Mark's description of Jesus' "looking around at everything," περιβλεψάμενος πάντα, seems significant since verse 11 is redactional. Both Luke and Matthew omit verse 11, and much of the language is characteristically Markan.[65] Even if Mark inherited this from some traditional material, he nevertheless shaped it in its final form. Jesus' inspection is not that of a newcomer, since it must be assumed that he has been to the temple before, although Mark makes no mention of any other visit to the temple. It has been suggested that Mark depicts Jesus as looking around intently at the temple in order to show his careful planning of the demonstration. While this may be true, it seems even more that Mark is setting the ominous tone for the subsequent conflict.[66] The silence that greets Jesus' entry to the temple is striking, considering how quickly the acclaim dissipated.[67] Like in Mark's parable of the sower, the welcome extended to Jesus withers immediately on the rocky ground, and here the rocks are the stone pavement of the temple (Mark 4:6).[68] Jerusalem's failure to welcome Jesus is illustrated in the subsequent story of the barren fig tree (11:12–14). Verse 11 functions as a pregnant pause, giving time for

---

[65] William R. Telford (*The Barren Temple and the Withered Tree* [JSNTSup 1; Sheffield: JSOT, 1980] 45) observes, "The reference to Jesus' disciples as οἱ δώδεκα is typically Markan, it is generally held, and not the product of a special 'Twelve Source.' The loose linkage of separate pericopes with the use of καί with the verb of motion ἔρχεσθαι or its compounds (καὶ εἰσῆλθεν ... καὶ... ἐξῆλθεν) as well as by the temporal (ὀψὲ ἤδη οὔσης τῆς ὥρας) and the topographical datum (εἰς Ἱεροσόλυμα ... εἰς Βηθανίαν), the repetition of the preposition first in the compound verb and then independently before the following noun (εἰσῆλθεν εἰς Ἱεροσόλυμα), and even the verb περιβλέπειν have all likewise been identified as characteristic of his redactional procedure, style and vocabulary."

[66] Timothy J. Geddert (*Watchwords: Mark 13 in Markan Eschatology* [JSNTSup; Sheffield: JSOT, 1989] 129) believes that Mark's account of Jesus' inspection of the temple is aimed at showing Jesus to be the "Lord" who has come to inspect his temple: "And what about the innocent-sounding description of Jesus' 'inspection' the day he entered Jerusalem, 'and he looked around at everything' (11.11)? In Jer 7 the same sentiment sounds ominous: 'Has this house, which bears my Name, become a den of robbers to you? *But I have been watching!*', declares the Lord'. Does Mark suggest that Jesus was able to see from the divine perspective ... and that readers are called to do the same? Mark not only drops hints, he drops hints that he drops hints." See also P. W. L. Walker, *Jesus and the Holy City: New Testament Perspectives on Jerusalem* (Grand Rapids: Eerdmans, 1996) 6 n. 15.

[67] Moloney (*Mark*, 220) observes, "Jesus is the only active figure in 11:11. After the crowd and the acclamation of 11:7b–10, there is an ominous silence and even a note of threat as Jesus, alone, enters Jerusalem and goes into the temple."

[68] James Edwards observes (*The Gospel According to Mark* [Grand Rapids: Eerdmans, 2002] 338), "Like the seed in the parable of the sower that receives the word with joy but has no root and lasts but a short time (4:6,16–17), the crowd disperses as mysteriously as it assembled."

the narrative tension and the reader's anticipation to build as the conflict between Jesus and the temple establishment draws near.

## 1.4.2 Jesus' Actions in the Temple (vv. 15–16)

Jesus' actions in the temple have drawn a great deal of attention among scholars, particularly as they question Jesus' intentions: did he seek to cleanse the temple or condemn it? E. P. Sanders, in his book *Jesus and Judaism*, puts Jesus' temple demonstration at the focus of his historical sketch of Jesus' life. Sanders argued that the episode in the temple represents one of the most certain accounts of the historical Jesus, which became the proximate cause of his death. Since the publication of *Jesus and Judaism* in 1985, a great deal of debate and work has centered on Jesus' temple demonstration. Much of this work, however, has focused on the historical questions surrounding this episode. For example, how could Jesus have made a significant demonstration in the temple, while at the same time avoid arrest from the guardians of the temple or the Romans? In this study, however, the focus is not to reconstruct the historical situation or what Jesus' intentions were, but rather to look at the place of Jesus' temple demonstration in Mark's narrative and to understand Mark's interpretation of this episode better, how he employs it to color his story of Jesus.

Mark explores four of Jesus' particular actions to narrate the temple demonstration. They are: (1) expelling the buyers and sellers; (2) overturning the money-changers tables; (3) overturning the seats of dove-sellers; (4) preventing transport of temple vessels (σκεῦος). The first and last actions have the practical effect of shutting down the temple, while the two central actions point to one of the reasons for Jesus' shutting down the temple, the greedy exploitation of God's people in God's house. The demonstration, however, goes well beyond social protest in Mark's account.

The expulsion of the πωλοῦντας and the ἀγοράζοντας makes the necessary procurement of animals – essential for the sacrificial cult of the temple – impossible. The temple cult required unblemished sacrifices, and so the buying and selling of animals was a natural part of temple operations. To exclude the business of buying and selling animals, for all practical purposes, is to bring the service of the temple to an end.[69]

---

[69] E. P. Sanders observes (*Jesus and Judaism* [Philadelphia: Fortress, 1985] 63), "There was not an 'original' time when worship at the temple had been 'pure' from the business which the requirement of unblemished sacrifices creates. Further, no one remembered a time when pilgrims, carrying various coinages, had not come. In the view of Jesus and his contemporaries, the requirement to sacrifice must always have involved

Scholars have often suggested that Jesus was simply cleansing the temple and not condemning it. Here, however, my focus must remain on Mark's narrative. Does Mark view Jesus' actions as a cleansing of the holy temple from trade, or is the demonstration of the Markan Jesus aimed to protest and end the cultic system itself?

Vincent Taylor's view, that Jesus was protesting the abuses of those who sold animals and changed coinage at the expense of pilgrims, is representative of the "cleansing" interpretation: "The action of Jesus is a spirited protest against injustice and the abuse of the Temple system. There is no doubt that pilgrims were fleeced by traders..."[70] If, however, it was Mark's aim to show Jesus cleansing the temple from the abuses of those who sold to the people, then why does he show Jesus driving out both the πωλοῦντας and the ἀγοράζοντας?[71] Why would those who are being fleeced, the ἀγοράζοντας, be on the receiving end of Jesus' demonstration, if the goal was simply to protest unjust business practices? An interpretation that reads this demonstration as a social protest fits Luke's account of the demonstration, ἤρξατο ἐκβάλλειν τοὺς πωλοῦντας (Luke 19:45b), far better than Mark's account. Luke makes no mention of the ἀγοράζοντας, which is undoubtedly for the purpose of highlighting that Jesus' actions are against corrupt trading. Had Mark wanted to show that Jesus was simply protesting shady business practices, why would he have Jesus expelling the innocent customers along with the corrupt traders?[72]

The overturning of the money-changers' tables and the seats of those who sold pigeons raises the same questions. The pigeons were the sacrifice

---

the supply of sacrificial animals, their inspection, and the changing of money. Thus one may wonder what scholars have in mind who talk about Jesus' desire to stop this 'particular use' of the temple. Just what would be left of the service if the supposedly corrupting externalism of sacrifices, and the trade necessary to them, were purged?"

[70] Vincent Taylor, *The Gospel According to Mark* (London: Macmillan & Co., 1963) 463.

[71] "His attack on the traders and money-changers, who were there in the Court of the Gentiles with permission of the temple authorities and who provided a convenient and probably essential service to worshippers visiting the temple from outside Jerusalem, was not simply (if it was at all) a protest against exploitation by unscrupulous traders. It extended also to their customers (τοὺς ἀγοράζοντας) and even to anyone who was carrying things through the area" (France, *Mark*, 437).

[72] "It should be noted, further, that the 'purification from whatever abuse manifest in the trade'interpretation would best account for the Lukan form of v. 15 which mentions the sellers only. The interpretation completely ignores that the expulsion of the πωλοῦντας was accompanied by that of the ἀγοράζοντας" (Tom Holmén, *Jesus and Jewish Covenant Thinking* [Boston: Brill, 2001] 316–17).

for the poor.[73] The multitude of pilgrims, who came from all over the Greco-Roman world, needed to exchange their foreign currencies for Tyrian coinage, the standard currency of the temple. The money was needed for donations to temple, the temple tax, and the many items necessary for their offerings. Pilgrims to the temple needed money-changers, as the business of money changing was necessary for the daily religious business of the temple.[74] Why, then, does Jesus overturn (κατέστρεψεν) the tables of the money-changers and the seats (τὰς καθέδρας) of the money-changers, who provided a necessary service for pilgrims?[75] Indeed, the word καταστρέφω typically means to destroy a place or building, and thus Mark describes Jesus' action with the provocative image of destruction.[76]

One of the most important services the money-changers provided pilgrims was the proper money to pay the half-shekel tax. This tax, required annually by every Jewish man, went to the general fund that paid for the daily whole offerings. As Neusner observes, "These daily whole-offerings, it is clear, derive from communal funds, provided by every Israelite equally. They serve all Israelites individually and collectively, as

---

[73] For an account of how the overthrowing of the seats of those who sold pigeons relates to the exploitation of the poor, see Matthew, *Temple-Criticism*, 143–45.

[74] Peter Richardson argues that the Tyrian shekels had the image of the god Melkart, with the Tyrian (Ptolemaic) eagle on the other side. Therefore, he suggests, Jesus overturns the tables of the money-changers out of protest for the blasphemous images. Richardson's thesis is focused on a historical reconstruction of Jesus' aims, whereas we are focusing on Mark's purposes for presenting the incident in the manner and context of his narrative. Since Mark does not give any hints at the images of the coins here (as he does for the Roman coin in 12:16) and places this action against the money-changers along with his action against those buying and selling and with those who sell pigeons, the overall thrust of the temple demonstration in Mark is not against idolatrous images. This is particularly clear in the teaching that immediately follows, which condemns the temple for being a den of thieves and failing to be a house of prayer for all peoples. If there was a desire to condemn an implicit idolatry, there were certainly many prophetic oracles that could have been highlighted in Jesus' teaching. See Peter Richardson, "Why Turn the Tables? Jesus' Protest in the Temple Precincts," in *Society of Biblical Literature 1992 Seminar Papers* (ed. E. H Lovering; SBLSP 31; Atlanta: Scholars, 1992) 507–23, especially 515.

[75] Derrett suggests that καθέδρα implies that those who sat, presiding over the sale of pigeons, were of the rank of teachers. This imagery may hint that those who possessed these seats had authority and were people of consequence, thus members of the temple establishment (J. D. M. Derrett, "The Zeal of the House and the Cleansing of the Temple," *Downside Review* 95 [1977] 84).

[76] Luke's account of the temple demonstration is toned down, as he does not even use καταστρέφω, while Matthew follows Mark (Matt 21:12).

atonement for sin."[77] This is based on Exodus 30:16, "And you shall take
the atonement money from the people of Israel, and shall appoint it for the
service of the tent of meeting; that it may bring the people of Israel to
remembrance before the Lord, so as to make atonement for yourselves." If
the money-changers served pilgrims for providing for the vital funds that
paid for the daily whole offerings, which brought expiation for sin, what
could Jesus' action against the money-changers mean? Of course, it could
be a protest against unjust profiteering, but even if this is the case, the
question is not whether Jesus' actions are provoked by the fleecing of the
people at the hands of the temple authorities but rather what Jesus' protest,
according to Mark, was ultimately signifying.[78] By overturning these
tables, was Jesus claiming that the temple was no longer the place for
atonement because of its corrupt stewards?

### 1.4.3  *Καὶ οὐκ ἤφιεν ἵνα τις διενέγκῃ σκεῦος διὰ τοῦ ἱεροῦ (v. 16)*

Verse 16 is unique to Mark and illustrates how much emphasis Mark gives
to Jesus' temple demonstration. This action, like the expulsion of the
πωλοῦντας and the ἀγοράζοντας, is not aimed at the temple authorities
alone, since he prohibits "anyone" (τις) from carrying a σκεῦος through the
temple. Before I explore the purpose of the prohibition, I must examine
what Mark intends the reader to understand by the term σκεῦος. Ford
accounts for six different meanings that σκεῦος can have in biblical Greek:
(1) household utensil; (2) agricultural implements; (3) military equipment;
(4) fishing tackle; (5) cultic vessel; and (6) luggage or baggage.[79] Ford
argues that σκεῦος means money bags, relating them to the money-changers
and the use of the temple as a bank. This interpretation would make more
sense if Mark put this prohibition right after the overturning of the money-
changers' tables. The other significant problem is that many things would
need to be carried through the temple, such as cultic vessels, which is one
of the meanings Ford gives for σκεῦος. Since the prohibition is against

---

[77] Although Neusner draws his conclusions from the Mishna, there is good evidence
that this understanding was current in Jesus' day, as it was based on Exodus 30:11–16.
We also know, for example, that the Essenes disagreed with the view of the Pharisees,
since they held that, in light of Exodus 30:11–16, the tax should only be levied once in a
lifetime and not annually (4Q159 2.6–7). That this was an issue in Jesus' day is reflected
in the story of Matt 17:24–27. See Jacob Neusner, "Money-Changers in the Temple: The
Mishnah's Explanation," *NTS* 35 (1989) 288–89.

[78] "None the less, it must be stressed here that in the light of the importance of the
temple tax to second-temple Judaism, the overturning of the money-changers tables was
indeed a very provocative act on part of Jesus" (Kim Tan, *The Zion Traditions and the
Aims of Jesus* [SNTS 91; Cambridge: Cambridge University, 1997] 167–68).

[79] M. J. Ford, "Money Bags in the Temple (Mk. 11, 16)," *Bib* 57 (1976) 249–53.

"anyone" (τις), and many people would be carrying all kinds of things through the temple – not just money bags – the prohibition in Mark's account makes no distinction. Therefore, to narrow the scope of what was prohibited from transport to only money bags would be to read more into the text than it can bear; this is why few scholars have followed Ford's reading of σκεῦος.[80]

Given that the context for the σκεῦος is the temple, it would seem most fitting that Mark intends σκεῦος to be understood as a cultic vessel. Kelber illustrates the viability of this reading: "Yet again, attention must be directed to the fact that it is *dia tou hierou* that a *skeuos* is forbidden to be carried. What other significance can *skeuos*, vessel, in conjunction with *to hieron*, temple, have but that of a sacred cult vessel?"[81] Kelber notes that over one third of the references to σκεῦος in the LXX denote a sacred cult object.[82] Since Mark says that Jesus prohibited "anyone," τις, from carrying a σκεῦος through the ἱερόν, the reader of Mark would see Jesus' action as going against the normal temple operations.

Tom Holmén, however, argues that the meaning of verse 16 is obscure: "As a matter of fact, today's scholarship has remained quite perplexed in trying to explain the meaning of the gesture accounted in this verse, while the other informative items have gathered a considerable amount of plausible suggestions as to their import."[83] The reason why Holmén claims that much more can be said about Jesus' other actions in the temple demonstration, apart from the prohibition of the σκεῦος, is that the expulsion of τοὺς ἀγοράζοντας and the overturning of the money-changers' tables, and the seats of those who sold pigeons, all relate to business within the temple. But the transport of the σκεῦος is not a matter of business and money, but simply a practical necessity for the daily operations of the temple. Therefore, Holmén finds verse 16 ambiguous, because Jesus' prohibition has no connection to social injustice. In other words, if Jesus were demonstrating solely against the financial exploitation of the temple authorities, why would he prohibit anyone from carrying the sacred vessels through the temple?

The answer is simple. Mark does not intend to portray Jesus' demonstration simply as a social protest but rather as a prophetic gesture foretelling the eschatological end of the temple. The only satisfactory conclusion a reader of Mark could make of Jesus' prohibition of the transport of a σκεῦος through the temple is that Jesus was acting against

---

[80] For one of the few who follow M. J. Ford, see Matthew, *Temple-Criticism*, 145–47.

[81] Kelber, *Kingdom*, 101.

[82] Ibid., 101 n. 43. Kelber cites Christian Maurer, "σκεῦος," (*TDNT* 7. 359).

[83] Holmén, *Jesus and Jewish Covenant Thinking*, 309.

the temple. Telford makes a similar claim: "Jesus' action then, according to Mark, was aimed directly against the sacrificial cultus, there being no more effective means of stopping the flow of sacrifices than by seizing the vessels in which gifts and offerings were received and carried by the priests (on behalf of worshippers) *through* the various Temple courts to the altar."[84] By stopping the flow of traffic and transport within the temple, Jesus brought the temple to a virtual standstill. Thus, Kelber observes: "Understood in a religious sense, the obstruction of the vessel's transport effects the cessation of the temple's cultic functions. In the view of Mark, therefore, Jesus not only puts an end to the temple's business operation, but he also suspends the practice of cult and ritual. At this point the temple no longer operates. It is shut down in all its functions."[85] What was the purpose of temporarily shutting down the flow of sacrifices? The purpose was for a prophetic sign. The shutting down of the temple cult, albeit temporarily, signified that soon the temple would be permanently silenced. I now turn from Jesus' actions to his words in the temple demonstration. This will shed light on Mark's understanding for why the temple is condemned.

### 1.4.4 Teaching (v. 17)

The opening phrase is a conventional Markan expression, καὶ ἐδίδασκεν καὶ ἔλεγεν (e.g., Mark 1:21; 2:13; 9:31).[86] The teaching consists of a conflation of two prophetic texts, Isa 56:7c and Jer 7:11. Although these citations from the prophets closely follow the LXX, Mark has subtly shaped them. The quotation from the latter part of Isa 56:7 is an assertion in Isaiah, but in Mark it is posed as a question: οὐ γέγραπται ὅτι ὁ οἶκός μου οἶκος προσευχῆς κληθήσεται πᾶσιν τοῖς ἔθνεσιν; In Jer 7:11 the phrase containing σπήλαιον λῃστῶν is posed as a question; however, Mark makes it an assertion: ὑμεῖς δὲ πεποιήκατε αὐτὸν σπήλαιον λῃστῶν. This rhetorical reversal highlights how the temple establishment has likewise reversed the order of things that God, according to Isaiah 56, has set down.[87] Thus, the assertion from the prophecy of Deutero-Isaiah that

---

[84] Telford, *Barren Temple*, 93 n. 102.

[85] Kelber, *Kingdom*, 101.

[86] Taylor, *Mark*, 463.

[87] "The verse part quoting Isa 56:7 contains an assertion, while in Jer 7:11 there is a question. In Mark 11:17b–c the reverse is true. The verse part quoting Isa 56:7 is embedded in a question, but the allusion to Jer 7:11 puts forward an assertion. So, what the Bible asserts (the Temple is a house of prayer), needs to be questioned now, but what it inquires ('has this house, which is called by my name, become a den of robbers in your sight?'), is now affirmed" (Holmén, *Jesus and Jewish Covenant Thinking*, 310).

God's house is to be a house of prayer for all nations must seriously be questioned in light of the temple leaders' policies. Moreover, Jesus' teaching makes certain that the temple has indeed been turned into a den of thieves, thus providing an answer to the question posed by God in Jeremiah. This is evidenced by the fact that the verb here πεποιήκατε, "have made," is stative. The rhetorical reversal, from assertion to question and vice versa, is unique to Mark and is intended to intensify the tone of judgment against the temple. In addition, by showing Jesus as having license to apply the oracles of the prophets to the temple, Mark highlights Jesus' authority, which will soon be questioned (v. 28).

Another element of Jesus' teaching that reflects Mark's style is the combination of two Scripture passages, Isa 56:7 and Jer 7:11. From the opening verses of Mark we have seen a proclivity for the conflation of texts with the combination of Exod 23:20 with Mal 3:1.[88] This pattern is typical of Mark and runs throughout his narrative (e.g., the combination of Isa 5:1–2 with Ps 118:22–23 in Mark 11:1–11; the combination of Dan 7:13 with Ps 110:1 in Jesus' answer to the high priest in Mark 14:62.[89] In the current example, the two different passages work well together by the natural antithesis between "house of prayer" and the "den of thieves."

Scholars have raised questions about the historical authenticity of v. 17 going back to Jesus.[90] Very few scholars doubt the authenticity of Jesus' actions in the temple, but they have less certainty about the teaching contained in v. 17. Again, I am not as directly concerned with the historical origins as I am with how Mark intended this verse to be understood.

It is worth remembering that there are many scriptural texts related to the temple, with no lack of passages concerning temple cleansing (e.g., Jehoash in 2 Kings 12; Hezekiah in 2 Chronicles 29; Josiah in 2 Chronicles 34). The selection of Isa 56:7 and Jer 7:11 must have been purposefully

---

[88] Marcus, *The Way of the Lord*, 13.

[89] Kee, "The Function of Scriptural Quotations," 165–88. Kee argues that the combining of two or more OT texts is a common feature of Mark, which he calls a "synthesizing process of Mark" (ibid., 177).

[90] Against the historicity of the passage, see, e.g., Sanders, *Jesus and Judaism*, 66–67 and A. E. Harvey, *Jesus and the Constraints of History* (London: Duckworth, 1982) 132. The skepticism of Sanders and Harvey have provoked a strong response, see, e.g., Evans, *Mark*, 174–79; Tan, *Zion Traditions*, 181–85; Hooker, "Traditions," 7–19. One of the main arguments of Sanders against the authenticity of v. 17 is the argument made by Harvey that the Hebrew text does not match the LXX version of Isa 56:7. However, Hooker demonstrates that Harvey misread the Hebrew text, which closely matches the LXX version.

chosen.[91] In quoting Isa 56:7, Jesus is pictured assuming the first person address of Yhwh. This not only grants Jesus a position of profound authority; it shifts the emphasis of the temple – it is now ὁ οἶκός μου. Thus, Jesus acts not only with the authority of God, but also as owner of the house. This motif will be played out in the subsequent parable of the wicked tenants, where Jesus describes himself as the son (heir) of the vineyard (12:6–7). The oracle of Isaiah therefore allows Jesus to make a subtle but bold claim to the temple, illustrating his authority over it.

Another striking aspect of the Isaiah oracle, chosen no doubt to complement Jesus' actions, is that this oracle describes the temple simply in terms of prayer, οἶκος προσευχῆς. There is no reference in this prophecy to the primary purpose of the temple – cultic sacrifice and atonement. "It is referred to in this context as a 'house of prayer,' rather than as a place of sacrifice."[92] The only acceptable sacrifice and atonement in Mark's story is Jesus', which stands out by the complete silence regarding the temple's function. Indeed, the only direct reference to cultic sacrifices that occurs while Jesus is in the temple actually confirms their displacement in Jesus' teaching. Jesus confirms the wisdom that love of God and neighbor "is much more than all whole burnt offerings and sacrifices" (Mark 12:33). Such a bold observation, made in the midst of the institution dedicated to burnt offerings and sacrifices, is aimed at diminishing the value of the temple for the Markan reader.

Jesus clearly asserts that the temple is to be an οἶκος προσευχῆς. Throughout the OT and NT, the term οἶκος, "house," is used for the temple. However, οἶκος serves as an important motif in Mark's story.[93] Instead of gathering at the synagogue (συναγωγή), Jesus and those who follow him are constantly gathering (συνάγω) at an οἶκος (e.g., Mark 2:1–2; 1:33; and συνέρχομαι in 3:20). Because the actions enclosed by a house parallel those enclosed by a synagogue, Elizabeth Malbon argues: "Thus, the Markan significance of 'house' (including 'his house' at 2:15) is to be understood in relation to the Markan significance of 'synagogue and

---

[91] Walker, *Holy City*, 6: "The Markan Jesus could have quoted other Old Testament passages which spoke of God's desire to 'reform' the Temple, but this one [Jer 7:11] spoke ominously of its destruction as the only solution."

[92] Howard Clark Kee, "Christology in Mark's Gospel," in *Judaisms and Their Messiahs at the Turn of the Christian Era* (ed. Jacob Neusner, William Scott Green, and Ernest S. Frerichs; Cambridge: Cambridge University Press, 1987) 199. He goes on to observe, "The only sacrifice mentioned favorably in Mark is that of Jesus himself. From Jesus there is no hint of regret or of ultimate restoration of the Temple and its cultus in Mark."

[93] Elizabeth Struthers Malbon, "OIKIA AYTOY: Mark 2:15 in Context," *NTS* 31 (1985) 282–92.

'temple.'"[94] The opposition between synagogue and house in the first half of the gospel is continued in the second half, with the temple taking the place of the synagogue. Jesus demonstrates and teaches in the temple, but he stays, significantly, at the οἶκος of Simon the leper in Bethany (14:3; see also the reference to his lodging in Bethany in 11:11). "But may it not be that the house," concludes Malbon, "which replaces the synagogue and stands in opposition to the doomed temple in Mark, does suggest the early Christian community?"[95] The call for a place of prayer has yet to be fulfilled, and this suggests that Mark believed the place of prayer to be none other than the Christian community, the true οἶκος of Jesus. Such an interpretation would have been an easy one for Mark's first readers, as the Christians gathered in their small communities in private homes.[96] The future tense employed in the oracle, that the temple "shall be called (κληθήσεται) a house of prayer," points to a future fulfillment, a time beyond the present story, a time that the Markan reader would have very well seen as his own.

The future tense of the oracle also highlights the eschatological character of this passage in its original context. The context of Isaiah 56 is the final time of salvation, the long-awaited deliverance that is revealed by the Lord (Isa 56:1). This prophecy concerns the eschatological hopes of restoration and renewal.[97] The climax of this deliverance is that those who are foreigners (Isa 56:3) will have an equal share in this salvation. Therefore, the house of the Lord shall be for πᾶσιν τοῖς ἔθνεσιν (Isa 56:7c; Mark 11:17). Mark is the only one of the gospel writers who records the distinctive phrase, "for all nations." The inclusion of the Gentiles, ἔθνη, is therefore particularly important for Mark. For instance, the climax of the Markan story comes with a Roman soldier's confession of faith (15:39). It is not accidental that the text quoted by Jesus in the temple is eschatological. This picks up the constant tone throughout Mark, that the fullness of time (πεπλήρωται ὁ καιρός) has arrived (Mark 1:15). The Jerusalem temple, unable to draw the Gentiles into prayer, is part of the old

---

[94] Ibid., 287.

[95] Ibid., 288.

[96] Sharyn E. Dowd, *Reading Mark: A Literary and Theological Commentary on the Second Gospel* (Macon, GA: Smyth and Helwys, 2000) 122. "For the Markan community prayer takes place, not in a temple 'made with hands,' but in the groups that meet together in homes – 'in the house' where the Markan Jesus teaches his often confused and frightened disciples."

[97] For the important connection between Isaiah 56 and the hope for the eschatological restoration of Israel that would include the nations, see Tan (*Zion Traditions*, 188–92) and Steven M. Bryan (*Jesus and Israel's Traditions of Judgment and Restoration* [SNTS 117; Cambridge: Cambridge University Press, 2002] 222).

age and is therefore doomed; the eschatological plans of God are now being ushered in by Jesus. The temple cannot be reformed, if for no other reason than there is no time left to reform – the eschatological time is at hand.

The context of Isaiah 56 provides a transition to Jeremiah 7. The eschatological gathering of the Gentiles "is followed at once, however, by passages strongly critical of the present condition of Israel (56:9–12; 57:1–12). Gentiles are to be welcomed in, but the present people of Israel, especially their supposed leaders and guardians (56:10f) are under judgment."[98] Just as the leaders of Israel are the object of judgment in the Isaian oracle, so too in Mark's narrative the leaders bear the blame for the Lord's "house of prayer" being turned into a "den of thieves."

Before I discuss the larger context in Jeremiah 7, from which the phrase σπήλαιον ληστῶν, following the LXX, is taken, I shall make an observation about Mark's rhetorical focus. Jeremiah 7 is closely connected to the previous oracle of Isaiah. The temple, according to Isaiah 56:7, was to be a "house of prayer." "But," the Markan Jesus asserts, "you have made it a den of thieves." Note that the temple is in sharp focus throughout both OT citations. The temple that should be a οἶκος προσευχῆς is instead a σπήλαιον ληστῶν. "To put it in another way: It is not a 'den robber' that is at issue here but a 'robber den.' The Markan text does not identify the people with 'robbers' but the Temple with the 'den.'"[99] The target of the teaching, just as with the actions, is the temple itself. Too often, because of the culpability of the temple establishment, interpreters focus on the Jewish leadership and miss the thrust of the narrative – the corruption and self-serving leadership is poignantly judged by bringing the temple institution to an end.

Jesus' accusation that the leaders (addressed simply as ὑμεῖς) have made the temple a σπήλαιον ληστῶν is taken from Jeremiah's speech against the temple, wherein he boldly threatened the temple's destruction.[100] There is a striking correspondence between the context of Jeremiah's speech and Jesus' demonstration in the temple. The parallels are so strong that they invite comparison. Indeed, Watty observes, "the context of the prophecy is as significant for the understanding of the quotation as the quotation itself."[101] Most importantly, both Jeremiah and Jesus give their address against the temple from the midst of the temple (Jer 7:2). The priests arrest

---

[98] N. T. Wright, *Jesus and the Victory of God* (Minneapolis: Fortress, 1996) 418.

[99] Holmén, *Jesus and Jewish Covenant Thinking*, 325.

[100] The citation of Jer 7:11 follows the LXX.

[101] William W. Watty, "Jesus and the Temple – Cleansing or Cursing," *ExpTim* 93/8 (1982) 238.

Jeremiah for his speech, sentence him to death, and hand him over to the princes, although they spare his life (Jer 26:8, 11). The chief priests respond to Jesus' words by plotting to kill him; however, they wait for fear of the crowds (Mark 11:18). The reference to the temple as God's house in Isaiah 56:7 (Mark 11:17) is repeatedly found in Jeremiah 7 (e.g. Jer 7:2,10,14,30 and most especially v. 11). One of the primary charges of Jeremiah is the almost universal greed, "everyone is greedy for unjust gain; from prophet to priest every one deals falsely." This accusation actually frames the antitemple speech of Jeremiah (Jer 6:13; 8:10). Note that the priests are named in Jeremiah, and they are the implicit target of Jesus' critique, as Mark 11:18 and 12:12 illustrate. Certainly, the charge of unjust gain fits well with the protest embodied in Jesus' actions as well as his words in the temple (e.g., Mark 12:38–40).

What is more, the Targum Jeremiah 8:10 substitutes for "prophet and priest" "scribe and priest" and calls them "robbers of money."[102] This tradition, which Hayward believes goes back to or just before the first century A.D., fits well with Mark.[103] The denunciation against the oppression of the alien (Jer 7:6) is reminiscent of Jesus' concern for the temple being a "house of prayer for all nations." Many small details correspond, such as mention of the oppression of the widow (Jer 7:6) with Jesus' concern for the oppression of widows (Mark 12:40, 42–43). Jeremiah's attack upon the value of the sacrificial cult, particularly his criticism of it in light of the importance of obedience and walking in God's ways (Jer 7:21–24), matches well with Jesus' similar affirmations in his dialogue with the scribe in the temple, where sacrifices are secondary to love (Mark 12:33). Jeremiah has God complain ἐξαπέστειλα πρὸς ὑμᾶς πάντας τοὺς δούλους μου τοὺς προφήτας, which is strikingly similar to Jesus' parable of the wicked tenants, where the owner (God) ἀπέστειλεν πρὸς τοὺς ... δοῦλον with other servants sent later (Mark 12:2,4). The sending (ἀποστέλλω) and the servants (δοῦλοι) are so similar that one wonders whether the Markan Jesus has adopted the words of Jeremiah 7:25 into his parable. This may not be the only narrative echo to Jeremiah 7 in the Markan temple scene; the withered fig tree in Mark 11:20 may be an allusion to Jeremiah 8:13: "When I would gather them, says the Lord, there are no grapes on the vine, nor figs on the fig tree; even the leaves are withered, and what I gave them has passed away from them." The inability of gathering figs and grapes is a motif that follows Jesus' temple

---

[102] Robert Hayward, *The Targum of Jeremiah* (The Aramaic Bible 12; Wilmington: Glazier, 1987) 74.

[103] Ibid., 38. See also Craig Evans, "Jesus' Action in the Temple: Cleansing or Portent of Destruction?" *CBQ* 51 (1989) 237–70, esp. 268.

demonstration (Mark 11:13,20 barren fig tree; 12:1–8 fruit of the vineyard). Thus, Geddert believes that "in chapters 11–15 of Mark, alert readers detect an astonishing number of allusions to Jeremiah 7."[104] These allusions led Richard Horsley to claim that Jesus patterned his demonstration in the temple on Jeremiah 7.[105] Given the allusions to Jeremiah 7 that are scattered throughout Mark's narrative, namely, the temple narrative of Mark 11–12, it seems clear that the interpretive context of Jeremiah 7 is vital for discerning how Mark understands Jesus' relationship to the temple.

Interpretation of Jer 7:11 has focused, with good reason, upon the crucial term λῃστής. Since this comes at the climax of Jesus' demonstration, it is paramount. First, as all agree, it must be observed that the term λῃστής does not simply mean thief but rather a robber (through violence).[106] This is the term that Josephus uses to characterize the insurgents, whom he blames for ushering in the violence that characterized and led to the Jewish revolt against Rome, which ended in the destruction of Jerusalem and the temple in A.D. 70.[107] Although the Greek term λῃστής means one who robs with violence, in first-century Palestine the term more typically denoted bandits and brigands, or from the Roman perspective, insurgents.[108] This is found both in Josephus and in the NT, where, for example, the brigands who violently rob the good Samaritan are called λῃσταί (Luke 10:36), and the two who are crucified with Jesus are referred to as λῃσταί, that is, insurrectionists (Mark 15:27). The problem is that λῃσταί, employed by Jesus in Mark 11:17, cannot simply refer to those engaged in dishonest economic activities, but rather brigands or insurrectionists perpetrating violence.[109] But how could this relate to the temple establishment?

---

[104] Geddert, *Mark*, 267.

[105] Richard A. Horsley, *Hearing the Whole Story: The Politics of Plot in Mark's Gospel* (Louisville: Westminster John Knox, 2001) 110.

[106] G. W. Buchanan, "Symbolic Money-Changers in the Temple?" *NTS* 37 (1991) 288: "The significance of the fact that the word used for 'brigand' here is not κλέπτης, a thief, but λῃστής, a highway robber or brigand, has been known for more than thirty years." See also his earlier article, "Mark 11:15–19: Brigands in the Temple," *HUCA* 30 (1959) 169–77.

[107] Josephus, *Ant.* 14.15 §415–16; 15.10 §§345–48; *War* 1.16 §§304–11.

[108] Marcus J. Borg, *Conflict, Holiness, and Politics in the Teachings of Jesus* (Harrisburg, PA: Trinity, 1984) 185–86.

[109] Thus Borg observes, "Contrary to the most common interpretation, 'robbers' almost certainly cannot refer to economic dishonesty on the part of the merchants, or to the inappropriateness of commercial activity in the Temple precincts" (ibid., 185).

Two answers have arisen in response to the interpretative problems surrounding λησταί. The first perspective is that Mark uses λησταί metaphorically.[110] This view, espoused by those who want to interpret Jesus' demonstration as a "cleansing" of the temple, focuses on the "robbing" connection of the term and sees the "violent" element as hyperbole. For example, Evans argues that the chief priests were clearly dishonest thieves, while he downplays the violence aspect as rhetorical overkill: "Moreover, the citation of this prophetic text is more rhetorical than it is descriptive of what actually was going on. It is suitable for the occasion because it refers to temple corruption in general, not because the temple priests of Jesus' time were actually behaving as brigands."[111] In this perspective, the problematic term is read in light of the economic injustice perpetuated by the temple establishment as the primary thrust of Jesus' actions in his demonstration.

The other interpretive perspective, perhaps more common, is that the term λῃστής is employed by Mark in view of the Jewish Revolt.[112] Josephus records how the insurgents used the temple as a fortress from which they fought the Romans.[113] Thus, Moloney observes, "These events, fresh in the minds of the readers of the Gospel of Mark (who are hearing of wars and rumors of wars: 13:7), provide contemporary meaning to Jesus' accusation. In the immediate postwar period, Mark's readers and listeners are aware that the temple, reduced to a σπήλαιον λῃστῶν by the leaders of Israel in revolt, has been destroyed by the Roman armies."[114] Thus, the term reflects Mark's perspective, and that of his readers as to what the temple will later become.

The first position waters down the linguistic meaning of λῃστής, viewing it simply as metaphor; the latter perspective has stronger linguistic and historical weight. The metaphor argument is at first persuasive because of its connection to the social injustice of the temple establishment, a perspective clearly found in Mark (e.g., Mark 12:38–40). However, the second narrative is also quite viable, given Mark's narrative tapestry. What if Mark's perspective, that the temple was a den of violent brigands, was interwoven with the Markan narrative? One should almost suspect this,

---

[110] Evans, "Jesus' Action," 268; Tan, *Zion Traditions*, 183–85; Matthew, *Temple-Criticism*, 151.

[111] Evans, ibid.

[112] Buchanan, "Brigands," 176–77; Borg, *Conflict, Holiness, and Politics*, 185–86; Moloney, *Mark*, 225–26; Sanders, *Jesus and Judaism*, 66–67; Gaston, *No Stone on Another*, 85.

[113] Josephus, *War* 6.2 §121.

[114] Moloney, *Mark*, 225.

given how the Jewish Revolt would be seared on the consciousness of Mark and his readers, as Moloney observed. Is there any evidence for this?

There are several clues, scattered in the Markan narrative, that the post-A.D. 70 perspective of ληστής is written into Mark's story. First, Mark employs the term ληστής at two crucial points in the passion narrative. Second, who above all else has been the victim of the violent brigands holed up in the temple for Mark but Jesus? Could the accusation of being ληστής be related to the violent death of Jesus, according to the Markan story? There are some strong hints that this is precisely Mark's understanding. First, the immediate response of the chief priests and scribes to Jesus' demonstration is to seek a way to kill him (Mark 11:18). The attempt to seize him violently takes place again shortly thereafter in the temple (Mark 12:12 and 14:1–2). Indeed, in the parable of the wicked tenants, Jesus describes the temple establishment as robbing God (by taking the fruit of the vineyard) through violence to his servants and finally killing the heir of the vineyard, the owner's son, who obviously stands for Jesus (12:1–9). When Jesus is arrested in the garden, he questions why the leaders send out men armed with swords and clubs, "Have you come out as against a ληστής?" (Mark 14:48). The image is clear, a ληστής is one who is armed and dangerous, which is precisely the position of those who arrest Jesus.

It may be objected that all these occurrences come after 11:17, so how could the Markan reader be expected to understand 11:17 in such a way before reading further? However, the Markan reader already knows the end of the story, that Jesus is violently killed, as well as the story of A.D. 70. Second, in the three passion predictions, Mark has already forewarned the reader that the leaders of Israel would perpetrate a violent end upon Jesus (Mark 8:31; 9:31–32; 10:33). On two of those occasions, the perpetrators are named as the chief priests and scribes (8:31; 10:33). Thus Mark, who has already shown Jesus predicting his violent death at the hands of the chief priests and scribes, presents Jesus as condemning the temple leaders, λησταί, precisely because they will kill him. Indeed, the plotting of Jesus' death had already occurred in the early part of Mark's story (Mark 3:6). Thus for Mark, what the temple became in A.D. 66–70 (during the Jewish Revolt) it had earlier become through the violent opposition to Jesus.

### 1.4.5  Fig Tree (11:12–14, 20–21)

Mark has carefully framed the temple demonstration with two interrelated episodes of Jesus cursing the fig tree (Mark 11:12–14 and 20–21). The scene is remarkable in a number of ways: for example, why does Jesus curse the fruitless tree? This action is particularly perplexing because it was not the season, ὁ καιρός, as Mark explains, for figs (v. 13). Just as

Jesus' search for fruit was out of season, so too does Jesus' cursing seem out of character. Indeed, this is the only negative mighty deed that Jesus performs in Mark's narrative. The Markan reader, accustomed to Jesus' authority to perform mighty deeds of exorcism, healing, and control of nature would still be surprised to see Jesus employ his authority negatively. This action becomes all the more stark as the reader realizes that this is the only mighty deed Jesus performs in Jerusalem (Mark 11–16). The framing of the temple demonstration with the fig tree is also unique to Mark. All this points to the salience of the fig tree for Mark's narrative flow. By framing the temple demonstration with this poignant and perplexing problem of the fruitless fig tree, Mark has carefully juxtaposed Jesus' condemnation of the tree with the temple, thereby making the two events mutually interpretive.[115]

Thus, the reader's experience of the fig tree would be significant, as Mark surely intended. For the discerning Markan reader, however, the significance of the fig tree is heightened when one becomes aware of the freighted vocabulary that Mark employs. After Jesus curses the tree, the narrator comments that the disciples heard Jesus, καὶ ἤκουον οἱ μαθηταί (11:14b). This narrative note seems odd, since the Markan reader would have assumed that Jesus' words were heard. However, by explicitly stating this, Mark is able to evoke one of his key themes. Earlier, Mark had forewarned readers for the need of discerning ears (4:23). Indeed, in the parable of the sower, the good soil is characterized as "those who hear," οἵτινες ἀκούουσιν (4:20). Is Mark therefore illustrating the need for a deeper discernment?

This is confirmed in vv. 20 and 21, when the story of the fig tree is resumed the following day. As Jesus and the disciples pass by the tree, they see (εἶδον) the fig tree withered away to its roots (ἐξηραμμένην ἐκ ῥιζῶν, v. 20). The image of withered away to roots may echo the seed sown on rocky ground, which withered for lack of roots (διὰ τὸ μὴ ἔχειν ῥίζαν ἐξηράνθη, 4:6). After seeing the withered tree in v. 22, Peter remembers (ἀναμνησθείς), Jesus' words and points out their efficacy upon the now-withered tree. Geddert explains well the significance of this clustering of Markan key words, "These three key words, 'hear,' 'see,' and 'remember,' are used 8:14–21 to teach the disciples about discernment." They recur here in a text that calls on the disciples and the readers to discern what is really being said."[116] Undoubtedly Geddert is correct to see

---

[115] "Any attempt, therefore, to elucidate the Markan significance of the temple 'cleansing' will prove abortive, unless the whole complex, fig tree – 'cleansing' – is taken into consideration" (Kelber, *Kingdom*, 99).

[116] Geddert, *Mark*, 263.

this cluster of key terms going back to 8:14–21, but it is important to note that 8:14–21 itself goes back to the Markan discourse of parables, particularly the parable of the sower.

When the disciples ask about the purpose of the parables, Jesus cites the oracle Isaiah received from God at his commissioning "so that they may indeed see but not perceive, and may indeed hear but not understand; lest they should turn again, and be forgiven" (4:12). Here we find, for the first time in Mark's story, the key motif of "seeing," "hearing," and "understanding" (συνιῶσιν and οἴδατε in vv. 12 and 13, respectively). It is significant that in 8:14–21 the motif of understanding (νοεῖτε and συνίετε in 8:17,21, respectively) recurs, but in the episode of the fig tree, that word is not found. What is missing may well be as important as what is resumed. Why did Mark choose to omit "understanding" from the narrative of the fig tree?

The answer may be that though the disciples "hear," "see," and even "remember," they fail to "understand" the significance of Jesus' action against the tree.[117] One of the disciples later confirms this, as Jesus and the disciples leave the temple, by the comment about the temple's wonderful stones (13:1). Clearly, this disciple, and perhaps all of them, did not understand the parable of the fig tree (despite "hearing" and "seeing" in 11:14,21). This, as I shall explain later, may be behind the narrator's call, in the midst of the following discourse on the end of the temple, for the reader to "understand" (ὁ ἀναγινώσκων νοείτω). In a warning addressed directly to the reader to discern what Jesus is saying and doing, the narrator is presumably asking the reader to do a better job discerning than the disciples (13:14).

Whether the disciples understand the cursing of the fig tree or not, Mark's key terms for discernment make it clear that the fig tree by no

---

[117] Contra Marshall (*Faith as a Theme*, 163–64): "The narrator goes to some lengths to indicate that Peter's outburst reflects on this occasion, not incomprehension, but a profound sense of portentousness of what he sees. Whereas in 8:18 the incomprehension of the disciples is typified as an inability to see, hear or remember the import of Jesus' deeds, here their positive 'hearing-seeing-remembering' ties both halves of the fig-tree narrative together..." There are two points that Marshall does not take into consideration. First, in 11:14, 20 the disciples "hear" and "see" and even this time "remember" but there is no narrative indication that this implies discernment. Indeed, Jesus upbraids them in 8:14–21 for having ears and eyes but not seeing or hearing with spiritual perception. So simply hearing and seeing is not enough for Mark. Second, the goal of seeing and hearing, which in Mark is always "understanding," is not found in the fig tree narrative. The motif of "understanding" was at the climax of hearing and seeing in 4:12 and 8:21, thus making its absence in 11:20–21 notable. This suggests that the connection between the fig-tree episode and 8:14–21 is the consistent failure of the disciples to understand the parabolic meaning of Jesus' words and deeds.

means lacks narrative symbolism. The special Markan vocabulary and the narrative sandwiching of the fig tree around the temple demonstration give ample clues to the reader that this episode is fraught with meaning. This call to see and hear beyond the empirical reminds the reader to view the fig tree symbolically. Indeed, Jesus' cursing of the tree is itself an enacted parable, one that does not bode well for the temple and its stewards.

A striking contradiction at the heart of this story is Jesus' condemnation of the fig tree for failing to bear fruit, even though it is not the καιρός for figs (v. 13b). The unusual expectation for figs alerts the reader to something beyond the ostensible search for food. The word used for season, καιρός, can have deeper connotations than mere time. Indeed, this word comes in the beginning of the gospel as Jesus' first words: πεπλήρωται ὁ καιρὸς καὶ ἤγγικεν ἡ βασιλεία τοῦ θεοῦ (1:15). Thus, καιρός evokes an eschatological time frame, which runs throughout Mark's gospel. There is one text in the Scriptures of Israel that speaks of fruit trees that perpetually bear fruit. In his vision of the new temple, Ezekiel sees trees that bear fruit every month because of the temple sanctuary. Ezekiel's eschatological vision of the temple, with its connection between perpetual fruitfulness and the temple sanctuary, provides a striking parallel with Mark 11:13. This text could help explain why Mark makes such a strong connection between the fig tree and the framing of the temple demonstration. The extraordinary search for fruit out of season is thus an eschatological quest.[118]

The failure to find fruit must therefore be read beyond the absent figs, but what is its figurative sense? The parable of the sower reminds the reader that fruitfulness in Mark's gospel represents a believing response to Jesus (4:20).[119] In the parable of the wicked tenants, which Jesus tells later while in the temple (12:1–12), the problem is the failure (because of the tenants) to collect the fruit of the vineyard; thus Mark affords the fruit of the tree great symbolism. Juxtaposed to the temple demonstration, this symbolism enlightens the meaning of the narrative. As Jesus fails to find fruit on the tree, he likewise fails to find the temple to be a "house of prayer for all nations." The tree's lack of fruit is a parable for the lack of prayer and faith that Jesus finds in the temple. This failure leads to the condemnation of the tree (11:14), the temple (11:15–17), and the tenants of

---

[118] Marshall, *Faith as a Theme*, 161, observes that καιρός evokes the eschatological character of this episode.

[119] Marshall, ibid., 160–61, observes that "the absence of fruit on the tree, despite external appearances, typifies the spiritual barrenness at the religious heart of the nation; 'fruitfulness' is Mark's metaphor for a believing response to Jesus' message (4:1–20; 12:1–12)."

the vineyard (12:9). This interpretation is strengthened once the traditional symbolism of the trees, in Israel's scriptural traditions, is recognized.

William Telford, in his classic study entitled *The Barren Temple and the Withered Tree*, has shown how the symbolism associated with fig trees is pervasive in the OT.[120] The fruitfulness of the fig tree is a sign of an eschatological blessing, whereas the withering of the tree comes from divine curse or judgment – Haggai 2 is a good example. In exhorting those who returned from Babylonian captivity to continue the rebuilding of the temple, he tells them to consider carefully how before "one stone was laid on another in the Lord's temple," the land was unfruitful (2:15–16). In his list of vegetation that has failed to bear fruit, Haggai mentions the fig tree (2:19). Therefore, the fruitfulness of the land is dependent on the temple. In addition to Haggai, other texts employ the fig tree as a symbol of eschatological judgment or blessing; it is thus likely that Mark has not taken any one OT text as the basis for Jesus' encounter with the fig tree. Rather, the general nexus of texts form an interpretive backdrop to Mark's story. The connection between the fruitfulness of the land and religious observance, epitomized by the temple cult, is deeply embedded in the OT – this is illustrated by the content of the covenant blessings and curses that make up the covenant between Israel and God in Deuteronomy 28. Many of the prophets' judgment oracles seem to be the application of the curses of Deuteronomy to an unfaithful people (e.g., Amos 4:9–10). Thus, Telford makes the following conclusion about the imagery of the fig tree in the OT: "It figures predominantly in the prophetic books and very often in passages with an *eschatological* import. Common to these passages are the twin motifs of *blessing* and *judgement*."[121] Given the stock imagery of the fig tree in the prophetic oracles of eschatological blessing or judgment, Mark seems to intend that Jesus' cursing of the fig tree be read against this OT backdrop.

Given the rich intertextual allusions to the OT motifs of fruitfulness (blessing) and barrenness (judgment), as well as the intratextual allusions that Mark makes to fruitfulness and its absence within his narrative (4:1–20 and 12:1–12), there can be no doubt that the cursing of the fig tree represents Jesus pronouncing a solemn eschatological judgment. It has correctly been pointed out that the Markan readers would have seen this reflected in the destruction of the temple in A.D. 70. Although this is undoubtedly true, I must also stress that Mark sees that the focus of eschatology should not be on the destruction of the temple but rather on

---

[120] See especially chapter five of Telford, *Barren Temple*, 128–63.
[121] Ibid., 161–62.

Jesus' life and mission. Jesus is the root and cause of the eschatological in-breaking, of which the destruction of the temple is but a sign.

For Mark, the importance of Jesus' eschatological judgment on the fig tree, and therefore the temple, is tremendous. This elucidates the old debate about the nature of Jesus' demonstration in the temple, whether it was a cleansing or condemnation. Any of Jesus' ambiguous actions in 11:15–16 are clarified by Jesus' subsequent teaching, which refers to Jeremiah's speech concerning the end of the temple. Mark, by framing the temple demonstration with the cursing of the fruitless fig tree, makes it clear that he intends his reader to understand the correlation between Jesus' actions in the temple and his response to the barren tree. The juxtaposition of the temple and the cursed fig tree make it clear that, for Mark, Jesus' deeds and words in the temple are a symbolic judgment of the temple. Indeed, what ultimately excludes any notion that the Markan Jesus is cleansing the temple is the eschatology that runs throughout both the foreground and background of Mark's narrative. In other words, Mark argues that Jesus could not possibly have tried to cleanse the temple, because there was simply no time to do so – the eschatological harvest time had come – and there was no time to wait for another season.

## 1.5 Conclusion

In the first half of this chapter I examined how Mark sets up Jesus' entry into Jerusalem's temple as a climactic moment. The narrative detail given to the entry account slows the story's tempo, which increases the reader's sense of drama, highlighting the significance of Jesus' arrival in the temple. Mark's rare use of the title κύριος in reference to Jesus as he makes the last leg of his journey to the temple heightens the narrative drama of this scene. Moreover, by bestowing the title κύριος upon Jesus, Mark evokes the prophetic oracles of Isaiah and Malachi, which open his story. The call to prepare τὴν ὁδὸν κυρίου now finds its most pertinent moment, as Jesus comes to the end of his "way," which is none other than the temple. Thus, the narrative motif of ὁδός, which began with the prologue and intensified in the travel narrative to Jerusalem (8:27–10:52), finds its last narrative occurrence in the account of Jesus' entry into the temple (11:8). The intratextuality employed through the interweaving of this term is complemented by the intertextual allusions Mark draws from the "way" motif. The ὁδός theme takes up the Isaianic "way" of the Lord, his eschatological return to Zion and to the temple.

Mark employs a similar pattern in his motif of ὁ ἐρχόμενος (11:9). Once again, Mark has brought an intratextual motif to its climax at the entry narrative.[122] John the Baptist speaks of a stronger one who is "coming" (1:7); Jesus refers to himself as "coming" to proclaim the good news; he speaks of this directly to the disciples (1:38), allusively in the parable of the sower (4:3), and cryptically (4:21). In the entry narrative, Jesus' "coming" is celebrated by those who accompany him in the singing of Psalm 118. By bringing the "coming" motif into climax with the citation of Psalm 118, Mark evokes the intertextual connotations of the Psalm, thereby showing that the "coming" theme must be understood in light of its prophetic and scriptural antecedents. One wonders if the motif of "coming" echoes the prophecy of Malachi, where "the Lord whom you seek will come suddenly to the temple" (Mal 3:1), in addition to Psalm 118. This text from Malachi ties together the three key terms, κύριος, ὁδός, and ἔρχομαι. It appears that Mark wove these motifs into the fabric of his narrative, bringing them to the fore as Jesus enters the temple in order to show the prophetic and eschatological significance of Jesus' coming to the temple.

The possibility that Mark is evoking the prophetic oracle of Malachi, one of the last prophets before the coming of John the Baptist, is particularly attractive since Jesus' actions in the temple demonstration seem to have been scripted by Malachi. For Malachi warns about the Lord's coming to the temple (Mal 3:2) as he will come in judgment (3:5f), a judgment particularly focused upon the priests (3:3). The charge against them is that they are robbing God (Mal 3:8–9), a charge that resonates with the accusations Jesus will make against the temple authorities.

Mark's framing of the temple demonstration with the condemnation of the fig tree makes it evident, whatever the ambiguity of Jesus' actions, that Jesus is giving a prophetic condemnation of the temple. Once again we see the Markan method of combining intratextuality and intertextuality. The barren fig tree embodies the Markan motif of fruitfulness as a believing response to Jesus. In the parable of the sower, the reader is warned that the

---

[122] Joanna Dewey (*Markan Public Debate: Literary Technique, Concentric Structure, and Theology in Mark 2:1–3:6* [SBLDS 48; Chico: Scholars, 1980] 32) recognizes that anticipation and retrospection are common rhetorical techniques employed by Mark: "The same word or phrase is then used later in the narrative to recall to the reader's mind incidents that have gone before. Such devices help to interconnect the parts of a narrative, to give an episodic work a sense of unity." Building on Dewey's insight, I would add that Mark often employs repetition of key words or themes (intratextuality), while at the same time he connects them to words or motifs from Israel's Scriptures, particularly the prophets (intertextuality). This rhetorical strategy creates a rich narrative texture to Mark's story. One effect of this dual method of intratextuality and intertextuality is to show that the story of Jesus is the long-awaited climax of Israel's story (eschatology).

refusal to heed Jesus would lead to barrenness, which is now portrayed by the fruitless fig tree (11:12–14). The fig tree stands for the temple and those who have refused to heed Jesus. There are many OT allusions that stand behind the image of a fig tree. Whatever individual texts Mark may have been alluding to, the overall motif of obedience as bearing fruit and judgment as bringing barrenness is at least close to the surface of Mark's intertextual echoes. Besides these implicit scriptural allusions, Jesus' citation of Jeremiah 7 and Isaiah 56 bring the prophetic oracles of Israel to the narrative forefront and therefore color Jesus' confrontation with the temple in eschatological hues. Thus, the temple establishment is condemned for turning it into a den of thieves rather than a house of prayer. The intertextual employment of "den of thieves" and "house of prayer" will be subtly repeated later in Mark's story, as I will argue. Mark has shown that Jesus' eschatological coming to the temple ends in a condemnation of it as a "den of thieves." What is now left in the reader's mind is the question of what, if anything, will replace this temple. In other words, where will the "house of prayer" for God's people be found?

Chapter 2

# Lord of the Temple

## 2.1 Introduction

Jesus' demonstration in the temple is a watershed event in Mark's narrative. Everything from Mark 11:20 through 12:44 flows from Jesus' condemnation of the temple. Just as with the story of the withered tree, Jesus' cryptic comment about "this mountain" being cast into the sea serves to confirm the fate of Jerusalem's temple (Mark 11:23). Jesus' sayings about faith, prayer, and forgiveness (11:22–25) point out the key features that once gave the temple its unique identity and are, for Mark's readers, features that are embodied by the Christian community. This is the first hint in Mark's story that there will be a new temple. The temple authorities respond to Jesus' demonstration in the temple by questioning Jesus and asking him to explain by what authority he can act and teach so boldly in the temple (11:27–33).[1] Not insignificantly, the setting for Jesus' teaching and conflict with the leaders is the temple.[2]

Section one of this chapter will examine how these two pericopes – the saying about faith, prayer, and forgiveness (11:22–25) and the question on authority (11:27–33) – advance the Markan Jesus' stance toward the temple. Section two will focus on Jesus' teaching in the temple, which comes as a response to the question of his authority (Mark 12). Here I will examine how the parable of the tenants answers the question of Jesus' authority and advances the notion of a new temple, for which Jesus himself will be the cornerstone (12:10). Mark's depiction of Jesus' teaching in the

---

[1] Donahue (*Are You the Christ?* 121) sees this tension as stemming from Jesus' earlier critique of the Temple: "Thus Mark underscores the fact that the anti-temple activity of Jesus is responsible for the mounting opposition to him."

[2] The context for all the teaching and conflict in Mark 11–12 is the temple, which illustrates how important the temple is for Mark's narrative. Ben Witherington (*The Gospel of Mark: A Socio-Rhetorical Commentary* [Grand Rapids: Eerdmans, 2001] 327) notes how the temple serves as the unifying context for Mark's narrative: "What really unites the material in Mark 11–12 is the setting of the temple courts, whether we are talking about actions (referred to at the beginning and end of these chapters, 11:1–9 and 12:41–44) or teaching material."

temple confirms his authority over the temple and serves to deepen the reader's understanding of Jesus' identity. There will be four parts to this section: the parable of the wicked tenants (vv. 1–9); the reference to the rejected stone (vv. 10–12); the three questions posed to the Teacher (vv. 13–34); and the riddle concerning Psalm 110 and Davidic descent (vv. 35–37). Finally, I will show briefly how vv. 38–44 reinforce Jesus' condemnation of the temple and lead into Mark 13.

## 2.2 Question of Faith – Faithless Question (11:22–33)

### 2.2.1 New Place for Prayer, Faith, and Forgiveness (11:22–25)

The morning following the temple demonstration, Peter and the disciples see the tree Jesus had cursed the previous day. It is withered from its roots up (11:20–21). Jesus responds to Peter's surprise with a call to faith, which is followed by a short discourse on prayer, faith, and forgiveness (vv. 22–25). This instruction is united by a *Stichwort* connection, where the key words of "faith," "prayer," and "forgiveness" are progressively connected. The question, however, is how this discussion on prayer relates to Jesus' cursing of the fig tree.

#### 2.2.1.1 Difficult Transition

The transition between Peter's observation of the withered tree and Jesus' teaching on prayer is not self-evident. Iersel concludes that the connection is not clear, causing the reader to become disoriented by the sudden shift.[3] Along the same lines, John Painter claims that the teaching on prayer diverts attention from the theme and focus of the narrative.[4] Thus, many scholars suspect that Mark lost the narrative thread of his story out of deference to this traditional material, which he clumsily added to the withered-tree episode.[5] Conversely, Telford argues that the teaching on

---

[3] B. M. F. van. Iersel, *Reading Mark* (Collegeville: Liturgical, 1988) 359.

[4] J. Painter, *Mark's Gospel* (New Testament Readings, London: Routledge, 1997) 160. "Although these sayings divert attention from the larger theme being developed by Mark, they have been retained because they add something to the theme of faith which is important for Mark."

[5] Hooker, *Mark*, 269. "The conclusion to the story is quickly told, but various sayings have been added to it – chiefly by word association, for the story itself has little to do with faith, prayer, or forgiveness." Similarly, Evans (*Mark*, 186) concludes: "This hardly seems to have been the place for the evangelist to add a section on prayer for the disciples." On the contrary, once these sayings on prayer and forgiveness are seen in light

prayer is not simply a digression but a destructive disruption of the narrative. "The crux of the problem, however, lies in the reflection that if Mark himself either found these sayings already attached to the story and did not remove them, or, conversely, himself connected them to the story, then it is hard to see how he himself could have intended that the story be understood as a specific commentary on the cleansing account."[6] Thus, Telford concludes that it was a later redactor and not Mark who added vv. 22–25.

Are vv. 22–25 an interpolation, as Telford suggests, or did Mark place them here out of deference for earlier traditions, perhaps with the aim of building on the theme of faith? This question puts in sharp question the narrative logic of Mark 11:20–25. Is there a relationship between the withered tree and Jesus' teaching on prayer, and what does that have to do with the temple theme?

### 2.2.1.2 "This Mountain"

The key to solving this riddle is in identifying the reference to "this mountain" (v. 23). Scholars have rightly focused on this phrase in their treatment of the prayer pericope. Three interpretations of "this mountain" have attracted the most attention.

The first interpretation understands "this mountain" simply as an idiomatic or proverbial saying, which means therefore that no one particular mountain is intended.[7] The proverbial nature of this saying is evident in its use in Matt 17:19–20, Luke 17:5–6, and 1 Cor 13:2. Thus, R. T. France argues that: "The throwing of a mountain into the sea is as useless and destructive an act as causing the death of a fig tree, and is best seen as merely a proverbial type saying for the impossible."[8]

The problem with this first interpretation is that, although the mountain saying is used with an indefinite sense in the other traditions (e.g., Matt 17:19 and 1 Cor 13:2), the reference in Mark is unmistakably definite: τῷ ὄρει τούτῳ (so also in Matt 17:20). Thus, Mark's reference must be to a particular mountain.[9] It is interesting that France notes the parallelism between the withering of the tree and the casting away of the mountain but

---

of Jesus' condemnation of the temple, it will be clear why the disciples need to hear about the new locus of prayer and forgiveness – the Christian community.

[6] Telford, *Barren Temple*, 49.

[7] See Vincent Taylor, *Mark*, 467.

[8] France, *Mark*, 448.

[9] Thus Edwin K. Broadhead ("Which Mountain is 'This Mountain?'" *Paradigms* 2:1 [1986] 33) argues that "the reference is far from indefinite (*tō orei toutō*, "to this mountain"), but the mountain is unnamed."

fails to see that the tree is a particular tree, ἡ συχῆ (v. 21), which strengthens the proposition that "this mountain" refers to a particular mountain. But the question remains, to which mountain is Jesus referring?

The second interpretation would see the Mount of Olives as the reference. The Mount of Olives, it is argued, must be the mountain since it is the one closest to Jesus. Since the narrative setting of v. 23 is somewhere outside Bethany (11:12–13), which is earlier identified "at the Mount of Olives" (11:1), the phrase τῷ ὄρει τούτῳ should refer to the nearest mountain – the Mount of Olives.[10] Also, since the Dead Sea is almost within view from the eastern side of the Mount of Olives, the mountain thrown into the sea may be associated with the Mount of Olives.[11] Further, it is suggested that a reference to the Mount of Olives echoes the eschatological overtones of Zechariah 14:4 and 14:10.[12]

The third position argues that, given the larger context of Jesus' antitemple polemic, the mountain thrown into the sea is best seen as the temple mount. Marshall illustrates this position well: "A reference to the temple mount, on the other hand, is consistent with the preceding emphasis on the condemnation and supplanting of the existing temple cultus. In this connection, 11:23 exerts an 'imaginative shock' comparable to the withering of the fig tree. Faith in God is not directed towards the exaltation of the 'mountain of the Lord's house' above all hills (Mic 4:1; Isa 2:2) but towards its casting down into the sea."[13]

Both the Mount of Olives and the temple mount are plausible references. Joachim Gnilka states that the Mount of Olives would make the most literal sense, while a more pictorial or symbolic reading would see the temple mount as the reference.[14] In the latter interpretation, the mountain cast into the sea refers to the judgment upon the temple.[15] This would certainly fit the context of Mark's antitemple polemic. In order to decide which of these is more likely Mark's intention, we must look to the

---

[10] Sharyn E. Dowd, *Prayer, Power, and the Problem of Suffering: Mark 11:22–25 in the Context of Markan Theology* (SBLDS 105; Atlanta: Scholars, 1988) 73. See also M.J. Lagrange, *Evangile selon Saint Marc* (Paris: Gabalda, 1966) 923.

[11] Rudolf Pesch (*Das Markusevangelium* [HTKNT 2: Frieburg: Herder, 1977] 208) quotes Grundmann's suggestion that the Dead Sea could be seen from the eastern face of the Mount of Olives; therefore, Pesch believes the Mount of Olives is the reference.

[12] Lane, *Mark*, 410.

[13] Marshall, *Faith as a Theme*, 168–69.

[14] Joachim Gnilka, *Das Evangelium nach Markus* 2 (EKK 2; Zürich: Benzinger/ Neukirchen-Vluyn: Neukirchener Verlag, 1979) 134.

[15] Gnilka, *Evangelium Markus*, 134.

context for clues.[16] Indeed, this approach makes most sense as Mark deliberately leaves a gap in the narrative. By leaving the mountain unnamed, the reader is challenged to fill in the gap.[17] This gap illustrates that the author wants the reader to ponder the problem and search the wider context for clues to its solution.[18] I also hope to show that the temple mount reference is actually grounded in the narrative logic of Mark's gospel and would fit both the literal and symbolic senses that Gnilka has divided.

The temple mount and the Mount of Olives are set points of reference in Mark's narrative. The middle section of Mark's Gospel, known as "the way" narrative, has Jesus making his way "up" (ἀναβαίνω) to Jerusalem's temple (Mark 10:32, 33). This common idiom for making a pilgrimage "up to" the temple is cognate with the motif of the temple being placed on Mount Zion (e.g., Isa 2:2; Mic 4:1). Jesus' journey up to the temple is made ominous with the three sets of passion predictions, which brace the

---

[16] As Geddert (*Watchwords*, 116) reminds us, context is especially important methodologically for interpreting Mark: "Mark has given evidence over and over again that the *context* in which a pericope is placed is an essential clue as to how it is to be construed" (italics original).

[17] A gap occurs when an author holds back information that is relevant to the narrative; it could be about the world, a character, time, name, place, motive or simply a piece of information that the reader would need or desire to know in order to understand the flow of the story. The rhetorical power of gapping is that it plays on the reader's desire to comprehend. Thus, the need for closure drives the reader to find a way, by a closer reading of the context, to fill in the gap. Meir Sternberg (*The Poetics of Biblical Narrative: Ideological Literature and the Drama of Reading* [Bloomington: Indiana University, 1987] 236) notes how the desire for closure is the hallmark of a true gap: "To make sense is to make distinctions between what was omitted for the sake of interest and what was omitted for lack of interest: between what I called, for short, gaps and blanks. Only the former demand closure, while the latter may be disregarded without loss, indeed must be disregarded to keep the narrative in focus."

[18] Again, Sternberg (*Poetics*, 191–92) notes well how gapping causes the reader to plunge deeper into the text for meaning, and so serves as one of the most powerful rhetorical tools available: "Biblical narratives are notorious for their sparsity of detail … And the resultant gaps have been left open precisely at key points, central to the discourse as a dramatic progression as well as a structure of meaning and value. Hence their filling in here is not automatic but requires considerable attention to the nuances of the text, both at the level of the represented events and at the level of language; far from a luxury or option, closure becomes a necessity for any reader trying to understand the story even in the simplest terms of what happens and why." Sternberg's comments here about gapping in the David and Bethsheba story illustrate well the nature and power of gapping and also fit well with the purpose of gapping the name of "this mountain" in Mark's narrative. As I hope to show, this gapping is intended to lead the reader into a deeper sense of the ongoing importance of the motif of the temple's demise in Mark's story.

reader for the events in Jerusalem (e.g., 10:33). Jesus begins his procession into Jerusalem from Bethany, which is associated in 11:1 with the Mount of Olives.[19] When Jesus finally arrives at the temple, the hour is late, and Jesus leaves Jerusalem for Bethany. The observations regarding the late hour and Jesus' leaving Jerusalem suggest the preference Jesus has for Bethany/Mount of Olives over and against Jerusalem and the temple. Jesus' demonstration in the temple, which for Mark is clearly a rejection of the temple, is also followed by Jesus' departure from the city (11:19).

The geographical contrast between Jerusalem/temple mount and Bethany/Mount of Olives becomes explicit when the author sets the Mount of Olives against the temple mount in Mark 13:3, where Jesus sits κατέναντι τοῦ ἱεροῦ immediately after leaving the temple for the third and final time (13:1). Mark's narrative pattern clearly shows Jesus moving away from Jerusalem and the temple mount toward Bethany and the Mount of Olives.[20] This transposition occurs, significantly, after Jesus leaves Jerusalem (having celebrated the Passover in the city as required by Jewish custom) and takes refuge once again at the Mount of Olives (14:26). Thus, it is true that "in the narrative development of Mark," as Edwin Broadhead observes, "the Mount of Olives serves as the antithesis to all that is represented by Jerusalem and its temple."[21]

The Mount of Olives represents the positive pole over and against the negative pole of the temple mount. This polarization between the Mount of Olives and the temple mount represents the conflict between Jesus and the temple. Given, then, that the Mount of Olives is always viewed positively, it cannot be the referent of "this mountain," which is cast into the sea.[22] What is more, Mark usually identifies the Mount of Olives by name (11:1; 13:3; 14:26), whereas the temple mount is never explicitly named, although it is alluded to. It would be in keeping with Mark's style, then, for

---

[19] See Elizabeth Struthers Malbon, *Narrative Space and Mythic Meaning in Mark* (San Francisco: Harper & Row, 1986) 87.

[20] Broadhead ("Which Mountain Is 'This Mountain?'" 35) makes this point: "The ultimate movement of the narrative is away from Jerusalem/temple and toward the Mount of Olives and the future."

[21] Broadhead, ibid.

[22] Schnellbächer ("Temple as Focus," 95–112) builds on U. Mauser's insight that the wilderness and the sea are symbolic in Mark for evil, while mountains are always positive symbols. Thus, Schnellbächer sees the mountain thrown into the sea as signifying the temple's disqualification and corruption: "'Mountain,' on the other hand, symbolizes, as we have seen, a location above both 'wilderness' and 'sea,' reaching up into a sphere near to God which makes it a place of refuge from desolation (cf. 13:14), and a place of prayer and possible revelation. If we now assume, as suggested, that it is the Temple Mount, 'the high place par excellence' which is to be cast into the 'sea,' then this would be in line with Mark's argument as we have drawn it out..." (pp. 105–6).

him to allude to the temple mount without naming it. Just as the withered tree was a symbol of the temple's fate, so too the mountain cast into the sea reaffirms Jesus' condemnation of the temple.[23] Therefore, the mountain that is to be cast into the sea is the temple mount, which in Mark is the place that embodies rejection of Jesus and failure of faith.[24] "Thus, Mark uses these two opposing mountains to embody the stark opposition between Jesus and the temple at Jerusalem."[25]

The mountain-moving saying has a twofold purpose. First, it confirms that Jesus' demonstration in the temple and subsequent cursing of the fig tree betoken the end of the temple cultus. Thus, the mountain cast into the sea is similar to the withered tree: both signify the eschatological judgment of the doomed temple. Second, by Jesus' claim that the temple mount will be cast into the sea, Mark evokes elements from the prophetic oracles of Israel's Scriptures. Isaiah declared that no obstacle could block the "way" of the Lord in the new exodus to come – not even mountains (Isa 40:4; 45:2; 49:11).[26] Zechariah told the Davidic heir Zerubbabel that, in his endeavor to build the new temple, the great mountain obstructing his project would be removed (Zech 4:7). If Mark intends this albeit subtle reference, he would be suggesting that Jesus is a new Zerubbabel who is to build a new temple – and that the mountain in his way would be removed.[27] The irony, of course, is that the temple mount was suppose to be exalted in the last days (Mic 4:1–2); but now Jesus, in a profound twist,

---

[23] "And there is one final hinge that links the two stories [fig tree and saying about faith, prayer, and forgiveness] together – the saying in v.23 about the mountain being cast into the sea. As a saying about the power of faith, this seems strangely out of context; but if Mark understood 'this mountain' as the temple mountain, it begins to make sense" (Hooker, "Traditions," 8).

[24] Wright (*Victory*, 324–25) argues that the context must determine how "this mountain" is understood: "The evident proverbial nature of the saying should not disguise the fact that someone speaking of 'this mountain' being cast into the sea, in the context of a dramatic action of judgment in the Temple, would inevitably be heard to refer to Mount Zion." Myers (*Binding*, 305) also concludes that the context necessitates reading "this mountain" as the Temple Mount: "In its Markan narrative context, however, the 'mountain' can only refer to the temple."

[25] Broadhead, " Which Mountain Is 'This Mountain?'" 35.

[26] Watts (*Isaiah's New Exodus*, 334) believes Jesus is referring to the temple mount, and that the mountain-moving statement echoes Isaiah: "Finally, it is a feature of the 'Messianic Age' that all obstacles to God's returning people will be removed, particularly mountains (Isa 40:4; 45:2; 49:11; cf. 64:1–3)."

[27] Wright (*Victory*, 422) argues that the allusion to Zechariah 4:7 and mountain moving is strengthened once all the Markan allusions to Zechariah are taken into consideration.

claims that it is an obstacle in the way of the eschatological coming of the kingdom.[28]

Now that we have identified the referent of "this mountain," it will be easier to see how Jesus' teaching on prayer is connected to the cursed fig tree and the temple demonstration that precedes it.

### 2.2.2  New Temple

Jesus' response to Peter, which leads into his teaching on prayer, is an imperative call to faith, ἔχετε πίστιν θεοῦ (v. 22). This rather abrupt summons to faith makes sense, given the narrative logic of the fig tree's demise. Since the fig tree represents the temple, its tragic fate serves as a lesson of what is to befall the temple. The very assertion that the temple, the place of God's presence and Israel's prayer and forgiveness, is soon to be lost would immediately shake the disciples' faith. Myers explains: "One could not simply repudiate the temple without provoking the most fundamental crisis regarding Yahweh's presence in the world. Jesus directly challenges this identification, arguing that to abandon faith in the temple is *not* to abandon faith in God."[29] Jesus' call to faith, in light of the end of the temple, is not unlike that of the prophet Habbakuk's: in view of the demise of Jerusalem and the temple in the hands of the Babylonians, "the righteous shall live by his faith" (Hab 2:4).

The motifs of faith, prayer, and forgiveness that follow the episode of the rejected tree are intended to show the disciples (and the reader) the way forward to a future without the temple mount.[30] Both the withered tree and the mountain cast into the sea represent the rejection of the temple and

---

[28] Telford (*Barren Temple*, 119) clearly identified the mountain with the temple mount, while citing R.E. Dowda's (*The Cleansing of the Temple in the Synoptic Gospels* [Ph.D. diss., Duke University, 1972]) earlier identification of the mountain thrown in the sea: "The function of this redaction is therefore to announce, we believe, that 'the moving of mountains' expected in the last days was now taking place. Indeed, about to be removed was *the* mountain *par excellence*, the Temple Mount. The Temple, known to the Jewish people as 'the mountain of the house' or 'this mountain' was not to be elevated, as expected, but cast down! As Dowda states: 'The temple is the mountainous obstacle which is to vanish before the faith of the gospel movement. The temple system, with its corrupt clericalism and vested interests, is to be removed in the eschatological era, which is now being experienced.'"

[29] Myers, *Binding*, 304–5.

[30] Pesch (*Markusevangelium*, 208) argues that Mark is writing after the destruction of the temple and therefore the teaching on faith, prayer, and forgiveness is intended to show how the new temple will not be man-made but rather it will consist of the Christian community, by virtue of their faith and forgiveness. Pesch believes that in Mark 8:27–10:52 the Markan Jesus' focus was the building up of such a community, which comes to the fore in the clash between Jesus and the temple in Mark 11.

thereby signal the eschatological judgment of God. The disciples must not despair that the temple, like the barren fig tree, is withering away, for there will be a new place for prayer and forgiveness – the Christian community.

Prayer is the center of the complex catchwords concerning faith, prayer, and forgiveness (vv. 24, 25). The discussion on prayer, which immediately follows the condemnation of the temple as a den of thieves that has failed to be a "house of prayer for all nations," suggests that Mark intended a further link to the preceding story.[31] Indeed, it is through the motif of prayer that the narrator makes a transition from the defunct temple to its replacement.[32] The temple is rejected because it failed to be a "house of prayer," but now Jesus suggests the community of disciples will be that "house."[33]

The use of the plural (ὑμῖν, twice in v. 24) in the imperative for prayer shows that this address is directed to the community. France observes, "The communal aspect of prayer is evident from the fact that vv. 22 and 24–25 are expressed in the plural (and the singular form of v. 23 derives from a ὃς ἄν which generalizes the statement); prayer is here presented as something which the community of disciples undertakes together, not a private transaction between the individual believer and God."[34] This communal thrust of the address suggests that it is the community gathered around Jesus that is to be the new locus of prayer and forgiveness, not the rejected temple.[35]

The temple, with its daily animal sacrifices, used to be the place of forgiveness, but Jesus has symbolically brought these sacrifices to an end

---

[31] Juel (*Messiah and Temple*, 135) suggests that "the juxtaposition of the saying on prayer with a story whose point seems to be that the temple establishment will be rejected because it has not made the temple into a 'house of prayer for all nations' may be quite important for the author."

[32] Dowd (*Prayer*, 55) observes: "It is precisely the rejection of the temple that makes the inclusion of the prayer logia at this point in the gospel not only appropriate, but even necessary."

[33] Marshall (*Faith as a Theme*, 163) notes how the motif of "prayer" and "house" have been characteristic in Mark of Jesus and the disciples, which prepares the reader to see Jesus "house" as the new "house of prayer for all nations": "Prayer is an activity in Mark almost exclusively associated with Jesus and the disciples (1:35; 6:46; 9:29; 11:24f; 13:33; 14:38; cf. 12:40), and the house is a regular setting for the instruction of the disciples (7:17; 9:28,33; 10:10) and the operation of the kingdom power (1:29–31; 2:1–12)."

[34] France, *Mark*, 448.

[35] Dowd (*Prayer*, 54) concludes that: "The prayer catechesis is addressed to the Markan community, represented in the narrative by the disciples. They are the 'house of prayer for all nations' that the temple had failed to become."

(vv. 15–16).[36] From now on, forgiveness will be found in the midst of Jesus' house, since the Father forgives when they forgive one another (v. 25).[37] The narrative purpose for Jesus' teaching on prayer is summed up by Francis Moloney: "The reader is being led to accept that there will be another temple, and within that temple faith, prayer, and forgiveness, not the cultic practices of Israel, will unite the believer with God."[38] The supplanting of the temple by the community, begun in this passage, will be taken up more vividly in Jesus' parable of the wicked tenants.

### 2.2.3  By What Authority? (11:27–33)

Three days after his triumphal entry, Jesus returns again to Jerusalem, πάλιν εἰς Ἱεροσόλυμα (Mark 11:27). By his use of πάλιν, Mark reminds the reader of the events of the previous day, namely, Jesus' provocative actions in the temple.[39] Indeed, this is the third time in chap. 11 that Mark narrates Jesus coming to Jerusalem (11:11, 15 being the first two). Since the description of Jesus walking in the temple area would have sufficed for geographical information, the repetition of Jerusalem may serve Mark's plot. The reader is already aware that Jerusalem was named, in Jesus' third passion prediction (10:33), as the place where Jesus would be put to death; thus, the repetitive naming of the city serves as an ominous drumbeat, a reminder that this is the place where Jesus will meet his end.[40] Mark's description of the religious leaders as οἱ ἀρχιερεῖς καὶ οἱ γραμματεῖς καὶ οἱ πρεσβύτεροι echoes the third passion prediction, in which the first two groups were listed as those who would condemn Jesus in Jerusalem (10:33). The three groups are also named in the first passion prediction (8:31). Mark has already noted that, in response to Jesus' demonstration, the οἱ ἀρχιερεῖς καὶ οἱ γραμματεῖς were seeking a way to destroy him (11:18). Therefore, the approach of these three groups in Jerusalem constitutes the beginning of the end for Jesus.

Once again, the stage for this confrontation between Jesus and the religious authorities is the temple, the target of Jesus' prophetic protest.[41]

---

[36] See Moloney, *Mark*, 227–28.

[37] See Dowd's account (*Prayer*, 123–29) of the role of forgiveness in the Christian community.

[38] Dowd, ibid., 228.

[39] Mary Ann Tolbert, *Sowing the Gospel: Mark's World in Literary-Historical Perspective* (Minneapolis: Fortress, 1996) 233.

[40] "The repetition at each entry of the name Ἱεροσόλυμα insistently reminds the reader that we have now reached the place where Jesus' predicted rejection and suffering is to take place" (France, *Mark*, 453).

[41] Edwards (*Mark*, 350) observes: "The temple in Jerusalem, in all its Herodian immensity and grandeur, with its commanding view of Jerusalem and the Mount of

The temple authorities find Jesus ἐν τῷ ἱερῷ περιπατοῦντος αὐτοῦ. For the first time in Mark's story they openly confront Jesus, asking, "By what authority (ἐξουσία) are you doing these things, or who gave you this authority to do them?" As Stephen Smith observes, the questions posed to Jesus here bring a key Markan theme to its climax: "The double question on authority (11:28) marks the climax to an on-going theme in the gospel: does Jesus posses divine ἐξουσία? (1:22,27; 2:10; 3:15; 6:7)."[42]

The reference to "these things" points back to Jesus' actions in the temple (11:15–17).[43] Throughout Mark's story the conflict between Jesus and the religious leaders has revolved around the issue of authority, and now, with his demonstration against the temple, Jesus has set himself against the most authoritative institution in Israel, thereby provoking its leading authorities.[44] "In the thoroughgoing temple context 'these things' can only refer back to Jesus' condemnation of the temple. Who gave him the authority to do what he did in and to the center of religious life?"[45] Jesus had questioned, at the very least, the divine sanction for the temple, given its current corruption. In turn, the temple authorities question the legitimacy of Jesus and his actions. Rather than attack the message of Jesus' demonstration, they question the messenger: by what authority does Jesus act against the temple?

---

Olives and its unrivaled historical and theological significance, becomes the inevitable stage for the challenge to Jesus' authority."

[42] Stephen H. Smith, "The Literary Structure of Mark 11:1–12:40," *NovT* 31:2 (1989) 114.

[43] The use of the plural would also allow for "these things" to go back to Jesus' entry into Jerusalem, where his actions of riding the ass, and his acceptance of being acclaimed with palms and the singing of Psalm 118 would also been seen by the temple leaders as actions that claim remarkable authority. However, what would be foremost in the mind of the reader is Jesus' actions against the temple. Thus Gaston (*No Stone on Another*, 88) concludes: "The anit-cultic implications of Jesus' action in the temple are confirmed by a consideration of the controversy story concerning Jesus' authority to do 'this', Mk 11:27–33. It is perhaps significant that it should be representatives of the temple who feel threatened (cf. 12:12) and so ask about Jesus' authority."

[44] Richard Horsley (*Hearing the Whole Story*, 100) believes that at the heart of the conflict in Mark's story is the issue of authority, particularly the authority of the Temple and its leading priests: "More subtly, perhaps, in Jesus' first act of healing or exorcism for the beleaguered people, and again in the ruler's first challenge to Jesus in Jerusalem, the conflict is framed in terms of power-authority (1:21–28; 11:27–33). Indeed, if we attend closely to the first several episodes of the story, Jesus' exorcisms, healings, and pronouncements at several points are simultaneously actions against the prerogatives and authority of the temple and its priestly aristocracy (e.g., 1:21–28,41–45; 2:1–12; cf. 7:1–13; 8:15; 10:2–9, later in the story)."

[45] Werner H. Kelber, *Mark's Story of Jesus* (Philadelphia: Fortress Press, 1979) 63.

The reader already knows the answer. From the outset, the narrator identifies Jesus as the Christ and Son of God (Mark 1:1). The narrator then confirmed this identification for the reader with the authoritative voice from heaven both at the baptism of Jesus (1:11) and at the transfiguration (9:7). Most recently, Jesus was depicted as the Lord, going up (ἀναβαίνω) to the temple as if in a royal cortege (10:32; 11:1–9). For the reader, the very question casts a shadow upon the temple authorities for refusing to understand and believe what God is doing through Jesus.

This conflict between Jesus and the religious leaders is focused on the question of Jesus' authority – the very issue that initiated the first controversy between them in Mark 2:1–12. Earlier in the story the crowds marveled at the authority Jesus displayed in his teaching and exorcism, in contrast to that of the scribes (Mark 1:22,27). A short time later, the issue of authority sparked the first controversy between Jesus and the religious leaders (Mark 2:7,10), which led to several episodes of conflict, known as "controversy narratives" (Mark 2–3:6).[46] The issue was raised by Jesus' declaration that the sins of the paralytic were forgiven. The question arose among the Jewish leaders as to who Jesus thought he was, since no one but God could forgive sins. Jesus then healed the paralytic in order to demonstrate that he had been granted such authority: ἵνα δὲ εἰδῆτε ὅτι ἐξουσίαν ἔχει ὁ υἱὸς τοῦ ἀνθρώπου ἀφιέναι ἁμαρτίας ἐπὶ τῆς γῆς (Mark 2:10). As Evans observes: "The linkage of ὁ υἱὸς τοῦ ἀνθρώπου, "son of man," and ἐξουσία, "authority," is to be traced to Dan 7:13–14."[47] In Daniel's vision it is the one like a Son of Man who inherits all ἐξουσία from God. Jesus' assertion to be the Son of Man, who has authority ἐπὶ τῆς γῆς, is a claim for a divinely sanctioned ἐξουσία. For Mark, ἐξουσία is clearly a key theme – the word is threaded throughout his narrative (Mark 1:22,27; 2:10; 3:15; 6:7; 11:28; 13:34).[48]

What is the significance, for Mark, in the link between Jesus' ἐξουσία and the ἐξουσία of the Son of Man in Daniel? By making Daniel 7 the intertextual backdrop, Mark gives clues to his reader as to the nature of Jesus' ἐξουσία.[49] Jesus' opening proclamation of the ἡ βασιλεία τοῦ θεοῦ

---

[46] It has become common to see Mark 2–3:6 as consisting of five controversy stories, e.g., Kelber, *Kingdom*, 18. For a discussion of the rhetorical unity of Mark 2–3:6 see Dewey, *Public Debate*, especially 109–22.

[47] Evans, *Mark*, 202.

[48] Ibid., 203. "Doubtless the matter of Jesus' authority, which introduces and marks Jesus' public ministry (1:16–8:26) and now leads directly into Jesus' mortal conflict with the authorities, represents a key theme in the evangelist's development of the Gospel as a narrative whole."

[49] It is not unlikely that the author is making an allusion to Dan 7:13 in Mark 2:10, given the significant role Daniel plays in Mark's story. Undoubtedly, there is an overt

in Mark 1:15 is now further explained as Jesus being the one who possesses the ἐξουσία of the kingdom. In Daniel, the motif of kingdom is permeated with eschatology; it is not accidental that "kingdom" and "authority" are interchangeable in LXX Daniel. In Mark the same is true. Jesus ushers in the kingdom, which is identical to his authority, both of which are signs of God's eschatological initiative.

How does this connect to the confrontation of Mark 11:27–33? Robert Guelich argues that, if Mark intended to link the ἐξουσία and Son of Man motifs, he would have done so in 11:27–33.[50] Since there is no explicit mention of Son of Man in the discussion of Jesus' authority (11:27–33), the link must not be important for Mark. However, Guelich does not take into consideration how the discussion of Jesus' authority continues in Mark's narrative beyond the pericope of 11:27–33. The Markan Jesus subtly addresses the nature of his ἐξουσία in the subsequent parable of the wicked tenants (12:1–12). Indeed, the issue of Jesus' authority resurfaces in 12:35–37 as well. Both of these pericopes relate directly to the question of Jesus' authority, and the focal point of each is Jesus' sonship (12:6,35,37). We have also seen that the account of the chief priests, scribes, and elders, along with the repetition of "Jerusalem," evokes the three passion predictions, each of which spoke of Jesus' suffering as the "Son of Man" (Mark 8:31; 9:31; 10:33). So the reference to Son of Man is not far below the surface. Although Mark does not employ the specific title "Son of Man" in the conflict scenes at the temple, he does link the issue of ἐξουσία to sonship. Thus, Mark connects Jesus' conflict with the authorities in the temple with the question of Jesus' sonship, just as he did in the earlier narrative in Galilee (2:10,28).[51] Mark, therefore, is not

---

allusion to Daniel 9:27 in Mark 13:14. There is also an allusion to Dan 7:13 in Mark 13:26, and this very passage is cited at the climax of Jesus' trial in Mark 14:62. Therefore, since Mark 7:13 plays such a pivotal role in the story, the linking of two key Markan motifs, ἐξουσία and ὁ υἱὸς τοῦ ἀνθρώπου in Mark 2:10 is most likely rooted in Dan 7:13.

[50] Robert A. Guelich (*Mark 1–8:26* [WBC 34a: Dallas; Word Books, 1989] 92–93) notes: "But one must again ask why 'Son of man' was limited to just 2:10,28 within this larger section, if the Son of man's authority is the key? More specifically, why is 'Son of man' missing in 1:21–28 and 11:27–33 where the question of 'authority' (ἐξουσία) is explicit, not to mention the other pericopes where Jesus' authority is implicitly involved?"

[51] Stephen H. Smith ("The Role of Jesus' Opponents in the Markan Drama," *NTS* 35 [1989] 163) notes how Mark shapes his narrative to give particular emphasis to this issue of Jesus' ἐξουσία as Son of Man: "'Εξουσία, indeed, is a word which re-emerges in the open controversies – both Galilean and Judean. The contrast of Jesus' authority with that of the scribes in this instance is rejoined in 2.10 where, in an apophthegmatic statement, Jesus declares, much to the chagrin of the scribes, that the Son of Man (= 'I'?) has

dropping the issue of ἐξουσία as it relates to Jesus' sonship in 11:27–33; rather, he is taking up the motif and developing it further, both to advance the conflict between Jesus and the authorities and to delve more deeply into the question of how Jesus possesses such ἐξουσία, that is, by his sonship.

The Jewish leaders had questioned Jesus' authority to forgive sins (2:7), heal on the Sabbath (3:2–6), and cast out demons (3:22). Now, Jesus' actions in the temple have provoked an open confrontation between Jesus and the Jewish leaders: by what authority does Jesus dare judge the temple and its rulers? The answer is clear: by the authority granted the Son of Man in Daniel 7. Significantly enough, this authority was given in the context of judgment. Whatever else one may make of the apocalyptic scene of Daniel 7, its basic thrust is the heavenly courtroom sitting in judgment (Dan 7:10). Thus, Jesus' actions in the temple condemnation were an exercise of the ἐξουσία, which in Daniel's vision was authority for eschatological judgment. In other words, Jesus' condemnation of the temple is the beginning of the eschatological judgment foretold in Daniel 7. Once again, we see how Mark takes an intertextual echo (Dan 7:13) and weaves it through the tapestry of his entire narrative, thus creating a vibrant intratextual pattern.

Jesus responds with a question of his own: was John's baptism from human beings or from God? (11:30). Jesus' ἀποκρίθητέ μοι underscores his own authority, while reversing the inquiry – now it is the temple establishment who must do the answering. It is interesting that John is invoked at this part of the story. After the temple demonstration, where the prophecy of Malachi was seemingly enacted, could mention of John be a further echo of Malachi, who claimed that Elijah would come before the terrible day of the Lord?[52] Would the mention of John strengthen this connection in the readers' minds? One thing is sure: the readers know that it was precisely John who both foretold and recognized Jesus' coming as of the "one stronger than I" (Mark 1:7–8). John's baptism of Jesus illustrated that Jesus' authority was "from heaven." Indeed, Jesus' question leaves only two choices for understanding the nature of John's authority; it was either "from human authority" or "from heaven" (11:29). By setting up this dichotomy, Jesus forces the conversation beyond the discussion of by what institutional authority he did or did not act upon in the temple. Rather, Jesus suggests that his authority comes from a higher source,

---

ἐξουσία to forgive sins. And just as ἐξουσία is the issue in the first Galilean controversy, so too in the first narrative of the Judean conflict cycle, where the question about Jesus' authority is climaxed (11.27–33)."

[52] Hooker (*Mark*, 272) makes this suggestion.

namely "from heaven," than that from which the Sanhedrin and temple
authorities draw their authority.[53] This is somewhat reminiscent of the one
like a Son of Man receiving authority in the "clouds of heaven" (Dan 7:13)
– a heavenly authority he clearly claimed to exercise "on earth."

The leaders deliberate among themselves, as they do not believe
(πιστεύειν v. 31) John's claim to be sent from God. Because they fear the
people, they do not want to admit this and consequently avoid giving an
answer (v. 33a). Jesus responds, "Neither will I tell you by what authority I
do these things" (v. 33b). Although the dialogue ends in deadlock, the
narrative portrait of the chief priests, scribes, and elders has been
advanced. They have refused to believe in John the Baptist and,
subsequently, in Jesus.[54] This sets up their role in the following parable as
the wicked tenants who reject the messengers of God, John the Baptist
being the last in a long series.[55] From their refusal to accept John, the
reader will be better able to identify them as the wicked tenants. Indeed,
failure to see God's eschatological initiative in John's ministry likewise
blinds them from seeing God's eschatological judgment and the kingdom
that Jesus is ushering in, along the story line of Daniel's Son of Man.

The confrontation between Jesus and the stewards of the temple brings
the question of Jesus' authority to the forefront of the story. Indeed,
ἐξουσία is mentioned four times in this brief pericope (11:28[2x],29,33).
Jesus' refusal to give an explanation of his authority only heightens the
conflict. However, as the Markan reader knows, nothing is hidden except
to be made manifest, and this is precisely what Jesus does in his parabolic
teaching that follows.

---

[53] The implication is that since John's authority came from heaven, so too does Jesus'
authority. See further Gnilka, *Evangelium Markus*, 137; Pesch (*Markusevangelium*, 211)
argues along similar lines, seeing that prophets are invested with authority from God
alone; thus Jesus' authority, like John the Baptist's, is prophetic.

[54] Gnilka (*Evangelium Markus*, 141) notes that in this text Mark is again paralleling
the Baptist and Jesus.

[55] "By recalling John's baptizing activity just prior to presenting the parable of the
Tenants (11:30–33), the author indicates to the audience John's role as one of the
servants sent by the owner of the vineyard to the tenants" (Tolbert, *Sowing the Gospel*,
244).

# 2.3 Teaching in the Temple (Mark 12)

## *2.3.1   The Parable of the Wicked Tenants (vv. 1–9)*

The pericope that focused on the question of Jesus' authority ends without resolution (11:27–33), since Jesus refuses to speak "to them" (αὐτοῖς) about his authority (11:33). The next pericope begins with Jesus speaking in parables "to them" (αὐτοῖς), which leads the reader to see that Jesus has the same audience – the Jewish leaders (12:1). This is confirmed in 12:12 when they desire to arrest him because of the parable, ὅτι πρὸς αὐτοὺς τὴν παραβολὴν εἶπεν, where again the αὐτούς refers back to the leaders identified in 11:27. What Jesus refuses to say to them in straight dialogue, he will say to them (αὐτοῖς) in parables. Thus, Jesus does provides, albeit parabolically, the source and nature of his authority. Indeed, the parable of the wicked tenants is a subtle but powerful account of Jesus' authority, which simultaneously serves to discredit the authority of his opponents.

The chief priests and stewards of the temple demand to know by what authority Jesus can claim to judge the temple (11:28). Jesus hinted, in his reference to John in 11:30, that his authority was from heaven. Now, in the parable of the tenants, Jesus will push this suggestion a step further by casting himself in a most privileged role: that of the son of the vineyard's owner. Because of his sonship, Jesus is God's unique and most privileged agent.

As Mark develops the theme of Jesus' sonship, the temple remains firmly in the foreground of the story. Thus, Jesus continues to assert his right to judge the temple because he is the son of the true owner of Mount Zion. Indeed, this parable will take up the themes of authority, the temple, and judgment, which have become the focus of Mark's narrative since Jesus' entry. The parable of the wicked tenants functions as a hinge for Mark's narrative, joining the previous topic of eschatological judgment upon the old temple to the vindication of the rejected stone that will be a new temple.

There are two parts to Jesus' parable teaching. In the first part, Mark relates the story of a vineyard and its fruit, and the ensuing struggle for the vineyard's produce (12:1–9). Through the parable, Mark further develops the conflict between Jesus and the Jewish leaders over who has authority over the temple. The second part of Jesus' parable teaching is a quotation from Ps 118:22–23. This quotation functions as a second parable – the stone rejected by the builders (12:10–12), a statement that is crucial because it is the most explicit reference in Mark's narrative to a new temple that will replace the old.

The parable of the wicked tenants consists of three episodes: (1) the building of the vineyard; (2) the sending of the servants to receive fruit from the tenants; and (3) the sending of the owner's son, which ends with his murder at the hands of the tenants. The first episode sets the stage for the story, calling to mind the familiar story from Israel's Scriptures: Isaiah's song of the vineyard (Isa 5). In Isaiah 5, God is depicted as the builder and cultivator of a vineyard, much like the man in Jesus' parable. Indeed, the vineyard was a common symbol for Israel (Ps 80:8–18; Isa 27:2–6; Jer 2:21; 12:10; Ezek 19:10–14; Hos 10:1). The Markan account of the parable of the wicked tenants follows the general story line and vocabulary of Isaiah 5.[56] Of all the synoptic accounts of this parable, as well as that in the gospel of Thomas, Mark's account is closest to Isaiah 5, which makes the story of Isaiah 5 particularly important for Mark's understanding of this parable.

Isaiah 5:1–7 is a juridical parable, inviting the reader to see the justice of Israel's prophetic condemnation.[57] The Markan Jesus takes up the Isaian story of the vineyard for the same purpose: prophetic judgment. However, the vineyard story is tailored by Mark to fit the new circumstances surrounding Jesus' encounter with the temple and its stewards. It is worth emphasizing that, despite the modifications in detail, the overall purpose of this parable is to demonstrate the prophetic judgment the leaders of Israel have brought upon themselves by turning the temple into a den of thieves and by refusing the summons of John to repent and prepare for the eschatological coming of the kingdom. Thus, this parable continues the theme of eschatological judgment begun in Jesus' demonstration in the temple.

### 2.3.1.1 *Building the Vineyard (v. 1)*

One of the salient features of both vineyards is the building of a tower, καὶ ᾠκοδόμησεν πύργον (Isa 5:2 LXX and Mark 12:1). The imagery of the

---

[56] Some of the language Mark employs directly echoes the LXX, for example, the building of the tower (καὶ ᾠκοδόμησεν πύργον), while at other times Mark makes a small change, such as changing the first person ἐφύτευσα (LXX) to the third person ἐφύτευσεν (12:1). At other times, however, Mark seems to depart from the LXX and follow the MT, for example, Mark's account employs third person verbs for the owner whereas the LXX has these verbs in the first person. Mark's language seems to be rooted in both the LXX and the MT but, regardless of the precise source for Mark's account, what is important is that Mark's account follows closely the OT story of Isaiah 5. For an account of Mark's language as rooted in both the LXX and MT, see Evans, *Mark*, 224–28.

[57] On the juridical nature of the Isaiah 5, see J.T. Willis, "The Genre of Isaiah 5:1–7," *JBL* 96 (1977) 337–62; G. A. Yee, "The Form-Critical Study of Isaiah 5:1–7 as a Song and a Juridical Parable," *CBQ* 43 (1981) 30–40; G. T. Sheppard, "More on Isaiah 5:1–7 as a Juridical Parable," *CBQ* 44 (1982) 45–47; Craig Evans, "On the Vineyard Parables of Isaiah 5 and Mark 12," *BZ* 28 (1984) 82–86.

tower in Isaiah, as in Micah 4:8, is a symbol for the temple in Jerusalem.[58] Not only does the tower serve as a symbol for the temple in Isaiah and Micah, but this tradition was very much alive in Second Temple Judaism. A fragment from Qumran, 4Q500, interprets Isaiah's account of the vineyard as related to Jerusalem and the temple.[59] Craig Evans observes, "That such tower symbolism was current in the first century is supported by passages in 1 Enoch which refer to the temple as the 'tower.'"[60] Even later sources such as the Targums and Tosefta bear witness to the interpretive tradition of symbolizing the temple as a tower.[61] Since Mark places this parable in the context of Jesus' confrontation with the authorities in the temple following his demonstration there, it is clear that Mark intended to equate the temple with the tower in the parable.[62]

John Donahue has rightly observed that the owner of the vineyard plays the most central role of the story.[63] Given that all the verbs in 12:1 have the owner as their object, it is worth addressing this point now. Why does the owner have the primary role in the story from start (12:1) to finish (12:9)? The reason is that this parable is given in answer to the question of Jesus' authority. Authority, in the world of Mark's readers, is delegated by a hierarchy of power brokers. God is at the top of this hierarchy and it is to him that Jesus appeals as the source of his authority. Consequently, the owner of the vineyard features prominently in the story. At the heart of the parable are two rival claims to authority: that of the owner and his son

---

[58] Johannes C. de Moor ("The Targumic Background of Mark 12:1–12: The Parable of the Wicked Tenants," *JSJ* 19 [1998] 63–80, here 70) notes: "The tower is an early metaphor for the temple, not only in the Song of the Vine but also in Mic 4:8."

[59] See J. M. Baumgarten, "4Q500 and the Ancient Conception of the Lord's Vineyard," *JJS* 40 (1989) 1–3; Marcus, *The Way of the Lord*, 120: Craig Evans (*Jesus and His Contemporaries* [Boston: Brill, 2001] 400) concludes, "This fragmentary text appears to be part of a midrashic interpretation that views the vineyard of Isa 5:1–7 as a metaphor of Jerusalem and her Temple."

[60] Evans, *Contemporaries*, 399.

[61] See *Tg. Isa.* 5:1–7 and *t. Meil.* 1.16; *Suk.* 3.15. For further discussion see Marcus, *The Way of the Lord*, 120, and especially Evans, *Contemporaries*, 397–401.

[62] Thus W. J. C. Weren ("The Use of Isaiah 5,1–7 in the Parable of the Tenants [Mark 12,1–12; Matthew 21,33–46]," *Bib* 79 [1998] 17) concludes: "The detailed description of the laying out of the vineyard in Mark 12,1 does not merely serve the embellishment of the story. No, the fencing in of the vineyard, the hacking out of the winepress and the building of a tower get a proper function when they are understood as references to the temple." de Moor ("Targumic Background," 71) also sees the importance of the temple context: "Therefore it is in line with this Targumic tradition that the synoptics situate the parable of the wicked tenants in the temple where Jesus is addressing the chief priests and elders."

[63] John R. Donahue, *The Gospel in Parable: Metaphor, Narrative, and Theology in the Synoptic Gospels* (Philadelphia: Fortress, 1990) 54.

versus that of the tenants. The owner possesses true and legitimate authority, which he delegates to his son, who represents him to the tenants. By putting the owner at the center of his story, Jesus points out the source of his authority – God.

### 2.3.1.2  Sending Servants (vv. 2–5)

The owner of the vineyard sends out a servant to collect the proceeds of the fruit when it is time, τῷ καιρῷ (12:2). The word καιρός is used strategically in Mark's narrative. The Markan reader would probably recall that at Jesus' approach to the temple he curses the fig tree that is barren because it was not ὁ καιρός for figs (11:13). Moloney notes the narrative importance of ὁ καιρός: "Another expression found in the cursing of the fig tree returns in this parable, as Jesus tells of the owner's sending of a servant 'when the time came' (τῷ καιρῷ) to gather from the fruit of the vineyard (12:2). The link is unmistakable. The inability of Israel to see that the time (ὁ καιρός) was fulfilled and that the kingdom of God was at hand (1:14–15; 11:13) continues in Jesus' description of the tenants' dealing with the servant."[64] The motif of καιρός in Mark is intended to alert the reader that the eschatological time has now arrived; the eschatological harvest is at hand and failure to bear fruit will bring divine judgment.

The owner sends a δοῦλον (v. 2), and he is beaten and sent back empty-handed (v. 3). The owner sends yet another δοῦλον, who is hit upon the head and shamefully treated (v. 4).[65] The owner continues to send servants, indeed πολλοὺς ἄλλους, whom the tenants beat or kill (v. 5). The term δοῦλος refers to more than simply a literal slave; rather, it signifies the

---

[64] Moloney, *Mark*, 232.

[65] The meaning of ἐκεφαλίωσαν is a bit obscure, although most commentators agree (see, e.g., Moloney, *Mark*, 233 n. 89) that it generally means "wounded in the head." Evans argues, "The meaning of the ἐκεφαλίωσαν may be suggested by καὶ ἠτίμασαν, 'and treated him dishonorably,' that immediately follows. If these verbs are taken together in a complementary sense, then we may assume that to suffer something done to the head is to be treated dishonorably." Evans is arguing, I think correctly, from the thesis of U. Mell (*Die "anderen" Winzer: Eine exegetische Studie zur Vollmacht Jesu Christi nach Markus 11,27–12:34* [WUNT 77; Tübingen: Mohr-Siebeck, 1995] 104) who gives the example of David's servants that were sent as emissaries and whose beards were shaved and greatly dishonored, which the LXX 2 Kgs 10:2b–5 expresses by the word ἠτιμασμένοι. Thus, ἐκεφαλίωσαν is paired with καὶ ἠτίμασαν in order to convey the disregard the tenants have for the owner's envoys, in that they purposefully shame his representative. This shaming by the wicked tenants anticipates the kind of shameful treatment Jesus will receive during his passion in Mark 15:19 (Jesus is struck on the κεφαλή) and 15:29–32.

prophets whom God has sent to Israel.[66] The term δοῦλος is used for prophets in the LXX (Amos 3:7; Zech 1:6; Neh 9:26; 1 Kgs 18:13,22–27; 2 Chr 24:21; 36:15–16). There is a further reference to the sending of prophets and their suffering that may be related to this discussion. In 2 Chr 36:14–16, the leading priests are blamed for polluting the temple (36:14) despite the numerous entreaties of the prophets: "The LORD, the God of their fathers, sent persistently to them by his messengers, because he had compassion on his people and his dwelling place; but they kept mocking the messengers of God, despising his words, and scoffing at his prophets, till the wrath of the LORD rose against his people, till there was no remedy" (2 Chr 36:15–16).

A similar account is given toward the end of Jeremiah's oracle against the temple, from which the image of den of thieves the previous day was taken: "From the day that your fathers came out of the land of Egypt to this day, I have persistently sent all my servants the prophets to them, day after day; yet they did not listen to me, or incline their ears, but stiffened their neck. They did worse than their fathers" (Jer 7:25–26). The context for both 2 Chronicles and Jeremiah is the imminent destruction of the temple. The motif of the persistent sending the prophets (God's servants) with warnings that, if unheeded, would lead to the destruction of the temple strikingly parallels the Markan context of the parable of the tenants. The link cannot be accidental.[67] Thus, the owner's persistence in sending his servants is intended to evoke the image of God's persistent sending of the prophets before the end of the Solomonic temple. Now, the Markan Jesus is suggesting, the cycle has repeated itself, and a line of prophets has come, the last of which was John the Baptist, and now the second temple is about to come to its end.[68] The failure of the leading priests to heed the summons to repentance will lead to the judgment and destruction of Jerusalem's temple.

The rejection of the owner's servants paints a grim picture of the tenants. The tenants have usurped the vineyard for their own greed. They hold on violently to the vineyard's fruit. This portrait of the tenants is carefully drawn so as to cast the religious leaders opposed to Jesus as a band of robbers who are usurping the temple and its fruit. As Edward Horne observes, there is irony at play here: "In an interpretive twist, the

---

[66] Pace Taylor, *Mark*, 474.

[67] So de Moor, "Targumic Background," 71–72.

[68] Ibid., 72, "Again we observe that the present context of the gospel of Mark carefully prepares the way for the correct understanding of the parable. It introduces John the Baptist as one of the killed prophets in the immediately preceding passage (11:30–32; cf. 6:14–29)."

temple authorities are being placed in the position of the rebellious tenants instead of the position of the landowner."[69] By doing this, the Markan Jesus subverts the authority of the religious leaders. They are not the owners of the temple but rather stewards who have been found wanting. It is Jesus who is the real heir and the religious leaders who are the usurpers. Indeed, the tenants are clearly aligned with those who have made the temple a σπήλαιον λῃστῶν (11:17), for they are violent robbers.[70] With this, Mark underscores Jesus' authority while at the same showing how the tenants have long abused their stewardship and are now using their God-given positions to oppose God and his son.

### 2.3.1.3 *Sending the Son (vv. 6–8)*

Finally (ἔσχατον), the owner sends his son as an emissary to the tenants (v. 6). By describing the time of the son's sending as ἔσχατον, Mark evokes the eschatological mood that has marked Jesus' entire mission. Jesus too has been sent at the fullness of time (1:15). The son holds special favor with his father, and so is described as υἱὸν ἀγαπητόν (v. 6). Mark has prepared the reader to see the son as Jesus, for at both the baptism and transfiguration he has narrated the divine claim that Jesus is ὁ υἱός μου ὁ ἀγαπητός (Mark 1:11; 9:7).[71] Thus, the two most revelatory moments of Mark's story thus far have each climaxed with the acclamation that Jesus is God's beloved son. Indeed, Mark's opening statement, if authentic, proclaims Jesus as υἱοῦ θεοῦ (1:1). This theme, interwoven through Mark's narrative, anticipates the climax of Mark's story – the centurion's cry, "Truly this man was the Son of God" (15:39). The constant repetition

[69] Edward H. Horne, "The Parable of the Tenants as Indictment," *JSNT* 71 (1998) 113.

[70] "The tenants' killing the man's 'beloved son' (Jesus, 1:11; 9:7) after beating and killing the many servants he sent them (12:3–8) confirms the leaders as the robbers whom Jesus accused of turning the temple into a den of robbers (λῃστῶν, 11:17)" (Heil, "Temple Theme," 81).

[71] See Moloney, *Mark*, 233. Similarly, France, *Mark*, 460; Evans, *Mark*, 230; D. Lührmann, *Das Markusevangelium* (HNT 3; Tübingen: Mohr-Siebeck, 1987) 199. However, there has been some debate regarding the identity of the son. Some have suggested that John the Baptist is the son, since John was referred to just before the parable on the issue of authority, and the reference to a servant hit on the head (12:4) could be a reference to John's beheading (6:27–28), and finally John would be the last of the prophets/messengers sent by God. For this position, see A. Gray, "The Parable of the Wicked Husbandmen (Matthew xxi. 33–41; Mark xii. 1–9; Luke xx. 9–16)" *HibJ* 19 (1920–21) 42–52; David Stern, "Jesus' Parables from the Perspective of Rabbinic Literature: The Example of the Wicked Husbandmen," in *Parable and Story in Judaism and Christianity* (ed. C. Thomas and M. Wyschogrod; New York: Paulist, 1989) 42–80; C. S. Mann, *Mark* (AB 27: Garden City, New York: Doubleday, 1986).

of this theme at key moments illustrates that, for Mark, Jesus' identity is best understood in terms of his sonship. Again, this parable illustrates the true nature and source of Jesus' authority.

When the son approaches the tenants they say to one another, δεῦτε ἀποκτείνωμεν αὐτόν. These are the exact words of Joseph's brothers when they plot his death in LXX Gen 37:20.[72] The subtle allusion to Joseph's story enriches the parable in several ways.[73] First, Jesus is cast as the new Joseph, despised for being the beloved son and privileged heir (in LXX Gen 37:3 Joseph is the son that Jacob ἠγάπησεν). Conversely, this casts the tenants (religious leaders) as the envious brothers who seek the death of their father's beloved son.[74] Third, like Joseph, Jesus will be betrayed by a brother for money (Gen 37:28; Mark 14:10–11). Finally, the story of Joseph has a surprise ending that brings vindication to Joseph and good out of evil (Gen 50:20). Mark's story of Jesus will also end with reversal and surprise.

The tenants' plotting to kill the son is reminiscent of the religious leaders' plotting to kill Jesus, which has already occurred twice in the story (Mark 3:6; 11:18). This parallel helps the reader identify the wicked tenants as the religious leaders who are opposing Jesus. That the tenants recognize the son as the heir (ὁ κληρονόμος) and seek his inheritance (ἡ κληρονομία) is also important for Mark's purpose in relating the story (v. 7).[75] By describing the son as the heir, Mark underscores the nature and legitimacy of Jesus' authority. By narrating the tenant's intentions, Mark also further characterizes the corrupt religious leaders.

In v. 8 the tenants seize the son, kill him, and throw him out of the vineyard. The death of the son, who represents Jesus, takes up the three passion predictions that spoke of Jesus' death in Jerusalem (8:31; 9:31; 10:33–34). The story of the vineyard is a coded and condensed form of

---

[72] A. Weihs, "Die Eifersucht der Winzer zur Anspielung auf LXX Gen 37,20 in der Parabel von der Tötung des Sohnes (Mk 12,1–12)," *ETL* 76 (2000) 5–29, builds on the work of Pesch (*Markusevangelium*, 219) and Gnilka (*Evangelium Markus*, 147) to show the connections here with the Joseph story. See also more recently, Moloney, *Mark*, 233.

[73] See B. B. Scott, *Hear Then the Parable: A Commentary on the Parables of Jesus* (Minneapolis: Fortress, 1989) 252, and Evans, *Contemporaries*, 405.

[74] Moloney (*Mark*, 233) observes: "In a way reminiscent of the plot of Jacob's sons to the murder Joseph (see Gen 37:20), they regard the slaying of the beloved son as a means to acquire what should be his birthright. The vineyard, which the son should inherit, will pass to them (v. 7)."

[75] Tolbert (*Sowing the Gospel*, 248) notes that "the emphasis on 'heir' and 'inheritance' in the tenants' direct discourse, caused by the lexical similarity of the two terms in such close proximity (a form of polyptoton), should alert the audience to the importance of this new perspective on Jesus' identity." As I hope to point out, this identity is not new to the Markan reader, but its place here is to confirm Jesus' identity.

Mark's story of Jesus. Jesus is the son, the religious leaders the wicked tenants, and the conflict between them will lead to Jesus' violent end – but that is not the end of the story.

### 2.3.1.4  Judgment (v. 9)

In line with the juridical nature of this parable and its model parable in Isaiah 5, the violence of the wicked tenants provokes a pointed question, "What will the owner of the vineyard do?" (v. 9). The answer is unequivocal: "He will come and destroy the tenants, and give the vineyard to others." In the end, judgment comes for the wicked tenants. Here again, the motif of judgment comes to the fore of the story. Although this parable follows Isaiah's story in many ways, there are some significant differences that should be noted. The problem with Isaiah's vineyard is that it produces bad fruit – literally, "stinking grapes" (Isa 5:2,4). The Markan vineyard produces fruit; however, those placed in charge of the vineyard have stolen it. In v. 9, the vineyard is not destroyed but handed over to new custodians. In other words, the Markan parable locates the problem of the vineyard in its leadership. This fits well with Mark's account, which depicts the crowds in a positive, or at times neutral, light. Rather, the blame for the corruption is placed upon the leaders. Thus, the story of Isaiah is modified to fit the circumstances of Jesus' confrontation with the religious authorities.

Mark's account of this parable, given its present context, serves to answer the question of Jesus' authority. By narrating the story of Jesus and his conflict with the authorities in such a way, Mark gives a deeper characterization of both Jesus and the authorities. He illustrates that Jesus' authority stems from his divine sonship. Likewise, he further characterizes the greed and fratricidal tendencies of the religious leaders. Mark accomplishes this by evoking the stories of Israel's Scriptures (Isaiah 5, Jeremiah 7, 2 Chronicles 36, Genesis 37) and weaving motifs throughout his narrative (ἐξουσία, καιρός, υἱός, and plotting Jesus' death).

### 2.3.2  The Rejected Stone: Psalm 118 (12:10–12)

In vv. 10–11 Jesus suggests that the vineyard parable is illuminated by a quotation from Ps 118:22–23. This passage is about the stone rejected by the builders that in the end becomes the cornerstone. This seems to be an abrupt transition, moving from the world of the parable's vineyard to that of the Psalm. "Further, no logical connection seems obvious," according to Klyne Snodgrass, "for the imagery of the parable is agricultural, but the imagery of the quotation is architectural."[76] How does the story of builders and stones correlate with that of the tenant farmers and fruit? Indeed, Snodgrass observes that "quite possibly the most determinative issue for interpreting the parable is one's treatment of the stone quotation."[77] Any interpretation of the vineyard parable must explain the juxtaposition of the vineyard with the stone passage from Psalm 118.

First, it must be noted that the passage cited from Psalm 118 is a story in itself. The brief two verses quoted from the psalm tell a story of conflict, failure, and vindication in a nutshell. It is no expository passage with clear meaning; rather, the stone is employed as a metaphor to the preceding parable. Indeed, this quotation-as-narrative may explain the plural form of "parable" (παραβολαῖς) used by Mark to introduce the vineyard story (12:1).[78] However, it may well be that Mark understood the stone citation as a parable itself by which the larger vineyard parable is to be understood. This would seem to make sense as the vineyard imagery of tenant farmers and fruit are juxtaposed in the psalm quotation with builders and stone. The quotation, in other words, has enough imagery and story line to serve as a parable, which would explain Mark's introduction of the passage with the plural form, παραβολαῖς.

Matthew Black saw a link between the "son" of the vineyard story and the "stone" in the quotation based on the wordplay in Hebrew between בן and אבן. Another word should be added this paronomasia, "builders," הבונמ, which makes the wordplay threefold.[79] The implications of this wordplay, however helpful for historical reconstruction, do not provide a narrative bridge between the vineyard and stone quotation, as the link is lost in Mark's Greek text and his Greek-speaking audience.[80]

---

[76] Klyne R. Snodgrass, "Recent Research on the Parable of the Wicked Tenants: An Assessment," *BR* 8 (1998) 187–216, here 203.

[77] Snodgrass, "Recent Research," 202.

[78] Many commentators see no significance that Mark introduces Jesus' teaching in parables, but then only gives one parable, the parable of the vineyard (e.g., France, *Mark*, 458).

[79] For a discussion of this three-way wordplay, see Snodgrass, *The Parable of the Wicked Tenants: An Inquiry into Parable Interpretation* (WUND 27; Tübingen: Mohr-Siebeck, 1983) 113–18.

[80] The location of Mark's audience is very much debated; the traditional designation of Rome still has adherents (e.g., Donahue and Harrington, *Mark*, 41–46), while others argue for the Eastern part of the Roman Empire, not far from Galilee (Horsley, *Hearing the Whole Story*, 49–51) or the province of Syria (e.g., Joel Marcus, *Mark 1–8* [New York: Doubleday, 2000] 33–36). Richard Bauckham (*The Gospels for All Christians: Rethinking the Gospel Audiences* [Grand Rapids: Eerdmans, 1998]) has argued against any specific audience, claiming that the gospel was intended for a more universal audience. The common thread in all these positions is that Mark's audience is outside

Is there a link to be made (beyond the Semitic background of the tradition) between the vineyard parable and the stone citation from Psalm 118? I believe a link can be established in two ways.

First, both the vineyard and stone imagery have a common referent: the temple. As illustrated above, the building of a tower (ᾠκοδόμησεν πύργον) within the vineyard, as well as the wine press, evokes in Jewish tradition the temple (12:1). The image of building (ᾠκοδόμησεν) connects with the previous description of the temple as God's house (οἶκος, 11:17).[81] The building image of 12:1 also makes a connection with the builders (οἰκοδομοῦντες) in 12:10 who, in the context of the psalm, are building the temple (Ps 118:22).[82] Thus, the temple is evoked in 12:10 by the image of "stone" (λίθον) and "builders" (οἰκοδομοῦντες). Psalm 118 is clearly related to the temple since it is a pilgrimage psalm that celebrates the building of the temple and worship within it (Ps 118:19–27).[83] Therefore, the agricultural imagery in vv. 1–9 and the architectural imagery of vv. 10–11 coalesce, both representing the temple. Thus, the stone quotation has much to do with the vineyard imagery because it advances the temple plot line of Mark's story.

The second link is the connection between the plot of the two parables. The vineyard story climaxes with the violent rejection of the owner's beloved son. The stone in Psalm 118 is also subject to rejection. They are thus connected by a similar fate. Mark highlights this connection between the stone and son by employing a key word from Ps 118:22, "rejection" (ἀποδοκιμάζειν). The only other place where this term is found in the gospel is in Jesus' first passion prediction, where he predicts that he will be ἀποδοκιμασθῆναι by the chief priests, scribes, and elders (8:31).[84] The two places where ἀποδοκιμάζειν are found in Mark match so well that it must be part of Mark's narrative strategy. The reader knows that the

---

Palestine proper and is a Greek-speaking audience that needs Aramaic translated for them and is familiar with Roman words and customs. Thus the audience, very much Gentile in makeup, is part of the Hellenistic culture of the Roman Empire. This being said, this Gentile audience has some familiarity with the Scriptures and history of Israel and value both. See also Donahue, "The Quest for the Community of Mark's Gospel," in *The Four Gospels* (ed. Frans van Segbroeck et al.; Leuven: Leuven University Press, 1992), 819–34. For a recent review of the different positions, see Moloney, *Mark*, 11–15.

[81] So Heil, "Temple Theme," 81.

[82] See Weren, " Use of Isaiah 5," 17.

[83] See, e.g., Wright, *Victory*, 498.

[84] Robert D. Rowe (*God's Kingdom and God's Son: The Background to Mark's Christology from Concepts of Kingship in the Psalms* [Boston: Brill, 2002] 263) notes the importance of this for Mark's narrative: "The theme of rejection and vindication, which is explicit in Psalm 118:22, exactly fits Jesus' interpretation of his Messiahship in Mark 8:29–31... These are the only two occurrences of ἀποδοκιμάζω in Mark's gospel."

Jewish leaders will reject Jesus (8:31), and now the stone rejected by the builders is juxtaposed to the son whom the tenants violently murder. Thus, by taking the intertextual echo from Psalm 118 and weaving it into his larger narrative about Jesus (8:31) and the owner's son, Mark has identified Jesus with the heir of the vineyard and the cornerstone of the temple.[85]

The stone is a metaphor for Jesus and, as I have suggested, an extended metaphor that functions as a parable. In parables and metaphors, there are two referents being compared or contrasted.[86] For example, the wicked tenants are set in comparison to the chief priests, scribes, and elders. The story of the wicked tenants and the story of the Jewish leaders are juxtaposed and thereby mutually interpretive. Here we see how a parable is able to tell a story about something (Jewish leaders) by means of something else (wicked tenants). Hence, the rhetorical force of parables comes from the inner tension and play between the two referents or poles. In many readings of this parable, however, the stone is not compared to Jesus, it is identified with him. This makes the stone function as a symbol rather than as a metaphor. In order to understand the parable/metaphor of Jesus and the stone, their mutually interpretive stories must be juxtaposed and compared, not collapsed into one simple identification. Just as the story of the wicked tenants informs the story of the Jewish leaders and vice versa, the story of the rejected stone informs the story of Jesus. Examining the story of the rejected stone of Psalm 118 and comparing it to Jesus' story of rejection will be crucial for a better reading of the parable.

What is the story of this rejected stone? The description of the rejected stone in Ps 118:22 comes during the psalmist's arrival at the temple. To speak of a stone rejected by the builders but raised up by God to be the cornerstone (literally, the "head of the corner," κεφαλὴν γωνίας) while one was in the temple would immediately evoke the foundation stone of the temple.[87] This is particularly true since this is the very psalm sung during

---

[85] Marcus (*The Way of the Lord*, 114) believes Mark intended this identification: "This identification is cemented by the fact that the verb ἀποδοκιμάζειν ('to reject') occurs in only one other place in Mark, in 8:31, where Jesus uses it to prophesy his own rejection by the Jewish leaders."

[86] Janet Soskice's work (*Metaphor and Religious Language* [Oxford: Carendon Press, 1985]) is helpful in this area; she defines metaphor as "that figure of speech whereby we speak about one thing in terms which are seen to be suggestive of another" (p. 15).

[87] Jeremias believes that κεφαλὴν γωνίας signifies keystone rather than cornerstone. Jeremias' examples, however, come from later patristic sources such as Tertullian, for whom keystone was more prominent due to Roman architecture. Jeremias ignores the witness of 1 Peter's use of Ps 118:22 along with Isa 28:16, where 1 Pet 2:4–8 associates the stone of Psalm 118 with the foundation stone of Isa 28:16 and thus provides an

Jesus' procession up to the temple (11:9–10). What is more, this psalm is closely associated with the Feast of Tabernacles, which was the feast of the temple par excellence. If the stone is to be identified as a foundation stone that was previously rejected, there can be only two possible referents: the foundation stone of Solomon's temple or that of Zerubbabel's temple.[88]

The *Psalms of Solomon* relates a story of how Solomon employed his power over demons to force a powerful demon to move the "gigantic cornerstone" for the temple. After the demon placed the stone, Solomon exclaims: "I, Solomon, being excited, exclaimed, 'Truly the Scripture which says, I was the stone rejected by the builders that became the keystone, has now been fulfilled,' and so forth."[89] Although there is much debate concerning the dating of this testament, "there is general agreement that much of the testament reflects first-century Judaism in Palestine."[90] But this is far from certain.[91] It is significant that the cornerstone of Psalm 118 is identified as the cornerstone of the temple. However, the explanation in the *Psalms of Solomon* for the stone's initial rejection is its formidable weight, which necessitated demonic aid. This is a grave difference between this account of the stone and Jesus' use of Psalm 118, given that the main point of the stone in Mark 12:10 is that it is rejected. Therefore, although the connection between Ps 118:22 and the cornerstone of the temple is revealing, the legend regarding the stone in the *Psalms of Solomon* cannot be the basis for Mark's use of the stone.

While there is no evidence within the OT canon that the foundation stone of the Solomonic temple was ever rejected, there is compelling evidence that the cornerstone of the second temple, Zerubbabel's temple, was met with bitter disappointment and even resistance. Ezra records how the laying of the foundation stone for Zerubbabel's temple triggered a

---

example of how the rejected stone could be interpreted as the foundation stone. This is also pictured in Eph 2:20 where Christ is seen as the cornerstone ἀκρογωνιαίου of the foundation θεμελίῳ. Therefore, there is good reason to believe that the cornerstone was seen by Mark and the early Christians as the foundation stone of the temple. Joachim Jeremias, "κεφαλὴν γωνίας" *TDNT*, 3. 274–75. Ernst Lohmeyer (*The Lord of the Temple: A Study of the Relation between Cult and Gospel* [London: Oliver and Boyd, 1961] 46) pointed out the fluidity of the terms, cornerstone and keystone, even within the OT.

[88] The cornerstone of Herod's temple may also be considered. Herod had Zerubbabel's foundation and earlier work gutted when he rebuilt the Temple. See Carol Meyers, "Temple, Jerusalem" *ABD* 6. 364–65.

[89] *Pss. Sol.* 23:4.

[90] Cf. D. C. Dulings's introduction to the work in James H. Charlesworth, *The Old Testament Pseudepigrapha* (New York: Doubleday, 1983) 1. 942.

[91] Marcus (*The Way of the Lord*, 119) sees *Pss. Sol.* as postbiblical, dating from first to third century A.D.

mixed reaction among the people of Israel. First, he describes how the priests led the people in singing and giving thanks to God:

And when the builders laid the foundation of the temple of the LORD, the priests ... sang responsively, praising and giving thanks to the LORD, '*For he is good, for his steadfast love endures for ever toward Israel.*' And all the people shouted with a great shout, when they praised the LORD, because the foundation of the house of the LORD was laid. (Ezra 3:10–11)

The designation of the priests, Levites, and elders among the builders who lay the foundation (ἐθεμελίωσαν τοῦ οἰκοδομῆσαι) for the Lord's temple (τὸν οἶκον κυρίου) should be noted. In rabbinic traditions, "builders" is a common designation for scribes and scholars.[92] This may be due in part to the paronomasia between build, בנה, and "understand," בין.[93] There is evidence for calling leaders in the Jewish establishment as "builders" in the first century in Acts 4:11 and Qumran.[94] What is significant is that Ezra provides a far older tradition for the understanding of religious leaders as "builders" in the context of laying the foundation stone of the temple. It may be that the tradition of seeing the religious authorities as "builders" stems from Ezra 3.

Ezra writes that opposition to the new temple foundation was incited by the Jewish leadership, from among the very "builders":

But many of the priests and Levites and heads of fathers' houses, old men who had seen the first house, wept with a loud voice when they saw the *foundation* of this house being laid ... (3:12)

The glory of the "first house," τὸν οἶκον τὸν πρῶτον, is contrasted with "this house," τοῦτον τὸν οἶκον, the latter falling far short of the leaders' expectations. It is striking that the Jewish leaders are broken into a triparte group in Ezra (καὶ πολλοὶ ἀπὸ τῶν ἱερέων καὶ τῶν Λευιτῶν καὶ ἄρχοντες τῶν πατριῶν οἱ πρεσβύτεροι). This threefold grouping bears a resemblance to Mark's threefold breakdown of the Jewish leaders who confront Jesus (οἱ ἀρχιερεῖς καὶ οἱ γραμματεῖς καὶ οἱ πρεσβύτεροι).

The older group of priests, Levites, and elders weep in dejection at the humble beginnings of this new temple project, in contrast to the younger generation who did not know the former temple:

---

[92] Marcus, *The Way of the Lord*, 124; Snodgrass, *Parable*, 96.

[93] See J. D. M. Derrett, "The Stone That the Builders Rejected," *Studies in the New Testament* (Leiden: Brill, 1977) 2. 64–65. See also Marcus, *The Way of the Lord*, 125.

[94] Evans, *Contemporaries*, 404. "As in the Targum, religious authorities were sometimes called 'builders.' We see this in rabbinic literature, but more importantly we find it in Qumran where it is quite negative. Of special importance is the appearance of Psa 118:22 in Acts 4:11 where the builders are specifically identified as members of the Sanhedrin."

so that the people could not distinguish the sound of the joyful shout from the sound of the people's weeping, for the people shouted with a great shout, and the sound was heard afar. (3:13)

The sadness experienced by many of the leaders had serious repercussions. Soon after the foundation stone is put in place, the people stop building the temple.[95] Ezra explains that the "people of the land," whom he labels "the adversaries of Judah and Benjamin," "discouraged the people of Judah, and made them afraid to build" (Ezra 4:1, 4).

Since this setback comes on the heels of the great anguish of many leaders over the insignificance of the foundation stone (3:12–13), one must not think that only those outside the Israelites contributed to the discouragement. The prophet Haggai does not blame anyone but the Israelites for the putting off the building:

Thus says the LORD of hosts: This people say the time has not yet come to rebuild the house of the LORD. Then the word of the LORD came by Haggai the prophet, 'Is it time for yourselves to dwell in your paneled houses, while this house lies in ruins?' (1:2–4)

The people do not have time for the Lord's house because they would rather work on their own:

You have looked for much, and lo, it came to little; and when you brought it home, I blew it away. Why? says the LORD of hosts. Because of my house that lies in ruins, while you busy yourselves each with his own house. (1:9)

Haggai puts the blame for discouragement on the Israelites, without a single mention of the "adversaries of Judah and Benjamin."

There is good reason to believe that Haggai saw that the primary cause of Israel's abandoning the temple project lay in its humble beginnings, e.g., its small foundation. This is manifest in his second and central oracle (Hag 2:1–9). In this oracle the Lord, through Haggai, addresses those who saw Solomon's temple in all its glory, who also happen to be those who wept at the foundation ceremony:

Who is left among you that saw this house in its former glory? How do you see it now? *Is it not in your sight as nothing?* Yet now take courage, O Zerubbabel, says the LORD; take courage, O Joshua, son of Jehozadak, the high priest; take courage, all you people of the land, says the LORD; work, for I am with you, says the LORD of hosts. (Hag 2:3–4, italics my own)

The exhortation to take courage despite the seeming insignificance of this new beginning – particularly the foundation – is evidence that, for Haggai, the heart of the problem was the elders' inability to reconcile the humble

---

[95] The prophets Haggai and Zechariah are sent to admonish the people to resume building the temple. Cf. Ezra 5–6, especially 6:14, as well as Haggai and Zechariah.

beginnings of the new project with the glory of the old. Haggai addressed this point with a prophetic promise:

For thus says the LORD of hosts: Once again, in a little while, I will shake the heavens and the earth and the sea and the dry land; and I will shake all nations, so that the treasures of all nations shall come in and I will fill this house with splendor ... *The latter splendor of this house shall be greater than the former*, says the LORD of hosts. (2:6–9)

This oracle was surely directed at the discontent that was loudly voiced at the foundation ceremony and that played a key part in suspending the construction of the Lord's house. This is confirmed by the occasion of Haggai's oracle. The oracle is given "in the second year of Darius the king, in the seventh month, on the twenty-first day of the month" (Hag 2:1). This is the last and climactic day of the feast of Tabernacles, the liturgical day of the dedication of the first temple.[96] Haggai's exhortation to Israel to resume building the temple on this day would evoke strong emotions and memories from his audience. Certain dates can evoke powerful memories and symbols, and the Feast of Tabernacles surely evoked, for the Jews of Haggai's time, the task of building and dedicating the temple. This is important because Psalm 118 is closely associated with Tabernacles in Second Temple Judaism.

The prophet Zechariah also addressed the resentment garnered by the feeble beginning of the foundation.

Moreover the word of the LORD came to me, saying, "*The hands of Zerubbabel have laid the foundation of this house; his hands shall also complete it.* Then you will know that the LORD of hosts has sent me to you. *For whoever has despised the day of small things shall rejoice*, and shall see the plummet in the hand of Zerubbabel." (Zech 4:8–10, italics my own)

"The day of small things" mentioned in conjunction with the statement that Zerubbabel's hands had "laid the foundation" must refer to the day of the foundation ceremony recorded in Ezra 3. Here, Zechariah gives a sharper picture of the displeasure of those dissatisfied with the foundation stone, for their sorrow led them to despise the day the stone was laid. This passage corroborates the evidence from Haggai that those who saw the former glory of God's house rejected the new cornerstone laid by Zerubbabel.

The parable's juxtaposition of the story of the murdered beloved son with that of the rejected stone creates an explosive fusion. Both the son and the stone have their own stories, but these stories become mutually

---

96 According to Num 29:12, the feast of Tabernacles begins on the 15th of Tishri and lasts for seven days. Solomon celebrates the dedication of the temple in the seventh month, which is Tishri, for seven days; cf. 2 Chr 5:3; 7:9–10 and 1 Kgs 8:2,65.

interpretive by their proximity. These two stories become the heuristic tools by which the Markan reader is to understand the story of Jesus: he is the beloved son rejected by the wicked tenants but vindicated by the Lord.

The rejected stone provides a biblical paradigm for Jesus' story. As Israel returns from exile, the Davidic representative lays the foundation stone for the new temple. The crowds rejoice and praise this new work that God is doing in their midst; however, many of the leading priests, scribes, and elders despise this humble beginning. Locked in the old ways of being Israel, they reject the new plans the Lord has for them. The builders reject the would-be cornerstone of the new Zion, but the Lord himself promises that the work will be completed. [97] Despite the humble beginnings, the splendor of the new temple will be greater than that of the old. Appearances are deceiving, but the Lord will bless this inchoate start. Those who accept the simple start and see the work through to the end will be vindicated. That vindication will come when the glory of the Lord fills the new temple with beauty and splendor. So many threads from Ezra's story of the rejected stone are found in Mark's account that the emerging patterns must be purposeful: the Markan Jesus is making a new beginning that is met with initial resistance from the religious leaders; in time, however, his work will be blessed by the Lord, and a new and greater temple will emerge.

By quoting Psalm 118 in the temple, therefore, the Markan Jesus is claiming to be the new cornerstone of the eschatological temple. God is doing a new work, leading his people out of the exile of sin and death. Because of a beginning that is simple and inglorious, Jesus is cast aside by those who measure glory by outward appearance. Despite his rejection and death, God will raise him up to be the cornerstone of the new temple. Jesus is the new locus of God's healing and forgiving presence. He casts himself as the new Davidic Zerubbabel come at the turning point of Israel's story, empowered by the Spirit (Mark 1:10; Zech 4:6). The mountain that stands in his way shall be destroyed (Mark 11:23; Zech 4:7). He is the humble king who enters Jerusalem meek and riding on a young colt (Mark 11:7–11; Zech 9:9). In the new Zion that he inaugurates, the nations will gather and join themselves to the Lord (Zech 2:11; 8:21–23; 14:16–17; and Mark 15:39).

Because of their continual rejection of Jesus, the Jewish leaders have become the "adversaries of Judah." By resisting the rebuilding of the Lord's house, Haggai's threat that there would be no fruit in Israel (Hag

---

[97] "These links suggest the Old Testament context of the psalm quotation, with its references to the Temple liturgy, is in view in Mark 12:10–11 and that Jesus is being portrayed as the cornerstone of a new Temple" (Marcus, *The Way of the Lord*, 121).

1:10–11) has become tragically realized, as the barren fig tree illustrates. Ironically, those who are the builders of Israel are the very ones opposing the rebuilding of the temple.[98] They would allow Herod to rebuild Zion, but they would not allow the true rebuilding commissioned by the Lord of the temple himself.

### 2.3.3   Three Questions for the Teacher (12:13–34)

After Jesus tells the parable of the tenants, the chief priests, scribes, and elders send some of the Pharisees and Herodians to test Jesus (12:13). This begins a threefold series of questions given by the representative groups of Israel's leadership: Pharisees and Herodians, Sadducees, and scribes. Three elements give unity to this section (12:13–44): (1) they all occur on the same day; (2) they all occur in the temple; and (3) and they all illustrate Jesus' teaching. Jesus' condemnation of the temple provoked a challenge from the temple establishment concerning proper authority. From 11:27–12:44 this issue of authority is the plot line at the heart of the various stories gathered together here by Mark. Mark's purpose is to illustrate Jesus' authority and show how he silences the leaders of Israel in order to reveal their lack of authority.[99]

Mark gives particular unity to this section by depicting Jesus as either one who is "teaching" or one who is addressed as "teacher." In the three questions posed to Jesus, the different Jewish leaders address him as διδάσκαλε (12:14,19,32). In turn, when Jesus poses his own question, it is narrated as his "teaching" (διδάσκων, 12:35). The following section has Jesus' warnings about the scribes (12:38–44), which is introduced by the narrator as further "teaching" (διδαχή, 12:38). Mark also highlights that during Jesus' demonstration in the temple he was "teaching" (ἐδίδασκεν, 11:15), and that the crowds were amazed at his "teaching" (διδαχῇ, 11:18). Why does Mark give such emphasis on "teaching" in his temple narrative?

The issue of "teaching" is closely related to the question of authority. By demonstrating the authoritative power of Jesus' teaching and the threadbare teaching of the religious leaders, Mark advances again the motif of ἐξουσία. Indeed, at the outset of his story Mark contrasted the teaching

---

98 "If Jesus is in some sense building the real Temple, the objectors – ironically, since their own worldview focuses so strongly on the Temple in Jerusalem – are cast as those who resolutely opposed its rebuilding" (Wright, *Victory*, 30).

99 "Jesus has entered Jerusalem and its temple (11:1–11) and symbolically ended the traditional way to God through the cultic activity of the temple, replacing it with the promise of a new temple, a way of life marked by faith, prayer, and forgiveness (11:12–25). He now condemns and reduces the leaders of Israel to silence: chief priests, scribes, elders, Pharisees, Herodians, and Sadducees" (Moloney, *Mark*, 229).

authority of Jesus verses the scribes: καὶ ἐξεπλήσσοντο ἐπὶ τῇ διδαχῇ αὐτοῦ· ἦν γὰρ διδάσκων αὐτοὺς ὡς ἐξουσίαν ἔχων καὶ οὐχ ὡς οἱ γραμματεῖς (1:22). It is noteworthy that Mark connects διδαχή with ἐξουσία. Mark begins his story in 1:22 by telling his audience that Jesus' teaching authority exceeds that of the religious leaders, and now in the temple controversies, where Jesus' authority is in question, Mark illustrates Jesus' superior authority through his irrefutable teaching. The one who teaches with authority in the temple is himself the Lord of the temple.[100]

The material of 12:13–34 is indirectly related to the temple motif. Besides confirming Jesus' authority over that of his opponents, the particular content of Jesus' teaching is not of significant concern for my study of the temple motif. The question about paying the tax to Caesar is perhaps a response to Jesus' charge that the temple establishment is a den of robbers, since they are now determined to paint Jesus as the true insurgents against Rome. The question of the resurrection bears upon Jesus' claim that the son will be vindicated and thereby become the cornerstone for the new temple. And of course the question about the greatest commandment allows Jesus – while teaching in the temple – to declare inconsequential all ceremonial sacrifices of the temple. By setting this conflict within the temple, Mark intensifies the conflict between Jesus and the religious leaders. In the dispute regarding ultimate authority over the temple, Jesus silences the religious leaders within the temple itself.

His temple teaching concludes with a robust condemnation of the scribes for bearing a false religiosity while extorting the poor and widows (12:38–40). The scribes have failed to give to God what belongs to God (12:17) and, by taking advantage of widows, have failed to love their neighbor (12:31).[101] Such corruption further illustrates why Jesus

---

[100] Heil ("Temple Theme," 85) sums up this focus on Jesus' teaching as it relates to the Temple motif: "The notice that Jesus was still teaching in the temple (διδάσκων ἐν τῷ ἱερῷ, 12:35) continues the emphasis on his lordship over the temple, which he entered as 'the Lord' (11:3) who comes in the name of the Lord God (11:9), and which his teaching condemned as a place of inadequate worship (11:15–19). Jesus' teaching in the temple of his messianic lordship develops his vindication of himself, in the face of his enemies, by his resurrection after his enemies had killed him – an essential element of the Marcan temple theme."

[101] "Devouring widows' houses is a violation of the command to love one's neighbor as oneself. The contrast between God's demand for love of God and neighbor and the Jewish leaders' behavior highlights the fact that the section is not only a defense that Jesus' authority is from God, but an indictment of the Jewish establishment for not deriving its authority from God" (Dewey, *Public Debate*, 165).

condemned the temple as a den of violent robbers and why the authority of the leaders is bankrupt.

### 2.3.4  Teaching in Riddles (12:35–37)

Mark brackets the three questions posed to Jesus between two accounts of Jesus' royal and divine sonship (12:1–12 and 12:35–37), both of which are foundational to his authority over the temple. Jesus' question about the Davidic origins of the Messiah (12:35) based on Psalm 110 plays a crucial role in his claim of authority over the temple. I shall therefore give an analysis of this pericope (12:35–37).

#### 2.3.4.1  Problem of Davidic Descent

The problem is: the scribes teach that the Messiah is the son of David, but if he is David's son, how can David call him "Lord"? (12:35). The underlying premise is: a father is greater than his son, and it is therefore inappropriate for him to call his son "Lord." Although this premise may not carry much weight in modern times, it was clearly strong enough to go unquestioned by Jesus' audience. What is so fascinating about this riddle is not that the scribes could not answer but that no answer is ever given, either by Jesus to the disciples or by Mark to the reader. We are left as puzzled as the scribes, and that is perhaps part of Mark's rhetorical strategy.[102] It is easy to see why many scholars have characterized this passage as enigmatic.

The most straightforward reading of this story is that Jesus is denying that the Messiah is the son of David.[103] Although this reading might make

---

[102] Robert M. Fowler (*Let the Reader Understand: Reader-Response Criticism and the Gospel of Mark* [Minneapolis: Fortress, 1991] 195–209) highlights the important rhetorical effect of ambiguity in Mark's story: "Jesus thus uses ambiguity as a rhetorical tool to provoke response from his listeners" (p. 199).

[103] See, e.g., T. W. Manson, *The Teaching of Jesus* (Cambridge: Cambridge University Press, 1963) 266–67; Telford, *Barren Temple*, 257; Lührmann, *Das Markusevangelium* (Handbuch zum Neuen Testament 3; Tübingen: J.C.B. Mohr, 1987) 209. As Moloney (*Mark*, 243) states, "David cannot possibly be the father of the Messiah because he called him his 'lord' (v. 37a). A person cannot be 'father' of his 'lord.'" This is clearly a problem that those attempting to defend the designation and title Son of David have not squarely faced (e.g., Edwin K. Broadhead, *Naming Jesus: Titular Christology in the Gospel of Mark* (JSNTSup 175; Sheffield: Sheffield, 1999) 109–15. In my argument that follows, I suggest that there actually is an answer to the riddle; an answer that illustrates from Israel's scriptural traditions how a person can be a "father" while at the same time can call his son "lord" (David with his son Solomon). Those who argue that the straightforward reading of this riddle from Ps 110:1 is a repudiation of Davidic sonship must grapple with the fact that both Matthew and Luke, whose

sense of the riddle itself, its heuristic value plummets once the riddle is put in the context of Mark's gospel. Jesus saw himself as the Messiah, as Peter's confession makes clear (8:29). Telford argues that Mark intended to affirm Jesus as the Messiah while denying that he was the son of David.[104] It seems unlikely, however, that Mark would deny Jesus the title son of David in his messianic portrait, since several times in the gospel this title and its equivalent forms are attributed to Jesus. For instance, when questioned about his disciple's actions on the Sabbath, Jesus asserted the right to do so by claiming David as his precedent (Mark 2:25–26). Jesus even asked the religious leaders if they had read the story of David, thereby inviting the reader to compare Jesus and David (2:25).[105] On another occasion, just before his arrival in Jerusalem, Jesus accepts the title 'son of David.'[106] The blind Bartimaeus hailed Jesus as "son of David," and while many rebuked him, he was called forward by Jesus himself. Jesus rewarded him for his faith and cured his blindness, thus implicitly accepting the title.[107] If Jesus had wanted to reject such a title, he surely would have silenced Bartimaeus as he had silenced many others.[108]

---

genealogies highlight Jesus' Davidic descent, also contain this riddle (Matt 22:41–46 and Luke 20:41–44). Clearly, this riddle does not necessitate an out-and-out denial of Davidic descent.

[104] Telford, *Barren Temple*, 251–62. Many interpret this riddle as an attempt to make relative the significance of the title Son of David for Son of Man and Son of God for Jesus, (e.g., Pesch, *Markusevangelium*, 254–56; Lührmann, *Markusevangelium*, 208–9; Gnilka, *Evangelium Markus*, 171).

[105] Marcus (*Mark 1–8*, 245) notes that the Markan Jesus here is cast in the role of David, and that the OT story of David is being echoed in important ways: "It is important to Mark to show Jesus playing a Davidic role."

[106] Mark 10:46–52.

[107] Contra Moloney, *Mark*, 208–11. Moloney argues, based on the work of John Meier (*A Marginal Jew: Rethinking the Historical Jesus* [3 vols.; Anchor Bible Reference Library; New York: Doubleday, 1994] 2. 689–90) and James H. Charlesworth ("The Son of David: Solomon and Jesus," in *The New Testament and Hellenistic Judaism* [ed. P. Borgen and S. Giversen; Peabody: Hendrickson, 1997] 72–87), that the title Son of David refers to Solomon as a healer. (See also Bruce Chilton, "Jesus *ben David*: Reflections on the *Davidssohnfrage*," *JSNT* 14 (1982) 88–112.) Thus, Bartimaeus's use of the title is simply to evoke his belief that Jesus can heal him. Regardless of how one dates this rabbinic tradition of Solomon as healer, the title itself used in this manner still leaves open the notion of Jesus being of Davidic descent, just as Solomon was. Indeed, the answer to the riddle of Ps 110:1, as I shall argue, is that it is precisely the relationship between David and Solomon that provides the key to unlocking the riddle's dilemma. Therefore, an allusion to Jesus as a Son of David like Solomon, even with connotations of healer, I believe, strengthens the position put forth in this paper.

[108] E.g., Jesus silenced demons (1:25), the healed leper (1:44), his apostles (8:30); therefore Jesus' silence in the wake of Bartimaeus's confession of faith is loud.

Strong allusions to Jesus' Davidic claims are made in the royal procession to Jerusalem, where the crowds sing, "Blessed is the kingdom of our father David that is coming! Hosanna in the highest!" (Mark 11:10). Finally, if Jesus were attempting here to deny the messianic claim, why does he answer the high priest affirmatively during his trial (14:62) – an answer that sends him to the cross? This interpretation makes sense of the riddle at the cost of making much of the gospel senseless.

Another reading of the riddle claims that Jesus was not denying Davidic messiahship, but was redefining Davidic sonship. This reading then usually takes one of two directions: (1) Jesus is asserting that he will not be a warrior-king who will bring about a bloody political revolution; or (2) that Jesus is more than a descendent of David – he is the Son of God and or Son of Man.[109] According to the latter view, the answer to the riddle is to be found in the resurrection.

Donald Juel is representative of those who believe that the answer to the riddle is not revealed until the resurrection. According to Juel, it is through Jesus' death and resurrection that he is elevated to the right hand of God. Subsequently, "it is appropriate for David to call his messianic son 'Lord' in view of Jesus' installation at God's right hand."[110] The point of the riddle, then, is that "death and resurrection are not incompatible with what the Scriptures have to say about the Christ."[111] Unfortunately, the sole argument Juel gives to support this hypothesis is that it is the only explanation possible: "In fact, only if Jesus, the Son of David, has been elevated to that position does the alleged scriptural contradiction disappear."[112] Thus, the answer, according to Juel, can only be found outside the context of Mark's story.

Readings of this passage generally assume, as Juel claimed, that there is no possible way to reconcile how king David would call his son Lord. This has led some to believe that Mark denies any Davidic lineage or title for Jesus. On the other hand, because of the Davidic allusions in the rest of Mark's story, many commentators claim that Jesus is not denying Davidic descent, although the riddle points precisely in this direction. These scholars hold that Jesus is not actually denying Davidic sonship but rather critiquing its meaning – despite the fact that no evidence from Mark 12:35–37 is given in support of this position.

---

[109] E.g. Marcus, *The Way of the Lord*, chapter 7.

[110] Donald Juel, *A Master of Surprise: Mark Interpreted* (Minneapolis: Fortress, 1994) 98–99.

[111] Juel, *Master*, 99.

[112] Ibid.

The assumption of Jesus' question – that the son of David could not call him "Lord" – is fundamental to the positions above but ought not go unchallenged. What if a precedent for the contrary existed? What if there is evidence in Israel's Scriptures that David called one of his sons "Lord"? Such a case might just be the key to unlocking this enigmatic riddle. I propose that the best clue to this riddle comes from the very text used to pose it: Psalm 110.

### 2.3.4.2  *Psalm 110 and Solomon*

Psalm 110 is an enthronement psalm, sung during the coronation of the Davidic kings. By the first century this psalm, like many others, had messianic and eschatological overtones – hence Jesus' use of this text in reference to the Messiah. It is not hard to see how a psalm that spoke of a Davidic king conquering the nations and ruling from Zion would be conceived by first-century Jews as being messianic. The psalm not only promises kingly rule but priestly authority as well. This authority is solidified by a sworn oath from the Lord: "You are a priest for ever after the order of Melchizedek" (110:4). From a canonical perspective – the perspective Mark would have taken – who is this king who will rule the nations from Zion and reign as a priest-king in the tradition of Melchizedek?

According to the psalm title and the Markan Jesus, the psalmist is David. If this were the case, then the one being enthroned must be Solomon. However, that still does not explain why David would address his son, saying, "The LORD [Yhwh] says to my lord [Solomon]: Sit at my right hand…" Why would David ever address his own son Solomon as "Lord"? Under what circumstances would King David address another – albeit his own son – as king?

The first chapter of 1 Kings tells the story of the political intrigue regarding King David's successor. After Bathsheba reminded David of his oath that Solomon would reign after him, David swore to fulfill the oath that very day (1 Kgs 1:30). David then called for Zadok the priest, Nathan the prophet, and Benaiah the commander, and gave them instructions concerning Solomon's anointing and enthronement. Solomon was to ride David's ass and go down to the spring of Gihon where they were to anoint Solomon king (1:33–34).[113] Then Solomon was to process up to the throne

---

[113] Could Solomon's anointing at the spring of Gihon (1 Kgs 1:33,38,45) be alluded to in Ps 110:7, "He will drink from the brook by the way; therefore he will lift up his head"?

on David's ass, where he would be appointed ruler over Israel and Judah (1:35).[114] Upon hearing these instructions, Benaiah answered the king:

καὶ ἀπεκρίθη Βαναιας υἱὸς Ιωδαε τῷ βασιλεῖ καὶ εἶπεν Γένοιτο· οὕτως πιστώσαι κύριος ὁ θεὸς τοῦ κυρίου μου τοῦ βασιλέως· καθὼς ἦν κύριος μετὰ τοῦ κυρίου μου τοῦ βασιλέως οὕτως εἴη μετὰ Σαλωμων καὶ μεγαλύναι τὸν θρόνον αὐτοῦ ὑπὲρ τὸν θρόνον τοῦ κυρίου μου τοῦ βασιλέως Δαυιδ
(3 Kgdms 1:36–37 LXX)

Benaiah's words here resonate with the opening words of Psalm 109 LXX: εἶπεν ὁ κύριος τῷ κυρίῳ μου. The reference to both Yhwh and the king as κύριος bridges these two passages. The verbal links between Psalm 109 LXX and 3 Kgdms 1:36–37 LXX are furthered strengthened by the conceptual connections. The text of 3 Kingdoms 1 LXX is about the enthronement of David's son, Solomon; Psalm 110, whose title ascribes it to David, is also about enthronement. In Psalm 109 LXX, David recognizes his κύριος (Yhwh) as the one who blesses his κύριος (David's king – Solomon, 109:1), with authority and vindication over his enemies (109:2). The mention of the triumph over enemies is in line with Solomon's succession, which marks the immediate end of Solomon's enemies (3 Kgdms 1:41–2:35).

One detail in the account of Solomon's enthronement has particular importance for Jesus' question in Mark 12:35 – the response of David and his servants:

καὶ ἐκάθισεν Σαλωμων ἐπὶ θρόνον τῆς βασιλείας καὶ εἰσῆλθον οἱ δοῦλοι τοῦ βασιλέως εὐλογῆσαι τὸν κύριον ἡμῶν τὸν βασιλέα Δαυιδ λέγοντες Ἀγαθύναι ὁ θεὸς τὸ ὄνομα Σαλωμων τοῦ υἱοῦ σου ὑπὲρ τὸ ὄνομά σου καὶ μεγαλύναι τὸν θρόνον αὐτοῦ ὑπὲρ τὸν θρόνον σου· καὶ προσεκύνησεν ὁ βασιλεὺς ἐπὶ τὴν κοίτην αὐτοῦ
(3 Kgdms 1:46–47)

David recognizes the superiority of his newly enthroned son by doing obeisance on his bed. He then gives thanks to God for exalting his son Solomon while he is alive to witness it: καί γε οὕτως εἶπεν ὁ βασιλεύς Εὐλογητὸς κύριος ὁ θεὸς Ισραηλ, ὃς ἔδωκεν σήμερον ἐκ τοῦ σπέρματός μου καθήμενον ἐπὶ τοῦ θρόνου μου, καὶ οἱ ὀφθαλμοί μου βλέπουσιν (3 Kgdms 1:48). This is the only instance in the history of Israel that a son ascends the throne and is crowned king while his father is still alive.

Given this backdrop, it is easy to see how Psalm 109 LXX would be read as the enthronement of Solomon – which explains why David would call his son κύριος. Solomon ascended the throne and began to reign as

---

[114] It is very significant that Jesus rides into Jerusalem on a colt, shortly after being hailed as "son of David" (Mark 10:47–48), and then quotes the psalm that speaks of Solomon's enthronement while in the temple area.

king over Judah and Israel while his father David was still alive.[115] Thus, as Psalm 109 LXX claims, David addressed his son as king and Lord, and did so with great fatherly joy. There is thus a clear and simple answer to Jesus' question, found in part in the psalm he quoted and in the historical narrative of 3 Kingdoms 1 that records the enthronement of Solomon. The Markan Jesus had already warned that ambiguous statements would take a discerning ear: "Anyone who has ears to hear ought to hear" (Mark 4:23).

With the riddle now answered, the question remains as to what the Markan Jesus' intention was in posing this riddle in the first place. Most commentators have assumed that Jesus is employing the riddle to redefine his messianic vocation. The riddle's purpose, it is argued, is to extend the boundaries of messiahship beyond those typically ascribed to the "son of David." In many readings of the riddle, it is assumed that Jesus is importing aspects of messiahship that are new, or foreign to, the biblical concept of Davidic sonship. If the riddle is read, however, as revealing something significant about messiahship from within the Davidic tradition, then one does not need to look outside the pericope for clues about the nature of Jesus' messiahship but rather to examine closely the text at hand.

We have seen that Mark's overall purpose in initiating the discussion of Psalm 110 and the Davidic origins of the Messiah is to explain once again Jesus' temple actions in terms of the larger story of Israel. He leads his audience to the story of Solomon's enthronement and subsequently to a deeper understanding of his own authority to act and teach in the temple (Mark 11–12). There are two key aspects of Jesus' messiahship that are advanced by the employment of Psalm 109 LXX: (1) royal enthronement; and (2) priestly authority.

### 2.3.4.3 Royal Enthronement

The double reference to κύριος gives emphasis to this keyword, which establishes a vital connection to the larger Markan narrative. I noted earlier the significance of the use of κύριος as a title for Jesus in his entry into Jerusalem and the temple (11:3). In that story Jesus sequesters the colt with the claim that the κύριος had need of it. Mark's presentation of Jesus as κύριος just before his entrance into the temple is now juxtaposed to Jesus' teaching that the Messiah will be called David's κύριος (12:35–37). By showing Jesus as κύριος, Mark is able to underscore again Jesus' ἐξουσία

---

[115] 1 Chronicles 28–29 also narrate that David oversaw the installation and enthronement of his son Solomon to the throne. This narrative, along with 3 Kingdoms 1–2, may also be the inspiration behind this interpretation of Psalm 109 LXX.

in response to the question raised by the religious leaders against Jesus in 11:27–33.[116]

Psalm 109 LXX is focused upon the enthronement of the κύριος in Zion. This king is the representative of Yhwh, whose intimate relation with him is powerfully signified by sitting at Yhwh's "right hand" (v. 1). The use of the imperative form κάθου, "sit" (from κάθημαι) makes it clear that the psalm concerns the enthronement of a new king. "God's invitation to the Messiah (in Psalm 110:1) to 'sit at my right hand' suggests a heavenly kingship and authority, although it will be effective in judgment on earth: his enemies will be put under his feet."[117] The theme of receiving authority from God brings the reader back to the earlier discussion on John's authority, which ended with serious implications of Jesus' divinely given authority. Clearly, by employing this psalm at this point, Mark is highlighting again Jesus' heavenly sanction.

The idea of enthronement is followed by judgment (LXX Ps 109:5–6) – a shift similar to that in Daniel 7, a text that the Markan Jesus will link to this psalm at his trial (14:62). The context of heavenly enthronement and judgment upon enemies fits the Markan context well, where Jesus has judged the temple and its corrupt leaders and announced that God would vindicate him and judge his enemies (12:9). In an interesting reversal of position (v. 5), the Lord is described as being at the king's right hand, from where he conquers the king's enemies. The king is then described as sitting in judgment (κρινεῖ ἐν τοῖς ἔθνεσιν) in the midst of the nations (LXX Ps 109:6).

There are some further parallels between the Davidic king in Psalm 110 and Mark's picture of Jesus in the unfolding narrative. The phrase "in his teaching" (ἐν τῇ διδαχῇ, 12:35) links the pericope of the condemnation of the scribes (12:38–39) to the Psalm 110 riddle, which is given while he taught in the temple (διδάσκων ἐν τῷ ἱερῷ, 12:35). Why does the narrator make this connection between the teaching riddle and the teaching concerning the condemnation of the scribes? Because Mark was subtly showing Jesus' reenactment of Psalm 110.

Mark describes Jesus as "seated" (καθίσας) in the temple, opposite the treasury. Such a depiction immediately following his citation of the

---

[116] Telford (*Barren Temple*, 255) sees the narrative emphasis Mark gives to κύριος as related to the question of his ἐξουσία: "What is also of note is that the story of the finding of the ass, as presented here, hints at, though it does not explicitly state, the question of Jesus' authority (ἐξουσία). Apparently it is enough for the disciples to say that ὁ κύριος has need of it for it to be immediately dispatched. For this reason, there is some resemblance between 11.3 and 11.27 ff., where the question of Jesus' ἐξουσία is likewise raised by the chief priests, scribes and elders."

[117] Rowe, *God's Kingdom*, 280.

enthronement psalm is quite suggestive. The new king has come to his city and his temple, and sits enthroned (κάθημαι) on Zion. As the crowned messianic king, Jesus pronounces judgment upon the scribes: "They will receive the greater condemnation" (12:40b). In case the reader misses these allusions, the whole scene is soon repeated as Jesus leaves the temple and is found seated (καθημένου) upon the Mount of Olives, opposite the temple mount, where he pronounces prophetic judgment upon the city and the temple that have rejected their true king (Mark 13:3).

Jesus' enacting of Psalm 110 is exactly what the disciples expected him to do. On the way up to Jerusalem, James and John approached Jesus with a request; "Grant us to sit (ἵνα ... καθίσωμεν), one at your right (δεξιῶν) and one at your left, in your glory" (10:37). The disciples expected Jesus to be enthroned as king of Israel upon his arrival to the city of the great king, Jerusalem. This makes sense, given Jesus' acceptance of the royal title Messiah at the beginning of the way (8:29).[118] The disciples must have reasoned: "Jesus is the Messiah, heading to the capital, and given his announcement that the "kingdom is at hand," he must plan on being enthroned at Jerusalem." What better Scripture passage for them to be contemplating on the way to Jerusalem then the psalm of enthronement, Psalm 110? It is important to note that Jesus did not deny that there would be thrones on his left and right, but "to sit at my right side [τὸ δὲ καθίσαι ἐκ δεξιῶν μου] or at my left is not mine to grant, but it is for those whom it has been prepared" (10:40). The echoes of Psalm 110 (LXX 109) are clearly audible. More importantly, Jesus envisioned himself in the psalmic code of enthroned Davidic kings.[119]

### 2.3.4.4 Priestly Authority

One of the most peculiar and striking elements of Psalm 110 (LXX Psalm 109) is the sworn oath by which Yhwh gives the Davidic kings a covenant

---

[118] "Language about the Christ derives from royal ideology associated with David. That is certainly true in Mark" (Donald Juel, *Messianic Exegesis: Christological Interpretation of the Old Testament in Early Christianity* [Philadelphia: Fortress, 1992] 144).

[119] The enthronement imagery of Psalm 110 plays a central role in the passion narrative. At the trial, when the high priest asks Jesus if he is "the Messiah, the Son of the Blessed One," Jesus responds affirmatively and promises that the high priest will see "the Son of Man seated at the right of the Power" [τὸν υἱὸν τοῦ ἀνθρώπου ἐκ δεξιῶν καθήμενον τῆς δυνάμεως] (Mark 14:62). The enthronement imagery is combined with the parallel imagery of Daniel 7:13. Cf. Wright, *Victory*, chap. 13, "The Return of the King." It is also important, but beyond the scope of this paper, to illustrate Mark's use of irony in his account of the mocking of Jesus' kingship, which is later poignantly demonstrated by his enthronement on the cross.

grant of perpetual priesthood, "You are a priest for ever after the order of Melchizedek" (110:4).[120] This is a significant privilege of the Davidic kings and therefore for the future Messiah. It is likely that, rather than teaching some novel notion of messiahship, Jesus' employment of this psalm presents an understanding of messiahship that is faithful to the deep and rich Davidic tradition. This is supported by Jesus' description of his mission in language borrowed from LXX Psalm 109, as seen in the James and John episode.

By citing the psalm that promises priestly office to the Davidic line and thereby the Messiah, Jesus is suggesting his own priestly authority. This would serve to answer the question concerning his authority over the temple, posed by the very scribes to whom the riddle is directed. "If a would-be king acted in the temple in such a way as to precipitate a confrontation with the present priestly regime, Psalm 110 was exactly the right text with which to claim legitimation for such an action."[121]

Is it likely, however, that a first-century Jew would envision the Messiah in terms of the royal priestly office of the obscure Melchizedek? Yes. There is substantial evidence that during the Second Temple era the Melchizedekian motif played an important role in messianic speculation.[122] An important example is Simon Maccabeus, who is made by the Jews and priests not only the ruler, but also a "high priest forever" (ἀρχιερέα εἰς τὸν αἰῶνα).[123] This language is patently taken from Ps 109:4 LXX, ὤμοσεν κύριος καὶ οὐ μεταμεληθήσεται· σὺ εἶ ἱερεὺς εἰς τὸν αἰῶνα κατὰ τὴν τάξιν Μελχισεδέκ. The author of Maccabees depicts Simon in the messianic language of Psalm 110. Simon is compared to Melchizedek because he both rules as king and officiates as high priest. That the Hasmoneans put themselves forward as priest-kings modeled after Melchizedek is an important precedent for the messianic interpretation of Psalm 110.[124] This sheds further light on Jesus' triumphal entry into

---

[120] This translation is questionable for the MT but, the LXX Psalm 109 clearly sees this psalm as granting priestly rights to the Davidic kings. For our discussion here, it is likely that the LXX tradition is what is being drawn on in Mark.

[121] Wright, *Victory*, 509. Although Wright does not see the answer to the riddle, his treatment of the riddle is perceptive in applying Psalm 110 to the larger temple narrative.

[122] Cf. Juel, *Messianic Exegesis*, 135–39; Wright, *Victory*, 508; 1 Macc 14:41; and especially Hebrews 5–7.

[123] 1 Macc 14:41. I owe this reference to Wright, *Victory*, 508 n. 115. See also Hay's important study of Psalm 110 from a New Testament perspective (David M. Hay, *Glory at the Right Hand: Psalm 110 in Early Christianity* [New York: Abingdon, 1973]).

[124] Cf. Juel, *Messianic Exegesis*, 137. He notes that the Testament of Levi contains language from Psalm 110, used by the Hasmoneans to legitimize their priestly rule of Israel by reference to Melchizedek. See also Hay, *Glory at the Right Hand*, 24–25.

Jerusalem – an entry that is remarkably similar to Judas Maccabeus's triumphal entry into Jerusalem (2 Macc 10:1–9).

By citing Psalm 110, there can be little doubt as to Mark's point in alluding to it, especially given the temple context.[125] The Markan Jesus is employing the psalm to explain his authority over the temple and the priestly leaders. This priestly authority relates not only to the judging of the old temple but also to the founding of the new temple. As seen earlier, Mark believed Jesus to be the cornerstone for the new temple. Could it be fortuitous that Jesus alludes to the Solomonic priestly role (which historically concerns temple dedication) established in Psalm 110, shortly after speaking of the rejected stone that will become the cornerstone of the new eschatological temple?

The imagery of priestly authority, after the order of Melchizedek, stems from the intimate relation between the temple and the Davidic kings. O. Keel gives a good summary of the priestly dimension of the Davidic kings, which will provide helpful background to our discussion:

> As builder of the temple, the king is responsible for its maintenance and for the cultus which is carried on in it. In the enthronement Psalm 110, the Israelite king is awarded the priestly office in an oath sworn by Yahweh (v. 4). The concentration of the kingly and priestly offices in a single person places the Israelite king in the succession of the ancient kings of Jerusalem. The prototype is Melchizedek, who was simultaneously king and priest of the highest god (Gen 14:18). The priestly activity of David and his successors is the subject of 2 Sam 6:14,18; 24:17; 1 Kgs 8:14,56. The king wears priestly attire (2 Sam 6:14), blesses the people, intercedes for the cult community, and presides over the rites. Indeed, he even offers sacrifice (1 Sam 13:9; 2 Sam 6:13,17) and approaches God like the high priest.[126]

Keel's list of priestly activity among the Davidic kings is useful and quite exhaustive. The two kings of Judah most often depicted in priestly terms are David and Solomon. It is also noteworthy that all the priestly depictions of David and Solomon are connected to the founding of the Jerusalem temple.[127] The priestly role of the Son of David, then, consists in

---

[125] Mark highlights that Jesus poses the riddle in the temple (Mark 12:35). The location could have been assumed, since the last temporal designation came in Mark 11:27, where it was narrated that Jesus was in the temple. Obviously, then, the temple setting is essential for Mark.

[126] O. Keel, *The Symbolism of the Biblical World: Ancient Near Eastern Iconography and the Book of Psalms* (New York: Seabury, 1978) 277–78.

[127] There are two incidents in David's life where he acts priestly: when he has the Ark taken up to Jerusalem, and later when he builds an altar on the threshing floor of Araunah the Jebusite, which later becomes the site for the temple that Solomon builds, according to 2 Chr 3:1. Solomon's priestly service is limited to the dedication ceremony of the temple (1 Kgs 8:14,56).

founding and dedicating the temple. As founder of the temple, the king is lord of the temple, high priest according to the order of Melchizedek. Both David and Solomon exercised their Melchizedek priesthood. David offered sacrifices and then "blessed the people in the name of the LORD," at which time bread and wine were distributed (2 Sam 6:18–19; 1 Chr 16:2–3). Solomon dedicates the temple in a similar ceremony (2 Chronicles 5–7).

At both ceremonies, the Levites led the congregation in psalms of thanksgiving and praise (1 Chr 16:4,7–42; 2 Chr 5:13; 7:3–6). This pattern of temple dedication recurs every time the temple is cleansed, as well as during its rebuilding by Zerubbabel. On each occasion cultic sacrifices were offered in huge proportions while people recited thanksgiving psalms. One refrain is constantly cited at every temple cleansing and dedication:

O give thanks to the Lord, for he is good;
for his steadfast love endures for ever!

This refrain is sung in the dedication services of David (1 Chr 16:34,41), Solomon (2 Chr 5:13,7:3), and Ezra (Ezra 3:11). The two marks of a temple dedication were the singing of thanksgiving psalms and extraordinary sacrifices.[128] To sum up, when the Davidic heirs exercised priestly authority, it was exercised in relation to the temple. The primary priestly activity is in blessing the people, distributing bread and wine, and presiding over the sacrifices. There may be a correspondence here to Jesus' celebration of the Passover with bread and wine, thereby inaugurating a new covenant and perhaps, given the previous Markan narrative, laying the foundation stone of a new temple.

### 2.3.4.5 Summary

Morna Hooker observed the importance of the temple setting for understanding Jesus' cryptic question in 12:35: "Why has Mark placed the pericope here? The message it conveys is that Jesus is to be acknowledged as 'Lord'. Once again, we are reminded of Mal. 3.1, which speaks of the Lord coming to his temple. It is perhaps significant that it is in the temple that Jesus comes closer to revealing his identity than anywhere else."[129] Mark's emphasis that this scene takes place in the temple (12:35a)

---

[128] The singing of thanksgiving psalms and the presentation of accompanying sacrifices occurs at all the temple cleansings and rededications: Hezekiah (2 Chr 29:3,30–31), Manasseh, after he repented (2 Chr 33:16), Josiah (2 Chr 34–35), Judas Maccabeus (2 Macc 10:7). The only kings in Scripture who perform priestly functions at temple dedications are David and Solomon.

[129] Hooker, *Mark*, 292–93.

confirms that the temple context is significant. Jesus' riddle based on Psalm 109 LXX allows Mark to give scriptural warrant for Jesus' exercise of authority – an authority both royal and priestly. Through the lens of Solomon's story, via Psalm 109 LXX, Mark brings Jesus' identity into sharper focus. Like Solomon, who rode into Jerusalem on a colt for his enthronement, Jesus has come in royal ἐξουσία to the temple as priest-king, wielding authority from God to condemn the corrupt temple and dedicate a new one. Jesus is the κύριος of the temple who has been given definite authority from heaven to execute eschatological judgment.

## 2.4 Conclusion

The morning after his temple demonstration, Jesus returns to the temple to continue teaching (11:20). Mark records a very full day of teaching for Jesus (11:20–12:44), whose subjects range from direct to indirect relation to the temple, including his protest of its corruption. All the teaching is set in the temple area – a point Mark emphasizes (11:27; 12:35,41). Rhetorically, Mark's emphasis on the temple setting for Jesus' teaching heightens the conflict between Jesus and the temple authorities. The question of Jesus' authority, provoked by his condemnation of the temple, provides the narrative means for Mark to further his portrait of Jesus' identity.

Certainly one of the primary thrusts of Jesus' temple teaching is his rejection of the temple. The mountain saying (Mark 11:23) is clearly connected to the enacted parable of the withered fig tree (Mark 11:20–21), illustrating in dramatic fashion that Jesus' protest in the temple points to the end of the temple. The motif of mountain-moving is an eschatological image used in the prophetic writings of Israel. Jesus takes the image of mountain obstacles and applies it to the least likely of references – the temple mount. Thus, the eschatological judgment upon the temple, a den of thieves, is confirmed again and again in Jesus' teaching. Through the withered tree (11:20–21), the mountain cast into the sea (11:23), and the tenants who will be destroyed (12:9), Jesus establishes beyond doubt that the temple and its leaders stand under divine judgment.

In the confrontations between Jesus and the religious leaders, Jesus' authority (ἐξουσία) to declare such a judgment is questioned (11:28) and triggers open conflict. However, Jesus takes control of the situation, questioning the leaders on the source of John the Baptist's ἐξουσία. The failure of the religious leaders to answer demonstrates their lack of integrity, which frees Jesus from giving them an answer. However, Jesus gives a veiled explanation of his ἐξουσία through his teaching in "parables."

The parable of the vineyard serves as a microcosm to the Markan story of Jesus. This parable and the Markan story of Jesus are mutually interpretive. The mention of John the Baptist just before the parable helps the reader see John as the last of the servants sent to the wicked tenants. Central to the parable is the owner's son, who stands for Jesus, identified by Mark as God's Son at every crucial juncture of his story. Peter Walker sees a key parallel between the plot of the vineyard story and Mark's story of Jesus in the temple: "This not only includes the strongest claim so far of Jesus' identity as the 'beloved son' (12:6, cf. 1:11), but also the declaration that God's desire is to receive 'the fruit of the vineyard' (12:2). The parable thus parallels closely the 'enacted parable' of the fig-tree. In both, God shows his desire to receive 'fruit' from his people Israel – indicated, respectively, by the fig and the vineyard."[130] Just as Jesus sought καρπός from the barren tree (11:14), so too the son is sent to receive the καρπός from the wicked tenants (12:2). Both searches are fruitless, thus underscoring the justice of Jesus' condemnation of the temple. Thus, the parable advances Jesus' charge that the religious leaders are λῃσταί who are stealing the fruit of Israel and will eventually murder the owner's son. Mark ends Jesus' teaching in the temple with specific examples of how the religious leaders are robbing God. That the scribes devour widows' houses and extort the poor for vain egotism is then made concrete in the closing story of the widow who gives her last coins to the temple (12:44).

The temple, like the vineyard, has been subverted from God's purposes. However, Jesus' rejection of the temple is counterbalanced by his teaching about a new one.[131] Although the Temple Mount will be cast into the sea for failing to be a house of prayer for all nations (11:17), the new community Jesus is forming will become the renewed locus of prayer, faith, and forgiveness. What the temple should have been, the Christian community will be: a place of prayer and faith where sins will be forgiven without animal sacrifice. The wicked tenants may violently reject the son and usurp the vineyard, but Jesus foretells that the rejected stone will become the cornerstone of a new temple. 1 Peter 2:4–8 interprets the stone

---

[130] Walker, *Holy City*, 7.

[131] Marshall (*Faith as a Theme*) captures this insight into the dual nature of Jesus' relation to the temple in Mark, as negative in terms of the old temple that must be condemned, and positive as the new temple Jesus is ushering in: "A replacement motif (cf. 12:9) is thus introduced to balance the rejection motif, and it is this that explains the ensuing discourse. In this double rejection-replacement motif, Mark draws a significant parallel between the fate of the temple and the fate of Jesus" (p. 163).

of Psalm 118 in terms of Jesus' rejection and posits that the Christian community built upon Jesus is the new house of God (1 Pet 2:5). Whatever relationship this letter has with Mark, it illustrates that Jesus was understood as the stone of Psalm 118 upon whom the new temple, the Christian community, is built. In light of Psalm 118 and its links to the foundation of the second temple, it becomes evident that the Markan Jesus is not only rejecting the temple but taking its symbolic import and purpose as the object of the new Christian community. In other words, the community is to become the new "house" of God, a place where the poor will be protected, love pursued, and a fruitful (faith-filled) response to God lived.

The riddle from Psalm 110 (LXX Psalm 109) serves to deepen the reader's understanding of Jesus' identity as well as his authority to condemn the temple and build a new one. This enthronement psalm illustrates the divine origin of Jesus' authority, explaining to the reader why Jesus is κύριος of the temple. The allusions to Solomon and to the Melchizedek priesthood, for those who have ears to hear, strengthens the sense of Jesus' authority to both judge the temple and found a new one. The entire Markan temple story begins with Jesus' royal entry into Jerusalem on a colt, paralleling Solomon's enthronement. At the end of Jesus' teaching in the temple, he points to Psalm 110 when teaching about the Messiah. That the psalm speaks of the enthronement of a priest-king is particularly striking given Jesus' location in the temple area – a location Mark stresses at precisely this point in the narrative (12:35). After Jesus discusses the enthronement psalm, he judges the scribes and sits (enthroned?) opposite the treasury. Mark's specification of the treasury, unique to this gospel, is powerful, given the unfolding story. Jesus accused the religious leaders of turning the temple into a σπήλαιον λῃστῶν, and now with Jesus seated in judgment opposite the treasury (the purse of the robbers), the reader witnesses exactly how the robbery takes place: the poor widow is fleeced. Jesus' time in the temple comes full circle with this scene, and there will be little surprise for the reader when Jesus exits the temple and explicitly declares that not one stone will be left upon another.

The Markan story of Jesus making his way to the temple, entering and judging it, and accusing the establishment of being robbers follows exactly the plot line of Malachi 3. In Malachi the "way" (ὁδός) leads to the temple, to which the "Lord" (κύριος) will suddenly come (3:1). The day of his coming will be a day of "judgment" (3:5). The charge against the priests and leaders of the temple (3:3) is that they are "robbing God" (3:8–9). Mark does not "tell" his audience that Jesus is following the script of Israel's prophetic traditions, but he subtly "shows" the reader these connections. These constant allusions to the prophetic traditions serve to anchor the story of Jesus in the larger story of Israel. The prophetic precedents to Jesus' teaching and actions also serve to ground his ἐξουσία in the traditions of Israel and not simply in some novel claim. Mark's point is emphatic: Jesus' coming to the temple is the eschatological καιρός, the fulfillment of the Scriptures of Israel.

In his compelling story, Mark draws fascinating parallels between Jesus and the temple. This rhetorical strategy will be the particular focus of my next chapter, in which I will explore why Mark employs the temple as the primary vehicle for understanding who Jesus is and what he is doing.

Chapter 3

# Prophetic Eschatology and Mark 13

## 3.1 Introduction

In the previous chapter, I illustrated how Jesus' teaching in the temple further advanced the motif of the temple's eschatological judgment as well as introduced the notion of a new temple. Both the mountain-moving saying and the parable of the wicked tenants served to reinforce the symbolic judgment of the temple, begun already in Jesus' demonstration and cursing of the fig tree. Statements that point to the coming of a new temple immediately follow each of these teachings about the end of the temple. The saying about faith, prayer, and forgiveness, which suggests that the old temple will be replaced by a new one – the Markan community – follows the mountain-moving saying. The cryptic saying about a new cornerstone, and thus a new temple, follows the owner of the vineyard's judgment upon the wicked tenants. Thus a clear pattern emerges; Mark follows judgment upon the old temple establishment with hints that a new temple will emerge.

Jesus' authority is a prominent issue in Mark 11–12, as discussed in the last chapter. The question of Jesus' authority relates to his twofold claim that the old temple is condemned and that a new one will soon replace it. Jesus' authority is confirmed by the double reference made to his sonship. In the parable of the wicked tenants, Jesus is cast as the owner's son; in the riddle taken from Psalm 110 the notion of Jesus' sonship is reinforced with Davidic overtones.[1] Thus Jesus, because of his identity as both God's and David's son, has the authority to condemn Jerusalem's temple and to inaugurate a new one. If the actions of Jesus in the temple raise the

---

[1] The issue of Mark's attitude towards Jesus' Davidic descent is much debated, and in the last chapter I argued that the riddle taken from Psalm 110 was not an attempt to reject Davidic sonship for Jesus. However, it should be emphasized that the issue of Jesus' Davidic pedigree is very much secondary for Mark. What matters most is that Jesus is the "Son of God"; thus, his Davidic sonship is subsumed in this far more important Markan title. For an excellent discussion on how the title "Son of God" is central for Mark's theology and how it relates to Mark's other titles for Jesus, see Telford, *Theology of Mark*, esp. 154.

question of his authority (Mark 11), his teaching in the temple (Mark 12) establishes his authority as son, all of which prepare the reader for the authoritative discourse Jesus delivers on the Mount of Olives (Mark 13), which is the focus of the present chapter.

In this chapter, I will examine how the twin themes of temple destruction and new temple are brought into sharper focus in the eschatological discourse of Mark 13. The previous chapters have shown that the Markan Jesus' critique of the temple often evoked eschatological claims. These eschatological claims climax in Mark 13, an enigmatic discourse whose nature and meaning can be more readily penetrated when considered in the light of Mark's focus on the temple.

For some time, modern scholarship regarded Mark 13 as a disruption to Mark's narrative.[2] It seemed to many that the eschatological discourse split apart what otherwise would be a seamless narrative between Mark 12 and 14. In light of the preceding arguments, however, it would be more helpful to say that Mark 13 serves as a bridge between the narrative of the temple's end, Mark 11–12, and Jesus' end, Mark 14–15. The key to what Mark intends to accomplish by his juxtaposition of the ends of the temple and of Jesus lies in the eschatological discourse of Mark 13. Hence, any study of the temple in Mark must come to terms with the role Mark 13 plays in the story.

This chapter will have four parts. First, a brief account of how this study understands the concept of eschatology will be given, especially as it relates to Mark's understanding of eschatology. Second, the issue of the historical context for Mark's Gospel and the context of the community to which he writes must inevitably arise in any serious consideration of Mark 13, and so a summary of the issues and relevance of the Gospel's historical context will be made. Third, I will describe the literary structure of Mark 13 and its immediate context within Mark's narrative. How one divides the literary units of the eschatological discourse will play no little role in deciding the outcome of any exegesis of this notoriously difficult text. Finally, I shall examine the elements of Mark 13 that relate to the temple theme. By offering an exegesis of the verses that pertain to the temple, I hope to show how Mark advances the temple motif prominent in the narrative since Mark 11.

---

[2] For a critique of earlier approaches to Mark 13 that do not take into account its larger narrative context, see Geddert, *Watchwords*, 16–18. This perspective is changing, and the trend is now moving towards seeing how Mark 13 fits into the wider narrative context. See, e.g., France, *Mark*, 497–500; Geddert, *Watchwords*, 18–20; Morna Hooker, "Trial and Tribulation in Mark XIII," *BJRL* 65 (1982) 78–99; Witherington, *Mark*, 337–38.

## 3.2 Eschatology in Mark

Because "eschatology," like the related term "apocalyptic," is a word that often has very broad and diverse usages in modern scholarship, it is necessary to briefly define how that term is understood in the present study.[3] The term, etymologically and conceptually, refers to an ending. It is the precise nature of that ending that is unclear. Some have believed that this ending is that of space and time.[4] However, this pushes eschatology into apocalyptic and is probably too radical, particularly for Mark's Gospel. In Mark's understanding of eschatology, for example, what good would fleeing to the mountains (13:14) and hoping that the tribulation would not happen in winter (13:18) serve if the end of space and time were at hand? So the question remains: what is coming to an end?

According to John Meier, it is the end of Israel's history; but this ending also marks a new beginning: "It is an end – but also a new beginning – brought about by God's wrathful judgment and extermination of sinners within his holy people and by the salvation of those who have proved faithful or who sincerely repent in the last hour..."[5] Meier notes that there is a particular view of eschatology in the prophetic corpus of the OT and some intertestamental literature that he calls "prophetic eschatology."[6] Prophetic eschatology has several prominent characteristics according to Meier: (1) the judgment (tribulation) upon sinners inside and outside Israel; (2) the gathering of the tribes of Israel at Zion or Jerusalem; (3) the liberation and renewal of Jerusalem, Mount Zion, and the temple; and (4) the defeat of the Gentiles and their humble pilgrimage to Jerusalem's

---

[3] For some definitions of eschatology and discussion of the basic issues surrounding the term, see, e.g., David E. Aune, "Early Christian Eschatology" *ABD* 2.597–605; Richard H. Hiers, "Eschatology," *Harper Collins Bible Dictionary* (ed. Paul J. Achtemeier; San Francisco: Harper Collins, 1996) 302; John T. Carrol, "Eschatology," *Eerdmans Dictionary of the Bible* (ed. David Noel Freedman; Grand Rapids: Eerdmans, 2000) 420–22.

[4] Johannes Weiss and Albert Schweitzer championed this view of eschatology. For a modern defense of their positions, see, e.g., Dale C. Allison, *Jesus of Nazareth: Millenarian Prophet* (Minneapolis: Fortress, 1998), esp. 34.

[5] Meier, *A Marginal Jew,* 2. 31. He notes that the nature of this new beginning can differ from author to author: "The extent to which the state of Israel after the end-and-new-beginning is in continuity with ordinary, earthly realities and the extent to which Israel is transferred into an idealized, magical or heavenly world vary from author to author. The greater the transformation of the whole cosmos, the closer one approaches to apocalyptic" (Ibid., 31).

[6] Ibid.

temple.[7] Meier's account of eschatology, particularly his account of prophetic eschatology, will serve as the working definition of eschatology for the present study. There are two striking features of Meier's observations that are particularly relevant to the study of eschatology in Mark's Gospel.

First, Meier's description of prophetic eschatology is important because of the significant number of citations and allusions made in Mark 11–16 to the prophets.[8] Indeed, the most eschatological section in this narrative, Mark 13, contains the most citations and allusions to the prophets. This implies that, when Mark gives the eschatological address of Jesus in Mark 13, he is relying heavily upon the prophets, and thus Meier's sketch of prophetic eschatology is especially helpful in comprehending Mark's eschatology.

Second, in Meier's list of the key characteristics of prophetic eschatology, one theme seems to unite them all – Jerusalem and its temple. The regathering of Israel is centered on Jerusalem; the temple and Mount Zion are to be renewed; and the Gentiles are to be defeated, the sign of which is their pilgrimage to the temple in Jerusalem. Meier himself notes this when he refers to "the Jerusalem eschatology of regathering."[9] This focus on Jerusalem and the temple finds striking correspondence to the present study. As this chapter hopes to show, the temple lies at the heart of Mark's vision of eschatology. This connection between eschatology and temple is not accidental, as the historical context for Mark 13 illustrates.

---

[7] Ibid., 2.31, 243–51, esp. 247–48, 251. N. T. Wright in many ways draws the same account of eschatology for his portrait of the historical Jesus as Meier does of "prophetic eschatology" (*Victory*, 201–9). Here is an example of Wright's summing up this eschatological hope of Israel: "The return from exile, the defeat of evil, and the return of YHWH to Zion were all coming about, but not in the way Israel had supposed" (ibid.). Wright's emphasis on "return from exile" has engendered much disagreement. Meier's description of the hope for the regathering of the twelve tribes makes much more historical sense than Wright's account of return from exile.

[8] Kee (*Community of the New Age*, 45) notes Mark's astonishing preference for the prophetic books: "Of these [57 quotations], only eight are from the Torah, and all but one of those appear in the context of the controversy stories in ch. 12 from Daniel, and the remaining 21 are from the other prophetic writings. An analysis of the allusions to scripture and related sacred writings gives the same general picture: of 160 such allusions, half are from the prophets (excluding Daniel), and about an eighth each from Daniel, the Psalms, the Torah, and from non-canonical writings." If we include Daniel in this count, then it is safe to say that the majority of Mark's quotations and allusions to the OT in Mark 11–16 are taken from the prophets. See also Kee, "Function of Scriptural Quotations and Allusions in Mark 11–16," 165–88.

[9] Meier, *Marginal Jew*, 2.251.

## 3.3 Historical Setting of the Markan Narrative

Any treatment of Mark 13, even a narrative reading, cannot ignore the historical questions that come with this text. It is not atypical, however, of narrative studies to ignore altogether the historical questions that come with reading ancient texts. This is especially true of the narrative school that arose with the New Criticism, itself a reaction to a reading that was excessively preoccupied with matters extrinsic to the text (an accusation often launched against form critics in their reading of Mark 13). Many adherents of the New Criticism, therefore, responded by focusing their attention solely upon the narrative world of the text, thereby ignoring the historical world that generated it. Thus, the text is often read as "autonomous" from a setting in time and space, situated in a closed world that is self-sufficient.[10] What is desirable, however, is a reading that avoids an overly extrinsic reading of Mark 13 but does not isolate this text from its historical context. At the end of the day the narrative critic must grapple with the vital question: what situation generated this narrative world?

For much of the twentieth century, scholarship generally dated the Gospel of Mark between A.D. 60–70.[11] The trend of the past two of decades has been to date the gospel close to A.D. 70. Therefore, Iersel is representative of many when he says, "There is every reason to think of a date just before or just after the destruction of the temple of Jerusalem in A.D. 70. But difference of opinion on the question whether Mark was written shortly before or shortly after that event is persistent and likely to continue."[12] Indeed, Iersel's observation that the debate on a pre-or-post-A.D. 70 date would continue has held true; there does not appear to be an imminent resolution.[13] This difference of opinion, however, should not obscure the rather solid consensus that has emerged that Mark's Gospel should likely be dated close to A.D. 70.

Dating Mark's Gospel to or around the time of the destruction of the Jerusalem temple coheres well with the findings of this present study. Given the prominent role the temple plays in Mark's story of Jesus, there

---

[10] A good example of a narrative approach to Mark's Gospel that follows the New Criticism is David Rhoads and Donald Michie, *Mark as Story: An Introduction to the Narrative of a Gospel* (Philadelphia: Fortress, 1982) 3–5.

[11] E.g., Taylor, *Mark*, 32; Lane, *Mark*, 12–21.

[12] van Iersel, *Reading*, 15.

[13] Two representative examples of the ongoing difference of opinion on dating Mark before or after the destruction of the temple are found in the recent work of Moloney (*Mark*, 11–15) who argues for a post-A.D. 70 dating based on the account of Mark 13 and Horsley (*Hearing the Whole Story*, 129–33) who argues on the basis of Mark 13 that the gospel must have been written before the destruction of the temple.

must be some reason propelling the narrator to highlight the temple so dramatically. Since the temple occupied a central place in the Jewish revolt of A.D. 66–70 – indeed, the conflict climaxed with the temple's fall to the Romans and its subsequent destruction – it would make sense to read the temple-dominated narrative of Mark in relation to the temple-dominated years surrounding the temple's demise in A.D. 70.

If Markan scholarship has an approximate time for dating Mark, what about its place of composition? Two general positions are held regarding this matter. The first, following the tradition found in Eusebius, places the Markan community in Rome.[14] Others, following the lead of Marxsen, place it in the Eastern part of the Roman Empire, somewhere not too far from Palestine where the destruction of the temple would have been especially relevant.[15] After surveying the data, Morna Hooker observes that "all we can say with certainty, therefore, is that the gospel was composed somewhere in the Roman Empire – a conclusion that scarcely narrows the field at all!"[16] I will take up the issue of whether we can narrow the field for the location and dating of the Gospel of Mark at the end of this chapter, after examining Mark 13 in some detail. For now, suffice it to say that the context that generated this narrative was the conflict that embroiled the temple sometime close to A.D. 70, in a place within the Roman Empire, where the demise of the temple would have some significance.

---

[14] For a survey of the different positions on the dating and location of Mark, see Marcus (*Mark 1–8*, 17–39) and Telford (*Theology of Mark*, 1–29). Examples of those who hold to the tradition of Rome as the place of origin for Mark's Gospel are Hooker, *Mark*, 8; Martin Hengel, *Studies in the Gospel of Mark* (London: SCM, 1985) 1–30; France, *Mark*, 35–41; Gundry, *Mark*, 1026–45; Evans, *Mark*, lxiii; Gnilka, *Evangelium Markus*, 1.34–35; Pesch, *Markusevangelium*, 1.112–14; Witherington, *Mark*, 20–27; Lane, *Mark*, 12–17; Donahue and Harrington, *Mark*, 43–46.

[15] E.g., W. Marxsen, *Mark the Evangelist: Studies on the Redaction History of the Gospel* (trans. R. A. Harrisville; Nashville: Abingdon, 1969) 54–116; Kee, *Community of the New Age*, 237–49; Moloney, *Mark*, 12–15; H. C. Waetjen, *A Reordering of Power: A Socio-Politcal Reading of Mark's Gospel* (Minneapolis: Fortress, 1989) 1–26; Marcus, *Mark 1–8*, 33–37; Gerd Theissen, *The Gospels in Context: Social and Political History in the Synoptic Tradition* (Minneapolis: Fortress, 1991) 237–49.

[16] Hooker, *Mark*, 8.

# 3.4 Literary Considerations of Mark 13

## 3.4.1  Tale of Two Temples

The profound relationship between Jesus and the temple is the interpretive backdrop for the Mount of Olives discourse. As shown above, Mark 13 is placed at a crucial junction in the narrative between Jesus' teaching in the temple, which focuses on the end of the temple and its leadership, and the passion narrative. These two poles, temple and passion, create the rhetorical tension that is fundamental to Mark's narrative strategy in Mark 13. This point is so important to the story that Mark gives the reader a significant narrative clue to help the reader follow the dense narrative logic. Scholars have noted that this intercalation illustrates how Mark anchors the eschatological discourse into the surrounding narrative.[17]

Mark frames the eschatological discourse by the stories of two women who give generous gifts at great personal cost. There are a number of parallels between the two stories. First, Jesus praises both women (the only times in the gospel where Jesus gives praise to someone), beginning with his solemn "Amen" formula (12:43; 14:9).[18] Second, the gift of each woman is specified: 2 copper coins (12:42) and 300 denarii (14:5). Third, despite the radical difference in value, both gifts come at a costly sacrifice for each woman. Fourth, in both stories the term "poor," πτωχός, is repeated (12:42,43; 14:5,7). Fifth, each woman stands in contrast to wicked men in their stories. The poor widow stands in contrast to the scribes who "devour widows' houses" (12:40), whereas the woman who enters the house and anoints Jesus stands in contrast to Judas who leaves the house in order to betray Jesus for money (14:10).[19] Sixth, the gift of each woman foreshadows Jesus' death. The widow's gift is literally "her whole life" (ὅλον τὸν βίον αὐτῆς, 12:44), while the other woman's

---

[17] Dewey ("Mark as Interwoven Tapestry," 233) notes the rhetorical function of this intercalation: "The anointing story and the story of the woman who gave her mite to the temple treasury (12:41–44) form a frame around the apocalyptic discourse of Mark 13. These two stories about women frame Mark 13 much as the two healings of blind men frame the way material of Mark 8–10." Other scholars have noted the significance of this intercalation: Malbon, *Company*, 53–55, 178–81; Geddert, *Watchwords*, 137; Moloney, *Mark*, 273, 281; Vernon Robbins, *Jesus the Teacher* (Philadelphia: Fortress, 1984) 179; Keith D. Dyer, *The Prophecy on the Mount: Mark 13 and the Gathering of the New Community* (New York: Peter Lang, 1998) 270.

[18] Dewey, "Interwoven Tapestry," 233.

[19] Malbon, *Company*, 180–81.

anointing of Jesus is for his "burial" (ἐνταφιασμός, 14:8).[20] Seventh, there is irony in both scenes. The widow's simple gift, although of less value than the "large sums" of the rich, is a greater contribution. However, her sacrifice is made for a temple that is corrupt and condemned.[21] On the other hand, the woman who anoints Jesus seems to have wasted a small fortune, "for this ointment might have been sold for more than three hundred denarii, and given to the poor" (14:5). Yet Jesus corrects this assessment and announces that she has done a beautiful deed (καλὸν ἔργον), for which she will be remembered wherever the gospel is proclaimed (14:9). Thus, both women give much, although the value of their gifts is misunderstood.

However, there is one significant difference between these stories – a difference all the more salient given the many parallels. The widow's gift is for the temple, whereas the other woman's gift is for Jesus. The beneficiary of each gift is doomed – the temple for destruction, Jesus for death. Within this parallel there is a sharp contrast. The reader knows that the end of the temple is to have the finality of the fig tree withered down to its roots and the mountain cast into the sea, whereas Jesus' death will end in victory, as foretold in the three passion predictions of Jesus' death and resurrection (8:31; 9:31; 10:34) and the parable of the rejected stone that would become the cornerstone (12:10). The object of both gifts is the temple – one old, the other new.

Why does Mark frame the eschatological discourse by these two gifts? As already shown, Dewey has argued that this serves to anchor the eschatological discourse in its narrative context.[22] While this is true, I propose that Mark's aim is larger than this rhetorical purpose. Certainly, the unique praise Jesus bestows on both of these women serves to highlight them as model disciples.[23] Beyond this parenesis, the stark contrast between the object of the two gifts, Jesus and the temple, must point to a further purpose. Vernon Robbins observed that an important difference emerges between these two stories: there is a different beneficiary in each story: the temple and Jesus.[24] He contrasted the nature of the gifts as well, stating that the widow's gift of financial support represents the old temple

---

[20] Malbon (*Company*, 54–55) notes "as Jesus' first action in the temple, the driving out of buyers and sellers, points to the temple's end, so Jesus' final action in the temple, or rather his reaction to the poor widow's action, points to his own end."

[21] Addison G. Wright, "The Widow's Mites: Praise or Lament? – A Matter of Context," *CBQ* 44 (1982) 256–65, esp. 263. On the employment of irony in these two scenes, see also Malbon, *Company*, 181.

[22] Dewey, "Interwoven Tapestry," 233.

[23] Moloney, *Mark*, 273, 281; Malbon, *Company*, 57.

[24] Robbins, *Jesus the Teacher*, 179.

in contrast to the new way of gospel service, which required not one's livelihood but one's very life. Therefore, the gifts point to Jesus' call for sacrifices that are not animal or simply monetary, but a sacrifice of oneself. The contrast between the two beneficiaries serves to deepen the tension between Jesus and the temple for Mark's story, with Mark suggesting that Jesus is the true temple for which sacrifice is of lasting value.

The argument that this intercalation sets forth Jesus as the new temple has been put forward by Timothy Geddert. Geddert claims that "taken together, Mark 12.41–44 and 14.3–9 prefigure the replacement of temples, a theme which Mark seems to have woven through his narrative."[25] It is important to note that while Mark contrasts Jesus and the temple through the parallel gifts of the two women, one of the aims of the narrative is to show that Jesus' identity is to be related closely to the temple. One of the things that Jesus and the temple share in common – a point that has overshadowed much of the narrative beginning with Peter's confession (8:29) – is an imminent end. The irony employed in the two scenes of the women's noble giving, however, hints at an underlying difference between the end of Jesus and the temple. The widow's gift, seemingly insignificant, is valuable. But for the reader it also ironic in that it is for the temple that has become a den of robbers, prophetically condemned and doomed to destruction. On the other hand, the woman's anointing of Jesus for burial, a significant gift that seems wasteful, is an act that will be recounted wherever the gospel is proclaimed. The irony is that although her gift is for Jesus' burial, Jesus' end will not be final. The Markan reader knows that Jesus will be victorious over death through the resurrection, and that the gospel will go out to the nations. The two temples are doomed, and the irony in these scenes hints that the one that looks fragile (Jesus) will be the one that will endure even death, whereas the temple that seems so secure and permanent – as Mark 13 will boldly put it – will not have one stone left upon another. Hence, the narrative both compares and contrasts Jesus with the temple in order to deepen the temple identity of Jesus. The narrative juxtaposition between these two gifts, one to the old and the other to the new temple, surrounds the eschatological discourse that bridges the end of the old temple (11–12) and the end of the new temple (14–15), with Mark hinting that one of these will endure the end to become the new eschatological temple.

---

[25] Geddert, *Watchwords*, 137.

## 3.4.2   Literary Structure of Mark 13

Mark 13 is the longest discourse in the entire gospel. Given the pace of Mark's story, the long monologue Jesus delivers in chapter 13 stands out among the short dialogues and perpetual action characteristic of Mark's narrative.[26] The subject matter of the Mount of Olives discourse is the longest pause in terms of time and space in the entire narrative, and so the subject of this discourse must be very important to the author. Far from slowing down the story, this discourse plunges the reader into the future tribulation and apocalypse, so that the nearness of the kingdom becomes palpable. Although Jesus gives the discourse sitting down, the reader feels a sense of urgency as the thrust of events brings the story forward into his own time.

Mark 13:1–4, in which the disciples ask Jesus for the signs and the timing of the temple's demise, sets the stage for the rest of the chapter. According to most scholars, the rest of the chapter, vv. 5–37, falls into three sections.[27] The first section, vv. 5–23, is framed with the Markan key word βλέπω.[28] Not only does the imperative βλέπετε frame vv. 5–23, but this frame is reinforced by the additional juxtaposition of its antithesis, πλανάω.[29]

v. 5 βλέπετε
    v. 6 πλανήσουσιν
    v. 22 ἀποπλανᾶν
v. 23 βλέπετε

This inclusio clearly marks out vv. 5–23 with their focus on watchfulness against false Messiahs who might lead astray even the elect.

The second section, vv. 24–27, contains the great cosmic signs that will be seen, culminating in the coming of the Son of Man. Verse 24, rhetorically distinguished from the previous section by the adversative ἀλλά, cites an Isaianic oracle that continues into v. 25. Verses 26 and 27 are joined to this oracle, each beginning with the connecting particles καὶ τότε. In addition to these rhetorical markers, the nature of the apocalyptic language and imagery found here supplies a unique theme that clearly singles it out as its own unit. How vv. 24–27 relate to the wider context of

---

[26] Lane (*Mark*, 444) observes that "the Olivet discourse is unique as the longest uninterrupted discourse of private instruction recorded by Mark."

[27] Marshall, *Faith as a Theme*, 146; Werner H. Kelber, *The Oral and Written Gospel: The Hermeneutics of Speaking and Writing in the Synoptic Tradition, Mark, Paul, and Q* (Philadelphia: Fortress, 1983) 100.

[28] See Geddert, *Watchwords*, 81–88.

[29] Moloney, *Mark*, 249.

the discourse is a question that will be taken up when I provide an exegesis of this pericope.

The third section, vv. 28–37, focuses on the signs of the eschatological time. The issue of when the eschatological time will arrive is addressed in vv. 28–37. There is more unity to this pericope than scholars allow, perhaps because commentators have been generally preoccupied with its tradition history. Although Mark 13 is often regarded as a loose collection of sources, it must be recognized that Mark has brought them together and united the material into a coherent narrative.[30] One key sign of this, often overlooked by commentators, is the word "know" (γινώσκω), employed five times throughout this unit, giving it cohesion and unity (13:28,29,32,33,35). Thus, vv. 28–37 are held together by the question of how one can "know" the arrival of the eschatological time.

It is difficult to discern where vv. 28–37 should be divided. This difficulty should serve to highlight their rhetorical unity, no matter where one would chose to demarcate the unit. The stumbling stone to a scholarly consensus on dividing this unit is v. 32.[31] Does it mark an end or beginning? The verse begins with the phrase περὶ δέ followed by the genitive. The only other time this phrase is found in the gospel of Mark is in 12:26, where it does not mark out a new literary unit. Indeed, from the other occurrences in the NT it is clear that περὶ δέ followed by the genitive ties together a different or adversative point of view to what directly precedes it. Thus, from simple rhetorical grounds, it is hard to justify making the phrase a strong adversative that would mark a new section.

In addition, there is evidence that vv. 33–37 are set apart by an *inclusio*. Verse 33 begins with the important thematic word βλέπετε, which formed the rhetorical division of vv. 5–23. βλέπετε in v. 33 is paralleled with γρηγορεῖτε in v. 37. Indeed, they form an *inclusio* that binds vv. 33–37 together. The change in wording from βλέπετε to γρηγορεῖτε makes the argument for an *inclusio* in vv. 33–37 a little less than certain. It may well be that v. 32 is intended to be a hinge verse, connecting 28–31 to 33–37. This is also suggested by the fact that "know" in verse 32 is found twice before (vv. 28 and 29) and twice afterward (vv. 33,35), thereby holding together two parables: the fig tree and the master's coming.

The stitching of the two parables (vv. 28–32 and 33–37) through the repetition of "know" suggests that Mark has carefully woven together the

---

[30] Recent commentators such as Moloney (*Mark*, esp. 252 n. 186) and Telford (*Theology of Mark*, 153) argue that the author of Mark was highly skilled and brought unity and coherence to the material he inherited.

[31] See George R. Beasley-Murray, *Jesus and the Last Days* (Peabody, MA: Hendrickson, 1993) 453–54.

traditions he inherited. This is crucial for any narrative reading of Mark 13 since this chapter, more than any other part of Mark, has the most complex tradition history. Because scholars have recognized the composite nature of this text and its complex source history, they have read this text with an eye for divisions and seams in the text. However, any attempt to read the text literarily with respect to its final form must move in the opposite direction, with an eye for unity and cohesion.[32]

Here the approach to the text can be likened to examining an oriental rug. The source and redaction critics look at the underside of the rug to find the seams and places where different sources are threaded together, whereas the narrative critic looks at the other side of the rug to discern the patterns and unity that have been woven out of the different sources.

Indeed, the more sources and tradition material one posits in this eschatological discourse, the more one must appreciate Mark's integrating them into a coherent discourse. Dewey captures this challenge well:

> Mark's problem, after all, was not to divide the Gospel into separate sequential units. Rather, Mark's task was to interweave and integrate disparate and episodic material into a single narrative whole, to bridge breaks rather than to create them. Mark is telling a story for a listening audience, not presenting a logical argument. Arguments may be clouded by the lack of a clear linear outline, but stories gain depth and enrichment through repetition and recursion.[33]

The need for such an approach to Mark 13 is pressing. The repetition of "know" throughout vv. 28–37, for example, indicates that Mark interweaves his material with key words, phrases, and repetitions in order to create what Dewey calls an "interwoven tapestry."

The vast majority of studies on Mark 13 since Timothy Colani's have focused on the historical questions surrounding the text.[34] Colani believed that much of Mark 13, namely vv. 6–30, originated from a source he called "the little apocalypse" and was later interpolated into the more original discourse of vv. 1–5 and 31–37. This idea, which liberated Jesus from eschatology, became quite popular and set scholars off in search of the sources behind the eschatological discourse.[35] The task before us, on the

---

[32] W. S. Vorster ("Literary Reflections on Mark 13:5–37: A Narrated Speech of Jesus," in *The Interpretation of Mark* [ed. William Telford; Edinburgh: T & T Clark, 1995] 269–88) claims that modern scholarship on Mark 13 has focused on the literary history and origins of the sources behind the discourse to the neglect of an exegesis that looks at the unified nature of the text and how it serves Mark's narrative purposes.

[33] Dewey, "Interwoven Tapestry," 224.

[34] For the history of interpretation of Mark 13, see Beasley-Murray, *Last Days*, 1–349.

[35] See Beasley-Murray's (*Last Days*, 13–109) account of this interpretive history of Mark 13.

other hand, is to step back in order to take in the patterns of coherence, meaning, and narrative artistry displayed in the final text. Whatever the history behind the discourse, Mark has woven the patterns together and created a new text with new contexts, the meaning of which can only be grasped by reading the new text in its integrity.[36] It is therefore imperative that one allows the context to determine the meaning of the newly formed text.[37] The most salient feature of Mark 13 is Mark's use of allusions and echoes to the Scriptures of Israel. Thus, any narrative analysis of Mark 13 must show how the world created by the text is created in large part through intertextuality and, when Mark's use of Scripture is carefully discerned, the narrative world of Mark 13 begins to come into sharp focus.

## 3.5 An Exegesis of Mark 13 as It Pertains to the Temple

### 3.5.1  *Judgment upon the Temple (vv. 1–4)*

Chapter 13 begins with a significant narrative marker: Jesus' leaving the temple, ἐκπορευομένου αὐτοῦ ἐκ τοῦ ἱεροῦ (13:1). This ends the long narrative stretch of Jesus' time in the temple that began in Mark 11:11 when Jesus entered the temple area, εἰσῆλθεν εἰς Ἱεροσόλυμα εἰς τὸ ἱερόν. But as Jesus makes this exit, one of his disciples turns the topic of conversation back to the temple. The disciple, left unnamed, addresses Jesus as teacher, διδάσκαλε. Such an address suggests to the reader that the disciple has not fully grasped just who Jesus is.[38] This is reaffirmed by the disciple's exclamation about the wonderful stones and buildings of the temple. Since Jesus had already judged the temple at his arrival, the reader knows what the disciples should realize: the temple is doomed. Therefore, the marvel of the disciples for the temple is mispent. Failing to perceive

---

[36] See the discussion of methodology in reading Mark 13 by C. Breytenbach, *Nachfolge und Zukunftserwartung nach Markus: Eine methodenkritische Studie* (Zürich: Theologischer Verlag, 1984) 32. See also Vicky Balabanski, *Eschatology in the Making: Mark, Matthew, and the Didache* (SNTSMS 97; Cambridge: Cambridge University Press, 1997) 55–58. I discovered Breytenbach's fine methodological discussion on reading Mark 13 through Balabanski's work.

[37] Malbon (*Company*, 4–5) sees this as one of the first principles of narrative criticism: "No sign has meaning on its own. Signs have meaning in relation to other signs. Analogously, no element of a literary work has meaning in isolation. Everything has meaning as part of a system of relationships."

[38] Moloney, *Mark*, 414 n. 180.

that the temple is soon to be destroyed and that the cornerstone of its replacement is in their midst, they still cling to the old ways.[39]

The inability of the disciples to discern the fate of the temple is strikingly paralleled by their failure to grasp Jesus' fate. The narrative's overarching focus during Jesus' journey to Jerusalem was his teaching on the imminence of his suffering and death.[40] The disciples failed to "understand" (ἠγνόουν) Jesus' passion predictions (9:32). The dominant theme of Jesus' teaching in the temple has been its demise, along with that of the nation's leaders. Indeed, as I pointed out earlier, Peter's remembering Jesus' word against the fig tree (11:21) did not convey understanding about the fate of the temple. Now, after Jesus' teaching about the end of the temple and the emergence of a new one, the disciples, as shown in the question, fail to comprehend the temple's fate. This failure of the disciples to "understand" is a prominent theme throughout Mark (4:13; 6:52; 7:18; 8:17; 9:32). Now it reaches its climax as the motif of "misunderstanding/understanding" will find its final occurrence in the midst of the eschatological discourse (v. 14).[41]

In short, the disciples' fixation and wonder at the temple illustrates their failure to understand the parable of the rejected stone. If they had grasped it, they would have known that a new temple was on the horizon, casting its shadow on Jerusalem's temple.

---

[39] Mark makes it clear to the reader that the temple has been replaced. First, the words about prayer and forgiveness in Mark 11:24–25 usurp the role of the temple as the place of prayer and forgiveness through sacrifice. Second, the Temple Mount is said to be a "mountain cast into the sea" (11:23). Finally, Mark 12:33 suggests that animal sacrifice is rendered obsolete.

[40] See N. Perrin's classic essay ("The Christology of Mark: A Study in Methodology," in *The Interpretation of Mark*, [ed. William Telford; Philadelphia: Fortress, 1985] 99) on this motif, where he shows how the threefold passion prediction structures this central section of Mark.

[41] This "misunderstanding" motif is the key to unlocking the meaning of the enigmatic aside "let the reader understand" (v. 14), which I will take up in commenting on v. 14.

Indeed, the "rejected stone" is evoked in Jesus' response to the disciple's observation of the temple's splendor. Mark employs a chiasm based on the key words "stone" and "building":[42]

A  Look, teacher, what wonderful *stones* (λίθοι)
   B  And what wonderful *buildings* (οἰκοδομαί)
   B'  Do you see these great *buildings* (οἰκοδομάς)
A'  There will not be left here one *stone upon another* (λίθος ἐπὶ λίθον)

This chiasm links the fate of the displaced temple stones with the rejected stone of Jesus' vineyard parable. Recall Jesus' question at the conclusion of the parable, "Have you not read this Scripture: 'the very stone (λίθον) the builders (οἱ οἰκοδομοῦντες) rejected has become the cornerstone?'" (Mark 12:10).[43] Mary Tolbert observes: "As the parable of the Tenants implies and the opening of the Apocalyptic Discourse confirms, for the rejected stone to become the new centerpiece, the buildings presently standing must first be completely dismantled and the tenants presently in control must first be destroyed; only then can the new edifice rise and the faithful tenants be installed."[44] Whatever else the discourse is about, the reader must not fail to read it in the context of Jesus' and the temple's intertwined fates, especially given Mark's implied conviction that only one of the rejected "temples" will be raised up.

### 3.5.1.1 Sitting in Judgment

Having announced the destruction of the temple, Jesus sat down (καθημένου) on the Mount of Olives opposite the temple (κατέναντι τοῦ ἱεροῦ) (Mark 13:3). Just a short while before this, at the end of his teaching in the temple, Jesus had sat down "opposite the treasury," καθίσας κατέναντι τοῦ γαζοφυλακίου (Mark 12:41). The word describing Jesus' posture here, καθίζω (κάθημαι in 13:3) can have connotations of a royal enthronement, a teacher seated giving a lesson, or a judge seated for

---

[42] Lambrecht (*Die Redaktion der Markus-Apokalypse: Literarische Analyse und Strukturuntersuchung* [AnBib 28: Rome: Pontifical Biblical Institute, 1967] 80–85) noted this chiasm and saw it as illustrating Mark's careful editing. See also Tolbert, *Sowing the Gospel*, 259.

[43] The "rejected stone" motif is carefully threaded through Mark's narrative more than one would at first glance suspect. The term rejected (ἀπεδοκίμασαν) describing the future cornerstone (12:10) is found in only one other place in Mark's gospel – Jesus' first passion prediction: "And he began to teach them that the Son of Man must suffer many things, and be rejected (ἀποδοκιμασθῆναι) by the elders and the chief priests and scribes …" (Mark. 8:31). Thus, we have another example of how Mark takes a key word from the Scriptures of Israel (intertextuality, Ps 118:22) and weaves it into his narrative tapestry (intratextuality, 8:31; 12:10).

[44] Tolbert, *Sowing the Gospel*, 260.

judgment.[45] These are likely the images Mark seeks to invoke, for in both cases Jesus is depicted as one who issues authoritative judgments. That Jesus sat opposite the treasury is itself provocative. At the outset of Jesus' time in the temple, the Jewish leaders questioned his authority (Mark 11:28), and in the dispute Jesus defeated them in an intense verbal exchange. Only after this account does Mark portray Jesus as one seated in authority, his rivals silenced. The sense of judgment is strengthened by Jesus portrayed as seated (12:41) immediately after his condemnation of the scribes (12:38–40) and his praise of the widow for her sacrificial giving (vv. 41–44). Moreover, just before Jesus' condemnation of the scribes he cited the opening verse of Psalm 110, which begins with the prominent image of enthronement, κάθου ἐκ δεξιῶν μου. That Mark describes Jesus as sitting in the temple area just after the discussion of Psalm 110 and as he announces judgment on the scribes may be meaningful.

Given Jesus' repeated criticisms of the temple, his final exit and his foretelling of its destruction, there is little doubt that Jesus' sitting opposite the temple is intended to embody his critique of its corruption. Therefore, this context leads the reader to understand the term κατέναντι as one implying hostility.[46] This imagery also fits in well with Mark's allusion to Daniel's vision of the Son of Man in the discourse (13:26), in which Daniel sees the Ancient of Days seated (κάθημαι) and giving judgment (Dan 7:9).[47] Both Jesus' posture and the content of his pronouncements dovetail into Mark's fundamental image of Jesus: that of Daniel's Son of Man seated in judgment.

### 3.5.1.2 Question and Answer

The entire discourse of Mark 13:5–37 is Jesus' response to the question of the timing of the temple's destruction and its accompanying signs. The question in v. 4 has two aspects, distinguished by the καί that divides the question into parallel halves:

---

[45] See BDAG, καθίζω 491–92. Also C. Schneider ("κάθημαι, καθίζω," *TDNT* 3.440–44) notes that this can evoke the image of both a judge or a king. Ephesians 1:20 is a good example of how καθίζω was used to evoke Jesus' royal authority as judge in light of Psalm 110.

[46] France, *Mark*, 507.

[47] It is worth noting here that in Mark 14:62 Jesus tells the high priest that he "will see the Son of Man sitting (κάθημαι) at the right hand of the Power, and coming with the clouds of heaven." In Daniel 7 the Son of Man is not pictured as sitting, but in Mark that is the emphasis of the vision. However, it should be noted that the image of thrones is prominent in Daniel 7, which also may be why Mark has combined it with Psalm 110. The significance of sitting in power is not lost on Mark.

πότε ταῦτα ἔσται
καὶ τί τὸ σημεῖον ὅταν μέλλῃ ταῦτα συντελεῖσθαι πάντα;

The subject of this question is the temple's destruction. It has, however, two aspects: (1) when will the temple end? and (2) what will be the signs of its demise? It is often observed by scholars that, although the question is focused on the temple, Jesus' discourse-response does not pertain to the temple, apart from a vague allusion to it in v. 14. Thus, Morna Hooker observes, "Commentators often echo the complaint of Victor of Antioch who, writing in the fifth century, remarked that the disciples asked one question, and Jesus answered another."[48] It is my contention, however, that the answer *does* follow the logic of the question, and that the temple is very much the focus of Jesus' subsequent discourse. The following exegesis aims to demonstrate that the temple is Jesus' focus as well as to explain why commentators have lost sight of the temple in reading Mark 13.

### 3.5.2 The Beginning of the Birth Pangs (vv. 5–8)

As noted above, βλέπω and πλανάω create an *inclusio* that frames vv. 5–23. The Markan term βλέπω is found also at the beginning of v. 9, which serves to mark vv. 5–8 as a subunit of vv. 5–23. This is confirmed in the way v. 8 concludes the list of catastrophic events begun in v. 5 "These (ταῦτα) are the beginning of the birth pangs." The ταῦτα here serve then, as a summation of the events that make up the beginning of the birth pangs: false prophets, wars, earthquakes and famines.[49] The call to take heed (βλέπω), which precedes the list of birth pangs, is a very important term for Mark. Geddert has argued persuasively that βλέπω is a call for discernment beyond what can be empirically seen.[50] Thus, more is to be seen behind the wars and natural disasters listed in vv. 5–8 than mere catastrophes and

---

[48] Hooker, *Mark*, 305.

[49] Brant James Pitre (*The Historical Jesus, the Great Tribulation and the End of the Exile: Restoration Eschatology and the Origin of the Atonement* [Ph.D. diss., University of Notre Dame, 2004] 269–70) argues that there is no break in vv. 5–8 but "rather, these verses are held together by the parallel parenesis against being led astray (βλέπετε μή τις ὑμᾶς πλανήσῃ) and being alarmed (μὴ θροεῖσθε· δεῖ γενέσθαι) (Mark 13:5,7), and by the summarizing statement: 'These (ταῦτα) are the beginning of the birth pangs' (Mark 13:8), which, in context, refers back not only to the natural catastrophes but to the wars, the rumors of war, and the coming of deceivers, as well as to the disciples' question about when "all these things (ταῦτα … πάντα) will take place (Mark 13:4)."

[50] Geddert (*Watchwords*, 60) sums up his analysis of the term, claiming "every usage of the term in Mark appears intended by the author to contribute to a carefully devised call for discernment concerning realities which lie beyond the observations of the physical senses."

human strife. Underlying these calamities is the eschatological judgment upon the temple and its corruption, which was borrowed from the language of prophetic critique against Jerusalem and its temple before it was destroyed in 587 B.C. Indeed, the list that comprises the birth pangs is common in the prophetic literature of Israel.[51]

### 3.5.2.1 False Prophets

The warning against those who will come in Jesus' name (ἐπὶ τῷ ὀνόματί μου) and lead many astray (πλανήσουσιν) in vv. 5–6 recalls the many prophetic texts that warn against being led astray.[52] In Jeremiah 14, after Jeremiah complains that the prophets of Jerusalem prophesy peace and security for the city, the Lord condemns the prophets who speak lies "in my name" (ἐπὶ τῷ ὀνόματί μου, a phrase repeated in Jeremiah 14:14–15):

And the LORD said to me: The prophets are prophesying lies *in my name*; I did not send them, nor did I command them or speak to them. They are prophesying to you a lying vision, worthless divination, and the deceit of their own minds. Therefore thus says the LORD concerning the prophets who prophesy *in my name* although I did not send them, and who say, 'Sword and famine shall not come on this land': By sword and famine those prophets shall be consumed. (Italics mine)

Jeremiah's use of "in my name" sheds light on the issue at hand in Mark 13:5–6. Just as false prophets in Jeremiah's time claimed divine authority for themselves and their words, false prophets will arise after Jesus who claim to be heirs of the Lord's own prophetic authority.[53] An earlier example of this is the man who cast out demons in Jesus' name (Mark 9:38–39).

The context of the citation from Jeremiah is also significant in that the false prophets are from Jerusalem and that they are claiming security and peace for the city as well as the temple. However, Jeremiah warns them of war (the sword) and famine that will befall Jerusalem (14:2 and 16 direct judgment upon Jerusalem, with v. 19 referring to the temple as "Zion"). A similar warning against false prophets in Mark 13:5–6, followed by a warning about war (13:7) and famine (13:8), give to Jesus' words the full, ominous force of Jeremiah's fateful proclamation.

---

[51] Pesch, *Markusevangelium*, 2. 280.

[52] Discussion on the phrase "in my name" among commentators usually focuses on whether it means a messianic claim or a claim to be Jesus himself (see Beasley-Murray, *Last Days*, 391–92). Evans (*Mark*, 305) notes the OT background for speaking "in the name of the Lord," but he does not connect the texts in Deut 18:5,7,20,22 with the prophetic traditions relating to false prophets speaking about the protection of Jerusalem, as drawn out in the discussion above on Jeremiah 14.

[53] See further Pitre, *Historical Jesus*, 271.

Several other prophetic oracles yield a similar pattern. In Isaiah 9, the prophets of the Northern Kingdom are accused of misleading the people to such an extent that the people's failure to repent results in the destruction of their kingdom and, ultimately, their being taken into exile (Isa 9:15–16). In Ezekiel 13–14 the Lord condemns Jerusalem and particularly the false prophets who have promised peace, when in actuality God was promising wrath and destruction for the city. The prophets have "deceived" (πλανάω) God's people (LXX Ezek 13:10; 14:9). Again, the context is a judgment against Jerusalem (LXX Ezek 13:16; 14:21–22), which entails famine and war (the sword) among other disasters (especially Ezek 14:13–22). In LXX Mic 3:5, the Lord also condemns false prophets who lead the people "astray" (τοὺς πλανῶντας) by promising peace for Jerusalem when its fate will be destruction. Here, as in Ezekiel, the temple is an object of the Lord's wrath: "Therefore because of you Zion shall be plowed as a field; Jerusalem shall become a heap of ruins, and the mountain of the house a wooded height" (Mic 3:12).

Three points are to be noted in the above examples. First, the false prophets are closely associated with a time of tribulation and wrath. Indeed, their misguidance is a contributing factor in the iniquity of God's people that ultimately brings about divine judgment. Second, these prophets who deceive and lead the people astray belong to the people of God. Third, these false prophets often rouse God's judgment against Jerusalem and its temple. All three of these elements are present in Mark 13:5–6.[54] This correspondence sheds light on Jesus' warning against false prophets: Jerusalem is again heading for divine judgment and one needs to be wary of being led into thinking otherwise, either by false hopes for peace or by deception that leads to moral corruption. Those who are not vigilant must be prepared to face God's wrath.

### 3.5.2.2  War and Rumors of War

Images of wars and strife are common to prophetic warnings and judgment oracles throughout the OT. However, France suggests that the formulation "when you hear of wars and rumors of wars, do not be alarmed" (Mark 13:7) parallels Jeremiah's words to the Jews about the imminent destruction of Babylon:[55]

Go out of the midst of her, my people! Let every man save his life from the fierce anger of the LORD! Let not your hearts faint, and be not fearful at the report heard in the land,

---

[54] The multiplication of thematic links between two texts can be evidence for intertextuality; see discussion in Hays, *Echoes of Scripture*, 30.

[55] France, *Mark*, 511; Evans, *Mark*, 306.

when a report comes in one year and afterward a report in another year, and violence is in the land and ruler is against ruler. Therefore, behold, the days are coming… (Jer 51:45–47)

There are two points of correspondence between this oracle and Mark 13:7–8: (1) parenesis against fear; and (2) rumors of war phrased in antithetical parallelism ("ruler against ruler" in Jeremiah with "nation against nation, kingdom against kingdom" in Mark).

The wider context of Mark's discourse echoes this oracle in three other ways. The notion of total destruction, in that "no stone shall be taken from you for a corner and no stone for a foundation, but you shall be a perpetual waste" (Jer 51:26) matches the image of "no stone left upon another" in Mark 13:2; and furthermore, the call to leave the condemned city in Jeremiah 51:6,45 is parallel to the call to flee to the mountains in Mark 13:14–15. Finally, the "day" and the "days" of the Yhwh's judgment are found in Jeremiah 51:2,47,52 as in Mark 13:17,18,20(2x),24,32. Taken individually, these allusions would be quite faint, but collectively they possess considerable force.[56]

It has been suggested that the statement that the wars and rumors of wars "must happen" (δεῖ γενέσθαι) echoes the book of Daniel,[57] although France claims that "δεῖ γενέσθαι is not specifically eschatological language; wars are sure to happen, and their occurrence is not to be seen as having any eschatological significance."[58] There are, however, two problems with this observation. First, this sentiment reflects modern thinking, not the thought of first-century Christians steeped in the Scriptures of Israel. In Jewish and much of ancient culture the causality for wars is often seen as theological as much as political. Second, while wars in themselves are not necessarily eschatological, France's argument takes the motif of wars in isolation when they are a part of a longer list filled with eschatological language and imagery. The larger framework of Mark 13 suggests that the wars described here have an eschatological purpose, as do the other events mentioned in the same context. Indeed, the list of dire events in Mark 13 begin with the call to discernment (βλέπω), summoning

---

[56] For the importance of thematic parallels for discerning intertextuality, refer to n. 39 above.

[57] Evans (*Mark*, 307) posits that the phrase is drawn from apocalyptic literature and cites LXX Dan 2:28. Lars Hartman (*Prophecy Interpreted: The Formation of Some Jewish Apocalytic Texts and of the Eschatological Discourse Mark 13 Par.* [ConBNT 1; Lund: Gleerup, 1966] 173) sees an allusion to Dan 8:19; Dyer (*Prophecy*, 103) sees allusions to Dan 2:28,29,45; 11:36. Moloney (*Mark*, 255) notes that δεῖ γενέσθαι means that the events are part of God's larger design. What better place to look for clues to that design than the prophetic eschatology found in the prophets?

[58] France, *Mark*, 511.

the reader to see the deeper reality behind these catastrophes.[59] Thus, Mark picks up the theological sense of δεῖ to characterize the calamities as falling into God's eschatological plan for the great tribulation.[60] Although this particular allusion to Daniel is by itself rather faint, it is strengthened by the other undisputed allusions to Daniel in this discourse. Furthermore, its likelihood is supported by another proximate allusion to Daniel, which I shall now examine.[61]

The phrase δεῖ γενέσθαι in v. 7 is completed by an even more important allusion to Daniel, one that is often overlooked: "This must take place, but the end is not yet (ἀλλ'οὔπω τὸ τέλος, Mark 13:7)." The phrase τὸ τέλος is found more frequently in Daniel than in any other book of the LXX OT (Dan 8:17–19; 9:26–27; 11:27,35,40; 12:4,9,13). In Daniel, it carries the technical sense of an appointed time set by providence. Hartman argues that the prediction of wars that must precede "the end" (τὸ τέλος) in Mark 13:7 is a strong echo of Daniel 9:26–27:[62]

And after the sixty-two weeks, an anointed one shall be cut off, and shall have nothing; and the people of the prince who is to come shall destroy the city and the sanctuary. Its end shall come with a flood, and to the end there shall be war; desolations are decreed. And ... he shall cause sacrifice and offering to cease; and upon the wing of abominations shall come one who makes desolate, until the decreed end is poured out on the desolator. (Daniel 9:26–27)

Hartman notes the thematic links between Dan 9:26 and Mark 13:7, as well as the rest of the discourse, which establish a vital relationship between

---

[59] On βλέπω as calling for discernment, see Geddert, *Watchwords*, 60.

[60] On the eschatological nature of δεῖ in Mark 13:7, see, e.g., Nineham, *Mark*, 225, 346; Anderson, *Mark*, 292; Beasley-Murray, *Last Days*, 396–97.

[61] Given the many strong echoes to Daniel in the latter half of Mark's Gospel, particularly in Mark 13 (e.g., 13:14), there are strong grounds for seeing faint echoes to Daniel as likely intertextual allusions. Hays (*Conversion of the Imagination*, 40) notes this phenomena in intertextual allusions: "Where we see evidence of such sustained and reflectively patterned reading of a particular text, we may assume that other possible echoes of that same text elsewhere in the same letter are likely to be theologically significant rather than merely the product of our own interpretive fantasy." There is strong evidence that this is the case for Mark's consistent and repeated use of Daniel (see esp. Kee, *Community of the New Age*, 45); however, to anticipate the conclusions of this chapter, it is also true that in Mark 13 there is a particular use of prophetic texts that focus on judgment oracles against Jerusalem and the temple. The thematic convergence of so many texts clearly points to a pattern. The kind of pattern that Hays argues for holds much import for understanding the theological thinking of the text that is making such echoes.

[62] Hartman (*Prophecy*, 148–50) argued for the importance of Daniel as a background for much of Mark 13, and he saw a close connection with Daniel 9:26–27.

Mark 13 and Daniel 9.[63] On the other hand, Beasley-Murray argues against a link with Daniel and Mark 13:7, claiming that there are no parallels in the language used in either text. However, Beasley-Murray does concede that Daniel 9:26 is "unmistakably in mind in v. 14 [Mk 13:14] ."[64] The fact that Dan 9:26–27 is used later in the discourse (Mark 13:14) should caution one against dismissing it here. In addition, the overall correspondence of themes between Daniel 9:24–27and Mark 13 is rather telling: (1) the coming of an anointed one (Dan 9:25); (2) wars (Dan 9:26); (3) the destruction of the city and temple (Dan 9:26)); and (4) the abomination (Dan 9:27). Moreover, there is a vital linguistic link between Dan 9:26 and Mark 13:7, the phrase τὸ τέλος, which is found twice in Dan 9:26 and once again in Dan 9:27. What is particularly worthy of note is that LXX Dan 9:26 describes that there will be war "to the end" (ἕως τέλους).[65] Since "the end" in Dan 9:26 is the destruction of Jerusalem and the temple, the connection with "the end" in Mark seems unmistakable, especially given that the context for Jesus' speech is his answer to the question about when the temple will be destroyed and what will be the signs previous to its destruction.

In Mark 13:8 the wars are described by the use of parallelism: "For nation will rise against nation, and kingdom against kingdom." This literary feature is taken from apocalyptic literature, its most striking parallel being the oracle of judgment against Egypt in Isaiah 19.[66] The oracle begins with the theophany of Yhwh on a cloud (19:1), followed by the pronouncement of divine judgment in the form of war: "And I will stir up Egyptians against Egyptians, and they will fight, every man against his brother and every man against his neighbor, city against city, kingdom against kingdom" (19:2). The entire judgment that is poured out upon Egypt is referred to as "that day" (τῇ ἡμέρᾳ ἐκείνῃ, LXX Isa 19:16,18,19,23,24). The point here is that the language employed in Mark 13:8 is borrowed from OT prophetic oracles about a day of judgment from the Lord.

---

[63] Ibid.

[64] Beasley-Murray, *Last Days*, 395.

[65] Hartman's case for Dan 9:26 relating to Mark 13:7 has recently been taken up and strengthened by Pitre, *Historical Jesus*, 274–75.

[66] This parallel is widely noted, e.g., by Dyer, *Prophecy*, 104 and Evans, *Mark*, 307–8. For references from Second Temple literature, see Pitre, *Historical Jesus*, 275.

### 3.5.2.3 Earthquakes and Famines

Earthquakes and famines constitute stock imagery from apocalyptic literature.[67] Earthquakes often accompany theophanies (e.g., Exod 19:18). Especially in the prophetic writings, earthquakes are associated with the Lord's coming in judgment (e.g., Jer 4:24; Mic 1:3–4; Hab 3:6, 10; Zech 14:5; Isa 29:6; Ezek 38:19–20; Joel 2:10–11).[68] In Jeremiah 4, an oracle against Jerusalem (the city and its temple are the object of the judgment, 4:3,5,11,14,16,31), the Lord is depicted as "coming like clouds, with his chariots like the whirlwind" (Jer 4:13). It is a "day" of judgment (4:9). War comes to destroy the land and Jerusalem (4:16), rendering the whole land desolate. In the midst of language evoking the return of creation to chaos, earthquakes are described: "I looked on the earth, and lo, it was waste and void; and to the heavens, and they had no light. I looked on the mountains, and lo, they were quaking, and the hills moved to and fro" (Jer 4:23–24). Earthquakes also feature in Joel's account of the day of the Lord (Joel 2:1). Again, the manifestation of clouds presages the Lord's judgment (Joel 2:2) and, as in Jeremiah, the earthquake comes in the midst of a return to chaos:

The earth quakes before them, the heavens tremble. The sun and the moon are darkened, and the stars withdraw their shining. The LORD utters his voice before his army, for his host is exceedingly great: he that executes his word is powerful. For the day of the LORD is great and very terrible; who can endure it? (Joel 2:10–11)

The final vision of Zechariah revolves around the day of the Lord against Jerusalem (Zech 14:1). The Lord comes against the city, and nations gather to battle against Jerusalem (14:2). Then, following a rare mention of the Mount of Olives, an earthquake like the one in the days of Uzziah is described, after which the Lord will come with his angels (14:5). It is not uncommon for scholars to acknowledge or even list the many examples of earthquakes mentioned in the OT. What is rarely acknowledged, however, is that most of the prophetic texts that mention earthquakes do so in judgment oracles against Jerusalem.[69]

The same is true for references to famine, even more common in prophetic oracles of judgment. Jeremiah employs the idea of famine as

---

[67] E.g., Lane, *Mark*, 458; Evans, *Mark*, 307–8. Although commentators note that earthquakes and famines are stock language for eschatology and apocalyptic, the pattern that these are found most often in oracles directed against Jerusalem is overlooked.

[68] "In the OT, earthquakes are sometimes associated with God's coming in judgment (e.g., Mic 1:3–4; Hab 3:6,10)" (Evans, *Mark*, 307).

[69] There are a few texts that employ earthquakes as divine judgment against a target besides Jerusalem, but they are the exception (e.g., Isa 29:6; Ezek 38:19–20), whereas Jerusalem is much more frequently the target in most references (e.g., Zech 14:5; Jer 4:24; Hab 3:6,10; Mic 1:3–4; Joel 2:10–11).

judgment against Jerusalem more than any other prophet.[70] Ezekiel also declares famine upon Jerusalem as part of the divine judgment issued for its wickedness. For example, in Ezekiel 5 the Lord is opposed to Jerusalem because its citizens have defiled the temple (5:11). One third of Jerusalem is given over to the sword, another third to famine, and the rest scattered in the wind (5:12). Famine is particularly emphasized:

"When I loose against you my deadly arrows of famine, arrows for destruction, which I will loose to destroy you, and when I bring more and more famine upon you, and break your staff of bread. (Ezek 5:16)

The motif of famine against Jerusalem is one that Ezekiel repeats often (Ezek 6:11–12; 7:15; 12:16; 14:13,21). Isaiah also announces famine as part of the judgment upon Jerusalem (Isa 5:13–14). Although there are some references to famine that are not signs of judgment against Jerusalem or Israel,[71] the vast majority of occurrences are directed toward Jerusalem, others are directed toward the ten tribes of Israel and only a few against pagan nations.

What is significant for our reading of Mark 13 is that, in the prophetic writings of Israel, the judgment oracles against Jerusalem frequently involve wars, earthquakes, and famine. There is no need to look for any one particular text as the source for Mark's material. What is important is that Mark 13:5–8 uses the eschatological language of the prophets, drawn primarily from their oracles against Jerusalem.

### 3.5.2.4 Birth Pangs

The final element of Mark 13:8 may be the most significant eschatological reference: "These are but the beginning of the birth pangs" (ἀρχὴ ὠδίνων ταῦτα). The image of "birth pangs" (ὠδίνες) is common in OT prophetic writings and usually associated with the "day of the Lord" and therefore describes suffering that comes with divine judgment.[72] Dale Allison

---

[70] Jer 11:22; 14:12,14–15; 18:21; 21:9; 24:10; 27:8; 29:18; 32:24,36; 34:17. All of these references have Jerusalem as the recipient of famine under divine judgment.

[71] Amos 4:6–9 is an example of an oracle that is directed against the ten tribes of Israel in the north, while Isa 14:30 is an example of one of the rare cases in which a Gentile nation is the object of famine as divine wrath.

[72] Many prophetic texts associate "birth pangs" with the "day of the Lord": Isa 13:6–8; 26:17–27:1; 66:7–8; Jer 4:9–31; 22:23; 30:5–7; 48:12–41; Mic 4:6–10. The "birth pangs" are very much at the heart of what Meier (*Marginal Jew*, 2. 31, 248–51) calls "prophetic eschatology," that is, the birth pangs speak of a time of tribulation and suffering, which are often followed by oracles of restoration and consolation. Not incidentally, Jerusalem and the temple are often the focus of both the tribulation and the restoration.

believes that Mark's use of ὠδίνες was a technical term in the first century for what later rabbinic tradition and many scholars have called the "messianic woes."[73] Brant Pitre has given one of the most recent and systematic studies of the great tribulation also known as the "messianic woes"; regarding this topic he makes an observation of how the motif of "birth pangs" in the OT has two key dimensions:

> If one closely examines the use of this image in the Old Testament and Second Temple Judaism, one finds that it is repeatedly linked not only to suffering in general, but to tribulations which (almost always) do one of two things: (a) accompany the destruction of a city or nation or (b) precede the coming of the Messiah.[74]

Building on Pitre's statement that the "birth pangs" are often linked to the destruction of a city, I would add that the city most frequently referred to is Jerusalem (Jer 4:31; 6:22–26; 22:23–27; 30:4–8; Isa 26:16–19; 24:10; Mic 4:10–14). Some of these examples are from oracles already discussed in reference to Mark 13:5–8. For instance, the oracle against Jerusalem in Jeremiah 4 closes with daughter Zion in anguish and travail, her birth pangs so severe that she is gasping for breath (Jer 4:31). We have already discussed Micah's judgment against prophets who lead the people astray and who eventually lead to the destruction of the temple and Jerusalem (Mic 3:5–12). This punishment is then likened to the pain of a woman in travail (4:10). Isaiah describes the chastisements sent from God upon his people (i.e., Jerusalem) as "birth pangs" (Isa 26:17–18). The destruction of other cities like Babylon (Isa 13:6–14:2; Jer 50:43) and Samaria (Hos 13:12–16) are also described in terms of birth pangs, but the city most often referred to in this way is Jerusalem.

Pitre's second point that "birth pangs" can also refer to the coming of the Messiah is important and merits further discussion. Pitre gives two OT

---

[73] Dale Allison, *The End of the Ages Has Come: An Early Interpretation of the Passion and Resurrection of Jesus* (Philadelphia: Fortress, 1985) 6 n. 6. In this work Allison gives a very nuanced analysis of the complex of ideas surrounding the expectation in prophetic eschatology and apocalyptic writings about a time of great tribulation. This idea is not always closely associated with a messianic hope, and so the later term "messianic woes" does not do justice to the diversity of traditions surrounding the idea of a coming eschatological tribulation. Albert Schweitzer (*The Quest of the Historical Jesus* [New York: Macmillan, 1961] 387–93) called the tribulation the time of "testing" (πειρασμός) and saw this as the key to Jesus' eschatological outlook. Besides Allison, other scholars take up Schweitzer's focus on the eschatological trial or tribulation, also known as messianic woes, e.g., Nineham, *Mark*, 346; Anderson, *Mark*, 292–93; Wright, *Victory*, 377–91; Mark Dubis, "Messianic Woes," *Eerdmans Dictionary of the Bible* (Grand Rapids: Eerdmans, 2000) 890–91; and most recently the significant work by Pitre, *Historical Jesus*.

[74] Pitre, *Historical Jesus*, 276.

examples, Mic 5:2–4 and Jer 30:5–9. These two texts are significant and will be cited in full:

But you, O Bethlehem Ephrathah, who are little among the clans of Judah, from you shall come forth for me *one who is to be ruler in Israel*, whose origin is from of old, from ancient days. Therefore he shall give them up until the time when *she who is in travail has brought forth*; then the rest of his brethren shall return to the people of Israel. (Mic 5:2–4, italics mine)

Thus says the LORD: We have heard a cry of panic, of terror, and no peace. As now, and see, can a man *bear a child?* Why then do I see every man with his hands on his loins *like a woman in labor?* Why has every face turned pale? Alas! That day is so great there is none like it; it is a time of distress for Jacob; yet he shall be saved out of it. And it shall come to pass in *that day*, says the LORD of hosts, that I will break the yoke from off their neck, and I will burst their bonds, and strangers shall no more make servants of them. But they shall serve the LORD their God and *David their king*, whom I will raise up for them. (Jer 30:5–9, italics mine)

As Pitre notes, both passages assert that the Messiah will come forth after the birth pangs of God's people.[75] While he is correct that the "birth pangs" are associated with the destruction of a city and the coming of the Messiah, it is important, particularly for the present study, to note that a specific city is in view. In Jeremiah, the "birth pangs" that precede the Messiah are clearly the same as those that describe the suffering and the destruction of Jerusalem (Jer 4:31). Likewise, the birth pangs in Mic 5:2–4 are related to the suffering and destruction of Jerusalem in Mic 4:9. In other words, birth pangs always refer to the suffering and destruction of a city or nation under divine judgment, and in two cases, this suffering – with reference to Jerusalem – is to precede the coming of the Messiah. Again, it is worth emphasizing that the primary subject of birth pangs is a particular city, Jerusalem. In cases where the birth pangs presage the coming Messiah, they are always associated with Jerusalem.[76]

These observations help explain Mark 13:5–8, which warns of false messiahs in its description of the birth pangs, since birth pangs may well be linked with the advent of the Messiah because of the tradition embodied by Jer 30:5–9 and Mic 5:2–4.[77] By identifying the false messiahs, wars and

---

[75] Pitre, *Historical Jesus*, 276–78.

[76] This is a point not explicitly made by Pitre, but it is not far from his thought as he notes the context of Mark 13 – the destruction of Jerusalem – as a significant link to many of the OT "birth pang" texts.

[77] Pitre (*Historical Jesus*, 278–79) makes this point: "However, in light of the fact that Jesus has *just predicted* the coming of *messianic pretenders*, the image of 'birth pangs' and the overall thrust of Jesus' warnings to the disciples is quite clear in context. He is, in effect saying: 'many persons will come saying, 'I am the Messiah' – but do not

rumors of war, famine, and earthquakes as the "beginning" (ἀρχή) of the birth pangs (ὠδίνων), Mark effectively paints all these things (ταῦτα) as divine judgment, using the language of Israel's prophetic tradition. Moreover, as already shown, these prophetic judgments were primarily delivered against Jerusalem. This coheres with the setting that Mark has established for the discourse – in a mode of opposition to the temple (Mark 13:1–4). Therefore, in light of the OT background concerning birth pangs and Jerusalem, these birth pangs refer to the imminent judgment that will once again befall Jerusalem before the revelation of the Messiah.

### 3.5.3  Proclamation to the Nations (vv. 9–13)

Verse 9 opens with the second use of βλέπω, which invites the reader to a new perspective on the sufferings to be endured in the "birth pangs." Whereas vv. 5–8 generally focused on external events, vv. 9–13 focus on what will happen to Jesus' disciples during the tribulation. I will examine this section in three parts. First, I will investigate Mark's description in 13:9, 11 of how the disciples will be handed over for trial. Here, I hope to highlight the significance of Mark's intratextual repetition, executed through terms such as "hand over" (παραδίδωμι) and "in that hour" (ἐκείνῃ τῇ ὥρᾳ). Second, I will focus on the proclamation of the "gospel" (εὐαγγέλιον) to "the nations" (ἔθνη) in v. 10, with a particular eye to crucial intratextual and intertextual echoes. Indeed, I hope to show why this verse is considered, at least by a few scholars, of central importance for the discourse. Finally, I will turn to the issue of interfamilial strife in vv. 12–13, which echo two pivotal texts from the OT and infuse the suffering and persecution of the disciples with eschatological overtones.

### 3.5.3.1  Delivered up for Trial (vv. 9 and 11)

Because v. 9 and 11 fit together so well, it is often thought that v. 10 is a Markan insertion that interrupts them.[78] Whatever the redaction history, vv. 9 and 11 now serve to frame the proclamation of the gospel

---

be deceived by them and do not follow them, for these are merely the *beginning* of the birth pangs of the coming of the true Messiah.'" Italics original.

[78] Gaston, *No Stone on Another*, 19–20; Lambrecht, *Redaktion*, 119–20; Lane, *Mark*, 461. Donahue and Harrington (*Mark*, 370) sum up well the arguments for v. 10 being a Markan redaction: "That Mark himself has inserted this sentence is suggested by the characteristically Markan vocabulary, the fact that the verse interrupts the smooth flow of thought from 13:9 to 13:11, and the unlikelihood that Jesus spoke so clearly about the Gentile mission (since there was so much dispute about it in the early church according to Acts and Paul's letters)."

commanded in v. 10, thereby highlighting this verse.[79] The repetition of "hand over" (παραδίδωμι) helps frame v. 10 by its repetition in vv. 9 and 11. The present order suggests that the disciples' witness to the "gospel" will cause them to be "handed over" and tried.

Verses 9 and 11 describe the persecution of the disciples in language that directly parallels Jesus' own passion.[80] Jesus warns that "they will hand you over (παραδώσουσιν ὑμᾶς) to councils (συνέδρια)," which corresponds to the way Jesus was handed over (παρέδωκαν) by the whole Sanhedrin (ὅλον τὸ συνέδριον) to Pilate for trial (Mark 15:1).[81] In v. 9, the disciples will be "beaten" (δέρω) – a word found twice in the parable of the wicked tenants (Mark 12:3,5). Jesus' followers are to share in his vocation of suffering and servanthood. If the cross has been the controlling symbol for the true understanding of Jesus' identity, the same is now true for both the disciple and the reader. Jesus' own perseverance is the singular model of that faithfulness which must endure to the end (Mark 13:13). However, Mark envisions this as much more than a moral example, for the suffering of Jesus and the subsequent suffering of the disciples both belong to the eschatological tribulation. In short, the disciples' participation in Jesus' suffering is a participation in the great tribulation. Jesus' example shows them that they can "persevere to the end" (13:13).

The disciples are promised the assistance of the Holy Spirit "in that hour" (ἐν ἐκείνῃ τῇ ὥρᾳ, v. 11), a phrase repeated at the end of the discourse (v. 32). The term ὥρα in Mark has a technical sense, conveying

---

[79] Taylor (*Mark*, 507) notes that παραδίδωμι functions as a catchword in v. 9 and v. 11, binding this unit together. Beasley-Murray (*Last Days*, 402) observes that thematically vv. 9–11 all share the theme of witness.

[80] C. B. Cousar ("Eschatology and Mark's *Theologia Crucis*: A Critical Analysis of Mark 13," *Int* 24 [1970] 321–25, 329) noted the narrative strategy of identifying Jesus with the disciples: "Behind and before the delivering over of the community into the hands of its persecutors stands the suffering Lord of the community, falsely accused before councils, hated, beaten, yet through endurance to the end bringing salvation. In the way of discipleship he leaves to his followers a no less difficult road to travel than he himself walked." Cousar is representative of many (e.g., France, *Mark*, 514) who see Jesus' suffering as a model for the latter suffering of the disciples, which, although true, falls short of the full meaning of this suffering as Mark sees it – that is, the suffering of both Jesus and the disciples is part of the eschatological tribulation.

[81] The repetition of "hand over" (παραδίδωμι) three times (Mark 13:9,11,12) is significant in light of its use in chapters 14–15. "Thus when it is predicted that the Christians will be handed over to councils and beaten in synagogues and will stand before governors (13:9), we are reminded that Jesus too was handed over (παραδίδωμι appears 10 times in Mk 14f) and was beaten and stood before Pilate" (Gaston, *No Stone on Another*, 478).

the "hour" of the great eschatological tribulation.[82] Very much connected to its use in Mark 13, "the hour" is repeated three times in the Gethsemane scene (Mark 14:35, 37, 41). As Judas comes to betray Jesus, he announces that "the hour has come" (ἦλθεν ἡ ὥρα) (Mark 14:41). Judas is subsequently called the "one who hands over" (ὁ παραδιδούς) and initiates a sequence of events that lead to Jesus' trial before councils (14:55; 15:1) and his being repeatedly handed over (see, e.g., 15:1,15, etc.). It is worth noting that the motif of being "handed over" is found in LXX Daniel 7:25, in which the saints are handed over (παραδοθήσεται, in Aramaic יהב) to the power of the fourth beast until the time of their vindication (7:26–27).[83] This scene takes place within the larger context of Daniel's vision of "one like a son of man" (7:11–28), a passage alluded to during two crucial points in Mark's narrative (13:14 and 14:62). Like the saints in Daniel's vision, Jesus and his disciples are to be "handed over" to persecution but will eventually be vindicated. This point will be vital for reading the use of Daniel 7 in Mark 13:24–27. It appears that, once again, Mark has deployed an intertextual echo (this time to Daniel 7:25) and through intratextual repetition woven it into the tapestry of his narrative. Moreover, the prophetic eschatology of Daniel, where tribulation and suffering precede time of restoration and vindication, is precisely the pattern Mark is following in his discourse, with tribulation (13:5–23) preceding vindication (13:24–27).

Commentators often note how the suffering of those who follow Christ are very similar to the suffering that Christ himself will endure in Mark's story. Thus, Mark is encouraging his readers by showing them that Jesus suffered just as they suffer. However, there is more here than some interesting parallels and parenetic teaching. Mark is associating the "hour" of tribulation that the disciples will undergo with the "hour" of Jesus' passion. He is also establishing important connections between the eschatology forecast in Mark 13 and the passion of Jesus – connections that will be further developed in my treatment of Mark 13:32–37 and the passion narrative. Indeed, the allusion to Dan 7:25 suggests that the

---

[82] See Raymond E. Brown, *The Death of the Messiah* (New York: Doubleday, 1994) 1. 167–68, 195. "Throughout I contended that 'watching,' 'trial,' and 'hour' were to be understood both on a historical level (what happened to Jesus on the last night of his life in Gethsemane with real enemies approaching who would arrest him and have him crucified) and on an eschatological level (the great period of final struggle with evil for the establishment of God's kingdom)." (p. 195).

[83] LXX παραδοθήσεται has πάντα as its subject, but πάντα refers back to the ἅγιοι that are being "worn out" in the first part of 7:25. See Hartman, *Prophecy*, 150. Dyer (*Prophecy*, 104) sees either LXX or MT Daniel as a possible link. However, for a recent defense of Hartman's case for an echo to Dan 7:25, see Pitre, *Historical Jesus*, 320–21.

disciples' suffering is part of the divine plan, placing both Jesus and them in the period of the fourth beast. This also means that the coming of the Son of Man and their eschatological vindication are at hand.

### 3.5.3.2 Gospel to the Nations (v. 10)

Set between the description of the disciples' trials is v. 10: "And the gospel must first be preached to all nations." Moloney observes that this verse comes at the heart of vv. 5–23: "The central theme of 13:5–23 is stated in v. 10."[84] The "gospel" (εὐαγγέλιον) embodies Jesus' teaching and mission and was the key term used to describe Jesus' first proclamation in Mark 1:14–15. The proclamation to "the nations" (τὰ ἔθνη) is a major motif in Israel's prophetic traditions, and particularly in Isaiah (Isa 42:6; 49:6, 12; 52:10; 56:3–8; 60:6; 66:18–23).[85] The motif of the "nations" coming to faith in God is so prominent in Second and Third Isaiah that it is God's ultimate accomplishment in the promised restoration. This is illustrated in the closing scene of the book, where ἔθνη is repeated four times (LXX Isa 66:18,19[2x],20).[86] The climax of the restoration is the gathering of the "nations" for the worship of God (66:18–23). In Isaiah, the inclusion of the Gentiles into the worship of God is an eschatological event, described in terms of "the new heavens and the new earth," that is, the new creation (66:22–23). Thus it is easy to see why Lohmeyer and Marxsen hold that the "insertion" of Mark 13:10 gives an eschatological tone to the witness and the sufferings of the disciples, which account for their proclamation of the gospel to the Gentiles.[87] After all, no mention of Gentile inclusion by an author so familiar with the Scriptures of Israel could be made without invoking the eschatological restoration promised by the prophets. Thus Mark 13:10, with its call for mission to the Gentiles, anchors the suffering

---

[84] Moloney, *Mark*, 257. For the importance of Mark 13:10 see Geddert, *Watchwords*, 146.

[85] Evans (*Mark*, 310) sees interest in Gentile outreach as rooted in the OT.

[86] Pitre (*Historical Jesus*, 323) underscores the significance of Isaiah 66 for Mark 13:10 (as well as 13:12, as we shall soon see): "Why this text is not more frequently discussed with reference to Mark 13:10 and 13 is difficult to explain, since it not only directly follows the oracle of hatred for the sake of the "name" (Isa 66:5) and the birth-pangs (Isa 66:7–14) but also is saturated with the language of "all the nations" (MT כל הגוים LXX πάντα τὰ ἔθνη), "to the nations" (אל הגוים LXX εἰς τὰ ἔθνη), "among the nations" (MT בכל הגוים LXX ἐν τοῖς ἔθνεσιν), and "from all the nations" (MT מכל הגוים LXX ἐκ πάντων τῶν ἐθνῶν) (Isa 66:18–20). Even more significantly, Isaiah explicitly depicts not only the ingathering of the nations but, moreover, a mission of proclamation to the Gentiles: 'And from them I will send survivors to the nations ... and they shall declare my glory among the nations' (Isa 66:19)."

[87] Lohmeyer, *Lord of the Temple*, 40; Marxsen, *Mark the Evangelist*, 175–76.

of the disciples in the eschatological framework of Israel's long-heralded restoration.

The inclusion of the Gentiles into the people of God, in the prophetic oracles of restoration, highlights that they will participate in Israel's worship of God.[88] This is important given Mark's criticism against the old temple and promise of a new temple built upon Jesus as the cornerstone, a place of prayer and forgiveness. Indeed, the only other time in the Gospel of Mark that the term ἔθνη is used (besides 13:10) is in 11:17, where Jesus condemns the temple, quoting Isa 56:7: "My house shall be called a house of prayer for all nations (πᾶσιν τοῖς ἔθνεσιν)." This text from Isaiah, like Isaiah 66 which we just examined, is undeniably eschatological, since it speaks of the final ingathering of Israel and the "nations" (56:8).[89] The question arises: does Mark intend a relationship between these two texts (11:17 and 13:10) that is significant for his temple motif?

Both 11:17 and 13:10 link ἔθνη to the temple.[90] In Mark 11:17, Jesus cites Isa 56:7 to assert that the temple was to be open to Gentiles as well as Jews. Indeed, Jesus was pictured criticizing the temple because it was corrupt ("a den of robbers") and had failed to advance the eschatological gathering of the Gentiles.[91] The second occurrence of ἔθνη is in the discourse on the temple's demise, in the midst of which Jesus commands his disciples to preach the good news to the "nations." In other words, the disciples are to fulfill the divinely intended purpose of the temple by becoming the means by which the Gentiles come to worship God. Here we have a convergence of vital themes: judgment of the temple for its failure to gather in the Gentiles, and the disciples' replacement of the failed temple by proclaiming the gospel to "all nations."

These themes are found in one other text of Mark's Gospel, which serves to strengthen this thesis. As Jesus dies on the cross the curtain of the temple is torn from top to bottom (15:38), immediately after which a Gentile centurion makes a most remarkable confession of faith: that Jesus

---

[88] Bryan, *Jesus and Israel's Traditions*, 221–22.

[89] "Jesus' interest in Gentiles coming to faith is strongly hinted at in his words uttered in the demonstration in the temple (11:17, quoting part of Isa 56:7)" (Evans, *Mark*, 310).

[90] Swartley (*Israel's Scripture Traditions and the Synoptic Gospels: Story Shaping Story* [Peabody, MA: Hendrickson, 1994] 167–70) notes the significance of the link between temple and "nations" as vitally important for Mark.

[91] Tan (*Zion Traditions*, 189–90) argued that Jesus condemned the temple because it would be unable to bring about the eschatological ingathering of the nations. Bryan (*Jesus and Israel's Traditions*, 222–23) has taken Tan's argument a step further, by suggesting that Jesus' condemned the temple for specifically failing to bring about the eschatological ingathering of the nations. "Jesus employs Israel's restoration traditions to indict the Temple for failing already to be the eschatological Temple."

is the Son of God (15:39). The centurion is a representative of the ἔθνη. His coming to faith at the cross, therefore, represents the beginning of the eschatological gathering of the "nations." Once again, the motif of the "nations" is linked to the temple, as the tearing of the temple veil marks the end of the Jerusalem temple, an establishment rendered redundant by the death of Jesus. With this third example of Mark's linking temple and mission to ἔθνη, it is clear that the eschatological inclusion of the Gentiles is a vital theme for Mark's story.

### 3.5.3.3 *Interfamilial Strife (vv. 12–13)*

The conflict spoken of in Mark 13:9,11 is intensified in the account of interfamilial strife given in 13:12–13. Most scholars recognize that the description of interfamilial strife is reminiscent of Micah 7:6.[92] In order to explore this observation further, both texts will be given in full:

And brother will deliver up brother to death, and the father his child, and children will rise against parents and have them put to death; and you will be hated by all for my name's sake. But he who endures to the end will be saved. (Mark 13:12–13)

Woe is me! For I have become as when the summer fruit has been gathered, as when the vintage has been gleaned: there is no cluster to eat, no first-ripe fig which my soul desires. The godly man has perished from the earth and there is none upright among men; they all lie in wait for blood, and each hunts his brother with a net. Their hands are upon what is evil, to do it diligently; the prince and the judge ask for a bribe, and the great man utters the evil desire of his soul; thus they weave it together. The best of them is like a brier, the most upright of them a thorn hedge. The day of their watchmen, of their punishment, has come; now their confusion is at hand. Put no trust in a neighbor, have no confidence in a friends; guard the doors of your mouth from her who lies in your bosom; for the son treats the father with contempt, and the daughter rises up against her mother, the daughter-in-law against her mother-in-law; a man's enemies are the men of his own house. But as for me, I will look to the LORD, I will wait for the God of my salvation; my God will hear me. (Mic 7:1–7)

Wright argues that there is more than just a simple echo of Micah 7:6 in the Markan text. He states that if one examines the wider context of Micah, it will become clear that the broader storyline of Micah is invoked by this allusion.[93] According to Wright, the overall coherence between the contexts of the two passages makes their link unmistakable. The following points of contact can be observed: (1) the context in Micah, as in Mark 13, is a judgment oracle against Jerusalem, a "day" of the Lord (e.g., Mic 4:6; 5:10); (2) Jerusalem's suffering on this "day" is also described as "birth

---

[92] Evans, *Mark*, 311; Moloney, *Mark*, 257; France, *Mark*, 518; Hartman, *Prophecy*, 168–69; Dyer, *Propehcy*, 106.

[93] Wright, *Victory*, 348.

pangs" (Mic 4:9; 5:3); (3) the failed search for ripe figs at harvest time is reminiscent of Jesus' search for figs in Mark 11:12–14 as well as the parable of the fig tree in Mark 13:28; (4) accounts of familial distrust and betrayal are common to both (Mic 7:6 and Mark 13:12); and (5) the call to endure (ὑπομένω) is issued in both LXX Mic 7:7 and Mark 13:13.[94] Despite these connections, only two words are shared between the two accounts (ἐπαναστήσονται and ὑπομενῶ), suggesting that their thematic similarities are not strong enough to place Micah 7 in the foreground of Mark 13:12–13. Thus, in spite of Wright's claims, this text from Micah can only be said to stand in the background of Mark's text.

There is another text from the OT, however, that may well stand as the principal text behind Mark's account of familial strife and universal hatred: Isa 66:5. Pitre has reconsidered this connection, listed some time ago by Hartman, as a significant reference behind Mark 13:10–13.[95] He makes a strong case for linking the two texts both thematically and linguistically. It would be helpful to give the broader context of this Isaianic passage:

> Thus says the LORD: Heaven is my throne and the earth is my footstool; what is the house you would build for me, and what is the place of my rest? ... He who slaughters an ox is like him who kills a man; he who sacrifices a lamb, like him who breaks a dog's neck; he who presents a cereal offering, like him who offers swine's blood; he who makes a memorial offering of frankincense, like him who blesses an idol. These have chosen their own ways, and their soul delights in their abominations ... Hear the word of the LORD, you who tremble at his word: Your brethren who hate you and cast you out for my name's sake have said, 'Let the LORD be glorified, that we may see your joy'; but it is they who shall be put to shame. Hark, an uproar from the city! A voice from the temple! The voice of the LORD rendering recompense to his enemies! Before she was in labor she gave birth; before her pain came upon her she was delivered a son. Who has heard such a thing? Who has seen such things? Shall a land be born in one day? Shall a nation be brought forth in one moment? For as soon as Zion was in labor she brought forth her sons. (Isa 66:1,3,5–8)

I will summarize the linguistic links between Isaiah 66:5 and Mark 13:12 highlighted by Pitre.[96] First, although Jesus' statement, "you will be hated" (ἔσεσθε μισούμενοι) is paralleled in Isaiah's "those who will hate us" (τοῖς μισοῦσιν ἡμᾶς), even more important is the reason for this hatred in both texts. In Mark the disciples will be hated "for my name's sake" (διὰ τὸ ὄνομα μου) and in the book of Isaiah those addressed are hated by their brothers "so that the name of the LORD may be glorified" (ἵνα τὸ ὄνομα κυρίου δοξασθῇ). In addition, this passage says "our brothers" (ἀδελφοὶ ἡμῶν) are to speak to those who hate us, which may evoke "brother will

---

[94] Hartman, *Prophecy*, 168; Wright, *Victory*, 348.

[95] Hartman, *Prophecy*, 168; Pitre, *Historical Jesus*, 321–23.

[96] Pitre, *Historical Jesus*, 322.

deliver up brother" (καὶ παραδώσει ἀδελφὸς ἀδελφόν) in Mark 13:12. Pitre also notes two other thematic and verbal links between Mark 13 and this Isaianic oracle: Gentile mission (ἔθνη, LXX Isa 66:18,19,20) and "birth pangs" (ὤδινεν, LXX Isa 66:7–8).

Because Pitre begins with Isa 66:5, he passes over a key point for our study. Isaiah's oracle opens with the Lord's questioning of the value of Jerusalem's temple (66:1), a challenge furthered by harsh rebukes against the value of sacrifices and offerings associated with it (66:2–4). This provides a strikingly thematic parallel with Jesus' critique of the temple and Jesus' praises for the scribe who realizes that love "is much more than all whole burnt offerings and sacrifices" (Mark 12:33). Moreover, Isaiah 66 opens with a harsh critique of the temple and closes with a call for a Gentile mission – a pattern replicated in Mark's discourse, which opens with the announcement of the temple's demise and climaxes in a call for mission to the nations (Mark 13:2, 10).

In summary, there are five significant elements in Isaiah 66 that parallel Mark's eschatological discourse: (1) the temple under judgment (Isa 66:1–4); (2) divine judgment described as "birth pangs" (66:7–9); (3) association of brothers and being hated (66:5); (4) the sake of the "name" (66:5); and (5) the call for mission to the Gentiles. The story line of Isaiah 66 anticipates much of Mark 13:1–13.

### 3.5.4 Understanding the Desolating Sacrilege (v. 14)

Verse 14 begins with the important textual marker "whenever you see" (ὅταν δὲ ἴδητε). This is parallel to "whenever you hear" (ὅταν δὲ ἀκούσητε) in v. 7. This parallelism moves the reader from "hearing" to "seeing," pointing to the intensification of the tribulation and the proximity of the temple's end. Indeed, the use of "whenever" (ὅταν) in v. 14 takes up the very language of an earlier question posed by the disciples in v. 4, of "whenever" (ὅταν) the demise of the temple would be.[97] All this heightens the need to understand correctly the "desolating sacrilege" (τὸ βδέλυγμα τῆς ἐρημώσεως) that will be seen, since it is the forerunner of the temple's demise. Although there is no explicit reference to the temple through the

---

[97] France (*Mark*, 519) notes this intensification by arguing that the sign is clear in v. 14,whereas it was ambiguous in vv. 5–13: "But now it is time for him to begin to answer their question more directly. ὅταν δὲ ἴδητε introduces a 'sign' more specific and visible than anything which has emerged from vv. 5–13, which indicates that we have moved from the period of delay towards that of fulfillment." See also Beasley-Murray, *Last Days*, 407.

bulk of the discourse in vv. 5–37, there is general agreement that the temple is being alluded to in this verse.[98]

### 3.5.4.1  Desolating Sacrilege and Daniel

What then is the "desolating sacrilege" (τὸ βδέλυγμα τῆς ἐρημώσεως)?[99] The general consensus is that, whatever Mark means by this cryptic allusion, he has the book of Daniel in mind.[100] What is not so clear, however, is how the key Danielic texts and contexts shed light on Mark's use of this phrase. Three texts from Daniel speak of the "desolating sacrilege," Dan 9:26–27; 11:31–35; 12:8–13. These three texts are all about the same event: the destruction of Jerusalem and the temple. This is most evident in the first passage, where a prince comes who "shall destroy the city and the sanctuary" and the destruction of Jerusalem and its temple is described as the "end" (συντέλεια) twice in LXX Dan 9:26 and four times in v. 27. This "end" will come with "wrath" (ὀργή) – the same term used earlier in the account of God's judgment upon Jerusalem and the temple executed through the Babylonians: δέσποτα, κατὰ τὴν δικαιοσύνην σου ἀποστραφήτω ὁ θυμός σου καὶ ἡ ὀργή σου ἀπὸ τῆς πόλεώς σου Ἰερουσαλὴμ ὄρους τοῦ ἁγίου σου (LXX Dan 9:16). In describing the Babylonian destruction of the temple, Daniel calls the temple "desolate" (ἔρημον v. 17): τὸ ὄρος τὸ ἅγιόν σου τὸ ἔρημον. The ruined city of Jerusalem is then described as a "desolation" (ἐρήμωσις, v. 18) (LXX Dan 9:17–18). In Dan 9:27, the sign that the prince would soon destroy the temple is that καὶ ἐπὶ τὸ ἱερὸν βδέλυγμα τῶν ἐρημώσεων ἔσται ἕως συντελείας (Dan 9:27). In other words, the "abomination that makes desolate" (τὸ βδέλυγμα τῶν ἐρημώσεων) is a sign that the temple's end is imminent. This fits well with the imagery in the book of Ezekiel, where the presence of "abominations" in the temple causes God to abandon the temple and destroy it. Thus, in Daniel 9 the key terms "wrath," (ὀργή) "desolation," (ἐρήμωσις) "abomination," (βδέλυγμα) and "end" (συντέλεια) are all associated with the destruction of the temple.

---

[98] Gnilka, *Evangelium Markus*, 195; Hooker, *Mark*, 305; Pesch, *Markusevangelium*, 2. 141, 145; Moloney, *Mark*, 258–61.

[99] For a summary of the various positions on this subject, see D. Ford, *The Abomination of Desolation in Biblical Eschatology* (Washington, DC.: University Press of America, 1979); W. A. Such, *The Abomination of Desolation in the Gospel of Mark: Its Historical Reference in Mark 13:14 and Its Impact in the Gospel* (Lanham: University Press of America, 1999); Beasley-Murray, *Last Days*, 407–16.

[100] Pesch, *Markusevangelium*, 2. 141, 145; Lührmann, *Das Markusevangelium*, 222; Gnilka, *Evangelium Markus*, 195; Moloney, *Mark*, 259; Evans, *Mark*, 317; Donahue and Harrington, *Mark*, 371; Tolbert, *Sowing the Gospel*, 263.

In the second account of the "desolating sacrilege," pagan forces penetrate the temple and take away the continual burnt offering, after which they set up the "desolating sacrilege" (τὸ βδέλυγμα τῆς ἐρημώσεως). This is followed by a time of suffering and purification that lasts "until the time of the end" (ἕως καιροῦ συντελείας) (Dan 11:35). Once again, the "end" (συντέλεια) relates to the destruction of the temple.

The third account of the "desolating sacrilege" places it in the contexts of a "day of tribulation" (ἡμέρα θλίψεως) (Dan 12:1) and the question of the "end" (συντέλεια) (Dan 12:4,6,9,13). Once more, the continual burnt offering will be taken away and the "desolating sacrilege" will be set up. This will be followed by an interval of time (12:11–12), at the end of which comes the long-awaited "days of the end" (συντέλειαν ἡμερῶν) (12:13). In conclusion, all three "desolating sacrilege" pericopes speak of the same event with small variations (Dan 9:25–27; 11:29–35; 12:1–13).[101]

There are six important elements shared by these accounts. First, all mention a "desolating sacrilege" (τὸ βδέλυγμα τῆς ἐρημώσεως) that profanes the temple (Dan 9:27; 11:31; 12:11). Second, in each the theme of "understanding" is at the forefront (Dan 9:22,23,25; 11:33; 12:8,13[2x] ). Third, in each case the "desolating sacrilege" triggers the cessation of sacrifices in the temple (Dan 9:27; 11:31; 12:11). Fourth, each pericope speaks of the "desolating sacrilege" in association with "the end" (συντέλεια) although, interestingly enough, the profanation of the temple is not itself the end but is followed by a time of suffering that precedes it (Dan 9:27; 11:32–35; 12:11–12). Fifth, suffering of the righteous for purification accompanies all three accounts of the "desolating sacrilege" (Dan 9:26; 11:32–35; 12:10). Sixth, each of the three "desolating sacrilege" pericopes follow the same time line: forces from a Gentile ruler curtail the daily offerings and set up the "desolating sacrilege" in the midst of a time of suffering and tribulation, after which the "end" comes and the temple is completely destroyed.[102]

---

[101] Although many commentators list all three passages of Daniel (Dan 9:25–27; 11:29–35; 12:1–13) as being alluded to in Mark 13:14, the context of these passages in Daniel is typically not explored (e.g., Gnilka, *Evangelium Markus*, 195; Beasley-Murray, *Last Days*, 408; Donahue and Harrington, *Mark*, 371; Evans, *Mark*, 317–18).

[102] The three texts in Daniel that speak of the "desolating sacrilege" speak to the historical situation in 1 Macc 1:54–59. Moloney (*Mark*, 259) sums up this historical backdrop: "The historical background for the event is supplied by 1 Macc 1:54–59. Returning to Syria after his victory in Egypt in 168 B.C.E., Antiochus Epiphanes stopped all sacrifice in the Jerusalem temple. He ordered that observance of the ancestral laws should cease, and he destroyed and burned copies of the book of the covenant. He set up a pagan altar, desolating sacrilege, on top of the altar of burnt offerings." Thus, for Mark

These three pericopes in Daniel should lay to rest the question of which text Mark 13:14 is taken from, because all three tell the same story – the destruction of the temple, accompanied with "tribulation" until the "end." The reference to "desolating sacrilege" in Mark 13:14, therefore, can be seen as invoking the contexts behind all three of its occurrences in Daniel (9:27; 11:31; 12:11). I propose that these Danielic texts and Mark 13:14 are mutually interpretive. In Daniel, the "desolating sacrilege" marks the imminent destruction of the temple, accompanied by a time of "tribulation" that will last until the "end." That Mark is familiar with Daniel's use of this expression is quite clear, which confirms that, at the heart of the discourse, the temple is undoubtedly in his mind.[103]

### 3.5.4.2 "Let the Reader Understand"

The case can be strengthened by another observation. In Daniel, the end of the temple and the suffering that surrounds it is repeatedly accompanied with a call for "understanding" (διανοέομαι).[104] Similarily, Mark follows his mention of the "desolating sacrilege" with the parenthetical exhortation, "let the reader understand" (ὁ ἀναγινώσκων νοείτω) (Mark 13:14). There continues to be much disagreement concerning the purpose of this parenthetical comment. There are four prominent interpretations: (1) Mark is informing his reader that he is intentionally ambiguous;[105] (2) Mark is asking that the lector note the grammatical complication of the

---

and his readers, Daniel's account would be read through the lens of the infamous desecration of the temple committed by Antiochus IV Epiphanes.

[103] A similar pattern is found in Ezekiel, where the Lord decries the "abominations" (βδέλυγματα, LXX Ezek 5:9,11) that have been set up within the temple (5:11) and therefore condemns Jerusalem and the temple, promising to make you "desolate" (ἔρημον LXX Ezek 5:14). Also, Jeremiah says that it was God's "wrath" (ὀργή) that made Jerusalem "desolate" (ἐρήμωσις) (LXX Jer 51:6). Or again, that because of their "abominations" (τῶν βδελυγμάτων) the land has become a "desolation" (ἐρήμωσις) (LXX Jer 51:22). See also Jer 4:7; 7:34; 22:5; 32:18, all of which describe the divine judgment bringing "desolation" upon Jerusalem. Once again, the way Mark tells his story of Jesus' critique of the temple parallels the past prophetic oracles against the temple and Jerusalem.

[104] E.g., Dan 9:25; 12:8,10.

[105] E.g., Geddert (*Mark*, 312) claims that Mark, by making v. 14 intentionally ambiguous, intends to leave the reader without answers: "It seems more likely that verse 14 is to be taken as a deliberately ambiguous reference, designed to make sure the readers do not claim to know more than Mark or Jesus. Neither Jesus nor Mark is intending to take a clear stand on how the desecration and destruction of the temple relate to the End of the age. They do not know."

previous clause;[106] (3) Mark is pointing to events of the reader's time for an understanding of the "desolating sacrilege;"[107] (4) Mark believes that one familiar with Daniel will understand his cryptic reference;[108] (5) Mark is signaling to his readers that the "desolating sacrilege" in Daniel is to be looked for in the political events of their time [a combination of (3) and (4)].[109] These positions need to be considered further if the crucial role of v. 14 in Mark's narrative is to be understood.

As a proponent of the first argument, Geddert claims that "let the reader understand" simply points to the yet to be resolved ambiguity of the "desolating sacrilege." Yet this is highly unlikely, since we would then need to read Mark's summon for "understanding" as a *caution* to the readers that they will not be able to understand what the Markan Jesus means by "desolating sacrilege" and consequently the ensuing narrative. Unless one is willing to accept this tortuous dissonance in the text as a part of Mark's style, such a reading is quite untenable.

The second position, represented by Gundry, reduces the most significant narrative interruption by the narrator to a simple grammatical footnote. What Gundry fails to see is that "understanding" is a prominent motif for Mark that, I believe, sheds light on his use of it in v. 14.

The third position holds that, with the interruption caused by the parenthetic comment, Mark lays aside his narrative world so as to call his readers to look to their times for an answer. While this view may have some historical relevance, it too quickly abandons Mark's narrative world, as I will argue below.

The third and fourth interpretations recognize that the Book of Daniel lies behind Mark's "desolating sacrilege," and so there are good grounds – especially in light of the above analysis of the coherence between Daniel and Mark 13:14 – to believe that the parenthetical comment serves to direct readers to Daniel. Indeed, "understanding" (διανοέομαι) is a major theme woven throughout Daniel, occurring over twenty times in the LXX Daniel.[110] Not coincidentally, each of Daniel's three pericopes concerning the "desolating sacrilege" includes a call for "understanding" (9:25; 11:33; 12:8,10). Given this, it is highly unlikely that the motif of "understanding"

---

[106] Gundry (*Mark*, 742–43) believes the most likely answer is that Mark is telling the public reader to "understand the masculine participle so as not to shift to the grammatically regular but predictively inferior neuter gender." This is unlikely and, moreover, would Mark interrupt his narrative to make such a minor grammatical point?

[107] E.g., Taylor, *Mark*, 512; Edwards, *Mark*, 396–400.

[108] E.g., Beasley-Murray, *Last Days*, 411; Evans, *Mark*, 320.

[109] Pesch, *Markusevangelium*, 2. 145.

[110] LXX Daniel 8:5,15,17,23,27; 9:2,13,23,24,25; 10:1(2x),11,12; 11:24,25,30,35; 12:8,10(2x) .

in Daniel – and its association with the "desolating sacrilege" – would be overlooked by Mark. Before I draw out the purpose behind Mark's highly probable allusion to the Danielic motif of "understanding," there remains to be examined how Mark's own motif of "understanding" fits in to Mark 13:14.

Mark employs the motif of "understanding" numerous times in his narrative (συνίημι 4:12; 6:52; 7:14,18; 8:17,21; νοέω 7:18; 8:17; 13:14; ἀγνοέω 9:32).[111] The last and most significant occurrence is 13:14. How does v. 14 relate to the use of "understanding" as a Markan theme earlier in the gospel? Why is v. 14 the last time this key term is found in Mark's narrative?

The first occurrence of "understanding" as a significant motif is in the discourse on parables in Mark 4. In response to the disciples' question to Jesus about the parable of the sower, the Markan Jesus quotes Isa 6:9 which brings together an important cluster of words for Mark: "seeing" (βλέπω), "hearing" (ἀκούω), and "understanding" (συνίημι) (4:12). This cluster of key words reappears when Jesus upbraids the disciples for not "understanding" (συνίημι in 8:17,21; νοέω in 8:17) the loaves and for failing to "see" (βλέπω) and "hear" (ἀκούω) in 8:18. This same combination of "hearing" and "seeing" has already been shown in Mark's account of the withered fig tree (11:14, 20–21). There, however, the disciples' "hearing" (ἀκούω, 11:14) and "seeing" (ὁράω) did not lead to true perception because the key words for "understanding" were conspicuously missing. Here, the subject they failed to understand is crucial – it was the temple's coming destruction that Jesus foretold.

The disciples' failure to understand the temple's demise was further illustrated in their admiration for its splendor (13:1) just as Peter pointed out (ἴδε) the withered fig tree to Jesus (whose significance they failed to understand, 11:21), so the anonymous disciple points out (ἴδε) the temple in its grandeur to Jesus (13:1). Not only were the disciples blinded to the meaning of the cursed fig tree; they were admiring the very structure whose end it foretold! Therefore, in Jesus' final, definitive discourse on the end of the temple – flagged with markers such as "whenever you *see*" (ὅταν δὲ ἴδητε, 13:14) and "whenever you *hear*" (ὅταν δὲ ἀκούσητε, 13:7) – Mark hammers out the last note to complete his chord: "Let the reader *understand*" (13:14). The hearing-seeing-understanding cluster (parallel to Isa 6:9) is now complete and, as a narrator, Mark has done everything within his power to prevent his readers from recapitulating the disciples'

---

[111] For Mark, συνίημι and νοέω are interchangeable; thus he can move from one to the other without any change in meaning (e.g., in 8:17 νοέω is juxtaposed to συνίημι). This is also true of βλέπω and ὁράω.

ignorance. Even if the disciples had failed to understand Jesus' teaching about the kingdom (Mark 4), the bread (Mark 8), his death (Mark 8–10), and the end of the temple (Mark 11–13), Mark's readers must be roused to vigilance: therefore, "let the reader understand." This aside, whose force is rivaled perhaps only by its Shakespearean counterparts, is right at home within the narrative world of Mark's story.[112] There is no need to look elsewhere for signs.

But how does the motif of "understanding" in Mark and Daniel serve our reading of Mark 13:14? In both Mark and Daniel, "understanding" is called for in relation to the "desolating sacrilege" and the end of the Jerusalem temple. Mark has woven together Israel's failure to understand God's plan in Isaiah 6 and Daniel's warning that the temple would be destroyed again in the future. Also brought into play are the disciples' failure to understand Jesus' teaching about his own end (Mark 8–10) and their failure to understand the temple's end (Mark 11–13). Hence, the intertextual echoes from Daniel and Isaiah, along with the intratextual echoes of the disciples' failure to understand, all converge in 13:14. Mark's readers must understand. Miscomprehension – or incomprehension – would be disastrous.

### 3.5.5 The Time of Tribulation (vv. 15–23)

#### 3.5.5.1 Eschatological Flight

The call to "understand" in v. 14. is followed by the summons for those in Judea to flee. The motif of fleeing, as so much of the language in Mark 13, is also apocalyptic in nature. The prototypical flight of course is that of Lot and his family to the hills when they abandoned the wicked city of Sodom (Gen 19:15–17.).[113] According to W. D. Davies and Dale Allison, "eschatological flight" from a condemned city under judgment is a

---

[112] Contra Tolbert (*Sowing the Gospel*, 263–64), who claims that the meaning of "let the reader understand" lies beyond Mark's narrative: "The reader or hearer of Mark is supposed to understand something about this reference to 'the desolating sacrilege set up where it ought not to be' that the narrative itself does not give. In other words, 'the desolating sacrilege' is an esoteric image, the proper interpretation of which depends on knowledge supplied, not by the story, but by information obtained from some external, initiated group. For modern readers, separated by centuries from that knowledgeable group, entering the ranks of the authorial audience of Mark 13:14. becomes an impossibility." Tolbert, much like Geddert, despairs of deciphering "let the reader understand" because he takes this as a reference to something outside Mark's narrative world. I believe this to be unnecessary once one grasps the motif of "understanding" in Mark as well as in Daniel. What the reader is to understand, then, is unveiled.

[113] Wright, *Victory*, 365–66.

common biblical motif.[114] For example, Jeremiah exhorts Benjamin to flee Jerusalem before it is attacked and destroyed (Jer 6:1–12).

Lane noted the correlation between flight in Mark 13 and Ezek 7:14–27, where the prophet warns that, in the "wrath" to come upon Jerusalem, God will bring the sword upon "him who is in the field" and "him who is in the city" famine will devour (Ezek 7:14).[115] This twofold distinction between the city and country is also found in the Markan Jesus' advice to flee from both the housetops and the fields without turning back (Mark 13:15–16). Ezekiel then foretells that the survivors will escape to the "mountains" (τὰ ὄρη) where they will mourn (Ezek 7:16), much like Jesus' warning to flee to the mountains (τὰ ὄρη, Mark 13:14). For Ezekiel, this wrath comes because of their "abominations" (τὰ βδελύγματα) and so Yhwh will allow the temple to be "profaned" and destroyed (Ezek 7:22–23). This will be a time of many disasters and a time in which rumor will follow rumor (7:26). The story line is a familiar one: Jerusalem and the temple will be destroyed and the people will suffer.

As in Jeremiah and Ezekiel, the city from which one is to flee in Mark 13 is Jerusalem. Within the context of Israel's prophetic literature, this implies that Jerusalem is marked for judgment. Much of the language used in Mark 13:14–20 to describe the "tribulation" that begins with the "desolating sacrilege" is eschatological in nature.[116] There is a particular cluster of this language in v. 19: "For in those days there will be such tribulation as has not been from the beginning of the creation that God created until now, and never will be." In this section (vv. 14–20) the phrase "those days" (αἱ ἡμέραι ἐκεῖναι, vv. 17,19) and its shorter form "the days" (τὰς ἡμέρας, v. 20 twice) frequently punctuate the account of the "tribulation" that follows the setting up of the "desolating sacrilege" in the temple. The phrase is clearly eschatological, denoting a time of divine judgment. It is used frequently in Isaiah, Jeremiah, and Ezekiel to describe a day of judgment upon a nation or city, but most often the city in view is Jerusalem.[117] Thus, by describing the tribulation that leads to the temple's

---

[114] W. D. Davies and Dale C. Allison, *Matthew* (3 vols.; ICC: Edinburgh: T & T Clark, 1997) 3. 347. I owe this reference to Pitre, *Historical Jesus*, 388.

[115] Lane, *Mark*, 470. See also Dryer, *Prophecy*, 108.

[116] "Apocalyptic language abounds as Jesus looks forward to 'those days' and describes them as a time of 'tribulation' (θλῖψις)" (Moloney, *Mark*, 262).

[117] The following are examples of the "day" or "days" of judgment invoking the image of God's wrath and judgment with Jerusalem as the target: Ezek 7:4,10,12; 13:5; 21:29; Isa 2:12,17,20; 5:30; 17:4; 39:6; Jer 4:9; 5:18; 7:32; 44:6. Other cities or nations can also be the subject of the "day" of judgment: Assyria (Isa 10:3); Babylon (13:6); Egypt (19:16); Egypt, Edom, Ammon, Moab, and Judah as well (Jer 9:25); Gog (Ezek 39:8). It is important to note that although the "day" or "days" of judgment are given

destruction as "those days," Mark is picking up the very language the prophets used to speak of God's judgment upon Jerusalem and the temple. The term "tribulation" (θλῖψις) in v. 19 has been seen as echoing Daniel 12:1, which uses that same word to describe the time of suffering before the temple is destroyed.[118] This connection is strengthened by what follows "tribulation" in both Mark and Daniel: "For in those days there will be such tribulation as has not been from the beginning of God's creation until now, and never will be" (Mark 13:19). Daniel 12:1 reads similarly: "And there shall be a time of tribulation, such as never has been since there was a nation till that time." The claim to a unprecedented punishment is also made for the plagues in the Exodus.[119] This kind of language is employed in Ezekiel and Jeremiah for the divine wrath poured out on Jerusalem and its temple (Ezek 5:9–10; Jer 30:7). In other words, the prophetic tradition often describes God's judgment upon Jerusalem in the language and imagery of the plagues that punished Egypt. Once again, the language employed in Mark's account is taken from prophetic oracles that address the temple and Jerusalem.

In sum, it is clear that much of the language of Mark 13:14–20 contains eschatological echoes going back to the prophetic traditions of Israel. Moreover, this eschatological language is common stock in the prophetic denunciations against the temple and Jerusalem. This is the same pattern found in my study of vv. 5–13. Although v. 14 marks the "tribulation" that vv. 5–13 anticipated (the beginning of the birth pangs), these two sections on "when you hear" (vv. 7–13) and "when you see" (vv. 14–23) both describe, albeit with different intensity, the tribulation and destruction that is to be poured out upon Jerusalem. The entire discourse resonates with the eschatological language of the prophets.

### 3.5.6 Seeing the Son of Man (vv. 24–27)

#### 3.5.6.1 Relation of Verses 24–27 to Verses 14–23

It is correct to see vv. 24–27 as a distinct unit, as argued above. However, this does not mean that vv. 24–27 should be read in complete isolation from their immediate context. It should not be forgotten that chapter 13

---

against many cities or nations, Jerusalem is far and away the most common target of the "day of the Lord."

[118] Taylor, *Mark*, 514; Donahue and Harrington, *Mark*, 372–73; Evans, *Mark*, 322; France, *Mark*, 527; Dyer, *Prophecy*, 108.

[119] Exodus 9:18,24; 10:6,14. Given that this tradition of tribulation unlike anything else in time is found repeatedly in the Exodus, the use of similar language in the prophets and Mark may have been intended to invoke the imagery of a new exodus.

comprises one long extended discourse in which the voice of Jesus is never interrupted.[120] The interpretive tradition has been to isolate vv. 24–27 from vv. 5–23 because it is believed they have different source origins and therefore refer to different events.[121] Whether one separates vv. 24–27 from the rest of the discourse depends largely on one's view of this pericope: does it describe the end of the world or the end of Jerusalem's temple? These two positions have often been characterized as a dichotomy between a literal reading of the OT imagery employed in this pericope (vv. 24–27) versus a metaphorical reading, but this distinction is problematic on two levels. First, more recent commentators recognize that one cannot read the OT imagery here in a strictly literal manner; yet they still argue for the parousia as the reference behind the pericope.[122] Second, Dale Allison has challenged N. T. Wright's argument that this language is simply metaphorical – surely the famines, earthquakes, wars, persecutions, and the "desolating sacrilege" are intended to have a literal sense. Rather than being tied down to either a literal or a metaphorical reading, it is better to see the language here as symbolic – which can be both literal and metaphorical.[123] For example, a reading that would reduce Jesus' healings

---

[120] "At no stage throughout the discourse is Jesus' voice interrupted" (Moloney, *Mark*, 248).

[121] One of the primary justifications for reading vv. 24–27 apart from the rest of the discourse is the historical-critical judgment that the unit itself is a fragment that Mark has inserted into the discourse. See Beasley-Murray, *Last Days,* 422. Thus, it originally had nothing to do with vv. 5–23. Although this may very well be true, it must be remembered that, whatever the prehistory of this periscope, Mark has placed it in this part of the discourse for a reason. The fragment is now contextualized. Any narrative reading of vv. 24–27 must be done from within its present context.

[122] For example, Moloney (*Mark*, 266) observes that the OT imagery from Isaiah should be read with the original context and intention in mind: "These cosmic events are not to be taken literally, but in the sense in which they were originally uttered by Isaiah."

[123] Here Allison's critique of Wright is very helpful and points forward towards a hermeneutic that may resolve some of the issues involved in the difficult hermeneutical issues surrounding the interpretation of Mark 13 and its eschatological language: "It is helpful here to keep in mind the distinction between metaphor and symbol. We need not choose between flat-footed literalism and metaphor, for there is the whole realm of real events that are symbolic. 'When it was noon, darkness came over the whole land until it was three in the afternoon' (Mk 15:33). The darkness is richly symbolic, but presumably Mark nonetheless thought it historical, not metaphorical" (Dale C. Allison, "Jesus and the Victory of Apocalyptic," in *Jesus and the Restoration of Israel: A Critical Assessment of N. T. Wright's Jesus and the Victory of God* [ed. Carey C. Newman; Downers Grove, IL: IVP, 1999] 132). Clearly, the image of darkness in 13:24–25 is meant to have a literal reference to the passion narrative (15:33). Thus, symbolism is a far better term than metaphor for what Mark is employing. This fits much better with Jewish thought of the first century.

to either a literal or a metaphorical sense would impoverish Mark's story, for Mark intends them to have the polyvalence of symbolic actions that contain both a literal reality (the actual healing) as well as a meaning beyond the action itself (e.g., the coming of the kingdom of God); thus they are best seen as symbolic.

My analysis of vv. 24–27 will have three parts. First, I shall examine how, in their final form, these verses relate to their wider context in Mark 13. Second, I shall briefly review the contextual significance of the OT citations and allusions made in this pericope, employing a symbolic hermeneutic that is open to both their literal and metaphorical dimensions. The exegesis of vv. 24–27 does not aim to be exhaustive but attempts rather to bring out the elements that relate to the temple motif. Finally, the results of the first two parts shall be brought to bear upon the question of whether this pericope relates to the temple or the end of the world and the final coming of Christ.

### 3.5.6.2  *A Contextual Reading of Mark 13:24–27*

The ἀλλά that opens v. 24 and the pericope of the cosmic signs is often read as a strong adversative that sets this pericope apart from the preceding verses (vv. 14–23).[124] However, this ἀλλά alone cannot bear the weight of isolating vv. 24–27 from the preceding verses; rather, it is better to say it distinguishes this unit without separating it entirely from vv. 14–23. The adversative ἀλλά is used 45 times in Mark, none of which serve to separate a literary unit or mark the beginning of an altogether new section. Rather, ἀλλά functions as a simple adversative that contrasts something that precedes it. For example, "He is not the God of the dead but (ἀλλά) of the living" (12:27). Indeed, ἀλλά is found four other times in Mark 13 to convey not a sense of separation but rather simple contrast,[125] e.g., the call not to be alarmed when hearing of wars and rumors of wars because "this must take place, but (ἀλλά) the end is not yet" (13:7). The simple adversative is found twice in v. 11: "And when they bring you to trial and deliver you up, do not be anxious beforehand what you are to say; but (ἀλλά) say whatever is given you in that hour, for it is not you who speak, but (ἀλλά) the Holy Spirit." Similarly in v. 20: "And if the Lord had not shortened the days, no human being would be saved; but (ἀλλά) for the sake of the elect, whom he chose, he shortened the days." Moreover, the adversative ἀλλά functions to conjoin what follows to something that precedes it, often to illustrate a contrast or make a negation. This is

---

[124] E.g., Gnilka, *Evangelium Markus*, 2. 200; Beasley-Murray, *Last Days*, 423; Moloney, *Mark*, 264.

[125] Mark 13:7, 11(2x) , 20, 24.

precisely its role in v. 24, where it sets up a contrast between what precedes it and that which it succeeds – but for this contrast to work it must set up a relationship with the preceding periscope. There are several linguistic parallels between vv. 24–27 and the preceding pericope that confirm this.

The adversative ἀλλά sets up a contrast between the false signs and wonders of vv. 21–23 and the true eschatological signs of vv. 24–27. In contrast to the false Messiahs and prophets (v. 22), there is the Son of Man and his angels. Whereas v. 22 warned the elect (τοὺς ἐκλεκτούς) of being led astray (ἀποπλανάω), v. 27 foretells that the Son of Man and his angels will gather (ἐπισυνάξει) the elect (τοὺς ἐκλεκτούς). The reader was admonished not to believe (μὴ πιστεύετε) the signs of the false Christs. Belief in Jesus has been a key Markan theme as well as an invitation to true discipleship.[126] "Seeing" (ὁράω) the Son of Man come in glory in v. 26 stands in stark contrast to the "seeing" (ἴδε) of the false prophets and those who claimed to be the Christ (vv. 21–22). Each pericope is also connected by the motif of the "elect" (ἐκλεκτοί, vv. 22,27), who are in danger of being "misled" (ἀποπλανάω, v. 22) but are "gathered together" (ἐπισυνάγω, v. 27) with the appearance of the Son of Man. Thus, ἀλλά serves to distinguish the appearance of false Messiahs from that of the Son of Man. The false Messiahs will lead the "elect" astray, whereas the Son of Man will gather them together. Most likely, then, Mark intended verses 21–27 to be read together, with one unit (vv. 21–23) contrasted with the other (vv. 24–27).

In treating of the adversative ἀλλά in verse 24, commentators often bypass the fact that the succeeding phrase sets it within a particular time: ἀλλὰ ἐν ἐκείναις ταῖς ἡμέραις. The phrase "in those days" creates strong links with vv. 14–23, since "the days" (τὰς ἡμέρας, v. 20 twice) and "in those days" (ἐν ἐκείναις ταῖς ἡμέραις, v. 17; αἱ ἡμέραι ἐκεῖναι, v. 19) is found four times in the discourse outside of v. 24, all of which come in vv. 14–23.[127] The temporal description "the days" or "those days" is found only after the appearance of the "desolating sacrilege" (v. 14), strongly suggesting that means that Mark uses them as technical terms – borrowed from the prophetic language of judgment – to refer to the "tribulation"

---

[126] See Marshall, *Faith as a Theme*, 147.

[127] R. T. France (*Jesus and the Old Testament* [London: Tyndale, 1971] 229) argued that "in those days" serves as a temporal link to vv. 5–22, "But this gives us no warrant for ignoring the very definite temporal link which Jesus made between the events of verses 5–22 and those of verses 24–27 ('in those days, after that tribulation', v. 24, accentuated by the Matthean addition of 'immediately'). This is a connection not in principle only, but in time, which is only made more explicit by verse 30."

brought about by the "desolating sacrilege."[128] Thus, the language of the "days" is frequent in vv. 14–23, and its deployment in v. 24 serves to bridge vv. 14–23 with vv. 24–27.[129] In other words, v. 24 introduces a *new moment* in the *same series* of events ("days"). The cosmic signs and appearance of the Son of Man (vv. 24–27) come "after that tribulation" (referring to vv. 14–23, begun with the appearance of the "desolating sacrilege") and is intended by Mark as the climax in the tribulation. France describes this temporal progression:

> So far everything has fallen short of the full answer, but ἀλλά at the beginning of v. 24 alerts us to a new stage of fulfillment. The setting remains ἐν ἐκείναις ταῖς ἡμέραις, but now we are moving beyond the θλῖψις of v. 19 to what must immediately follow it. And so we reach at last the destruction of the temple, described not in the prosaic terms of v. 2 but in the richly coloured and evocative language of OT prophecy.[130]

In short, Mark did not intend to separate the cosmic signs from the tribulation but rather to show that they come after the tribulation narrated in vv. 14–23.

Another important link between vv. 24–27 and the preceding pericope concerning the tribulation is the prominence of the book of Daniel in both sections. The allusion to Daniel in the "desolating sacrilege" (v. 14) and "tribulation" (v. 19) is followed in v. 26 with the dramatic account of the Son of Man coming on the clouds. The appearance of the "desolating sacrilege" from Daniel inaugurates the "tribulation," whereas the appearance of the Son of Man accompanies the cosmic portents in vv. 24–27. The allusions to Daniel in Mark's account of the tribulation (vv. 14–23) and the cosmic signs of the Son of man (vv. 24–27) further connects these passages.

### 3.5.6.3 Exegesis of the OT Echoes in Verses 24–27

There is a connection between the darkening of the sun, moon, and stars (vv. 24–25) and coming of the Son of Man on the clouds that is generally overlooked. It is the clouds that block out the light from the heavens and create the darkness. This conclusion is drawn from more than common sense: OT passages that speak of darkness often describe the Lord coming on the clouds in judgment.

In Jeremiah 4, the "day of Yhwh" (4:9) approaches with Yhwh coming on the storm clouds, bringing judgment: "Behold, he comes up like clouds,

---

[128] Pitre, *Historical Jesus*, 368.

[129] Lambrecht (*Redaktion*, 191–92, 275) notes that the use of "in those days" is a redactional hook used by Mark to link vv. 24–27 with the material of vv. 14–23.

[130] France, *Mark*, 530.

his chariots like the whirlwind; his horses are swifter than eagles – woe to us, for we are ruined!" (4:13). Jeremiah's account of this day of judgment can be characterized as a return to chaos, with the lights of the heavens darkened (4:23) and the mountains and hills quaking (4:24). Soon there is no human being left upon the land, and even the birds flee (4:25). The land reverts back to being "formless and void" (Jer 4:23) as it was before the creation (Gen 1:2). Finally, Jeremiah declares, "The whole land shall be a desolation" (Jer 4:27). The image of the Lord on the clouds is also related to the classic theophany at Sinai. In the Exodus tradition, the cloud of the Lord provided shelter (Isa 4:1–6), but in the prophets the cloud-theophany of Yhwh is a coming in judgment. This background is vital for understanding the complex of imagery in the darkening of the sun, moon, and stars and the subsequent vision of the Son of Man coming on the clouds. Preceded by the eschatological language of judgment, this coming can be for no other reason than judgment.

Indeed, the imagery of Mark 13: 24–25 is taken from two oracles of Isaiah, one against Babylon (Isa. 13) and another against Edom (Isa. 34). In Isaiah 13, the "day of Yhwh" brings war (vv. 2–5) and "pangs and agony" (v. 8). The land is made a "desolation" (v. 9): "For the stars of the heavens and their constellations will not give their light; the sun will be dark at its rising and the moon will not shed its light" (v. 10). After this people upon the land are as rare as fine gold (v. 12) and the land is uninhabitable (vv. 19–22). Clearly, the darkness constitutes a part of the imagery of divine judgment that reverses the work of creation. If creation is marked with blessing, then judgment ushers in the chaos that strips the blessing of life and light from the land. The judgment against Edom is similar. Imagery of violence (34:2–3) gives way to cosmic chaos: "All the host of heaven shall rot away, and the skies roll up like a scroll. All their host shall fall, as leaves fall from the vine, like leaves falling from the fig tree" (v. 4). The people of Edom are slaughtered so that none are left (vv. 5–9) and the land is to be a "waste" for generations (v. 10), uninhabitable except for wild beasts (vv. 11–17). Again, the image of darkness serves the larger motif of the reversal of creation. The question must now be raised: are there any clues in Mark 13 that this prophetic motif of chaos is in Mark's mind?

There are several textual clues. To begin with, Mark already mentioned creation when claiming that the "tribulation" was unlike anything else since "the beginning of creation" (ἀπ᾽ ἀρχῆς κτίσεως, v. 19). Also, the image of darkness is taken up again in the passion narrative, there to signify the chaos unleashed through the death of Jesus.[131] The reference to heaven and earth passing away (v. 31) may also be a continuation of the reversal-of-creation motif evoked in the darkening of the sun, moon, and stars in vv. 24–27.

What does the reversal-of-creation motif have to do with Mark 13 and the temple? The appearance of the "desolating sacrilege" is clearly located at the temple, "where he ought not be" (v. 14). Based on the texts from Daniel and 1 Maccabees that employ the same image of "desolating sacrilege," this indicates that the temple has been profaned. As shown above, "desolating sacrilege" literally means "the sacrilege that causes desolation" (τὸ βδέλυγμα τῆς ἐρημώσεως). It causes desolation because the profanation of the temple incurs God's judgment, which ultimately leads to the destruction of the temple. Although vv. 14–23 are the account of the tribulation that marks the profanation of the temple, the temple is never described as being destroyed – the very issue that launched this entire discourse. Thus, the reader is left waiting for the account of the temple's demise – and that account is given in vv. 24–26.

As argued above, the language of darkness and coming on the clouds, given the context of Isaiah 13 and 34 as well as Daniel 7, is clearly that of judgment. This fits in well with the image of Jesus sitting on the Mount of Olives in judgment against the temple. The question must be posed to those who hold that this pericope pertains to the final parousia: What in the narrative leads one to believe that vv. 24–27 are about the judgment of the world? Everything else in the narrative, especially given the antitemple polemic that runs through Mark 11–12, points to the temple as the object of Jesus' judgment. The motif of temple judgment in Mark's story and the eschatological language borrowed from the prophetic judgment oracles converge in Mark 13 in an ominous fashion: the temple is being condemned by Jesus in the language and imagery of the prophets. Indeed, when Jesus was in the temple, the "den of robbers" quotation (Jer 7:11) was put forward as the reason for his condemnation of the temple. The oracle of Jeremiah against the temple culminates with the declaration that the land will become a "waste" (Jer 7:34). If the darkening of the heavens signified the desolation of a land out of divine wrath, then certainly reading Mark 13:24–27 as a judgment upon the temple would make sense given the OT allusions made in this section and throughout the discourse.

The element of judgment that undergirds the darkness in vv. 24–25 furthermore coheres well with the image of the Son of Man coming with the clouds in v. 26. This imagery of the Son of Man is taken from the

---

[131] This will be pursued in more detail, especially with its relationship to the temple, in Chapter 4.

vision of Daniel 7, and judgment is at the heart of this vision. The beasts that represent pagan nations cause havoc and distress, but then Daniel sees thrones set up and the Ancient of Days taking his seat (Dan 7:9). The heavenly court is then assembled for "judgment" (v. 10). After the fourth beast is slain, authority and kingship are transferred to another figure: "I saw in the night visions, and behold, with the clouds of heaven there came one like a son of man, and he came to the Ancient of Days and was presented before him. And to him was given dominion and glory and kingdom, that all peoples, nations, and languages should serve him" (vv. 13–14a). This transference of the kingdom is repeated (vv. 22, 27), as is the idea of the courts sitting in judgment (vv. 22, 26). Given the context of the Daniel 7, it can be argued that one element Mark is invoking by his citation of this text is that of judgment – a judgment that also serves to usher in a new kingdom.

When the Son of Man appears with the clouds, Mark tells us that he comes "with great power and glory" (μετὰ δυνάμεως πολλῆς καὶ δόξης, v. 26). The combination of "power" (δύναμις) and "glory" (δόξα) is found in LXX Psalm 62:3: οὕτως ἐν τῷ ἁγίῳ ὤφθην σοι τοῦ ἰδεῖν τὴν δύναμίν σου καὶ τὴν δόξαν σου. The psalmist beholds the "power" and "glory" of Yhwh while in the temple (ἐν τῷ ἁγίῳ).[132] The image of "glory" (δόξα) is also found in the scene in Daniel 7, when the Son of Man is presented with all kingdom and authority (v. 14). This combination of "power" and "glory" occurs earlier in Mark's narrative, in a way that has striking similarities to Mark 13:26.

In Mark 8:38–9:1, Jesus moves from a discussion of discipleship to eschatological judgment and vindication:

For whoever is ashamed of me and of my words in this adulterous and sinful generation, of him will the Son of Man also be ashamed, when he comes in the glory of his Father with the holy angels. (8:38)

Immediately following this verse Jesus makes a parallel statement:

Amen, I say to you, there are some standing here who will not taste death before they see the kingdom of God come with power. (9:1)

In both verses the parallel is found in what is "coming" (ἔρχομαι): in 8:38 it is the Son of Man who *comes* in "glory" (δόξα), whereas in 9:1 it is the kingdom that comes in "power" (δύναμις). The parallel between the Son of Man and the kingdom is interesting. It is striking just how much the

---

[132] It is interesting that three other occurrences in the OT that match these two terms with synonyms all relate to the belief that God alone has the right to grant authority and kingdom (1 Chr 29:11; Dan 2:37; 4:30). Evans (*Mark*, 329) misses the connection between these texts in terms of God's prerogative to bestow authority and kingdom.

language of these two verses line up with Mark 13:26 and its context. There are six points of contact between 8:38–9:1 and its parallel in Mark 13:26–27: (1) both texts combine "glory" and "power" when speaking of the coming of the Son of Man; (2) both texts speak of the "coming" of the Son of Man and thus evoke Daniel 7; (3) "seeing" (ὁράω) is prominent in both text – some will "see" the kingdom coming with power (9:1) and "they will see" the Son of Man come with great power and glory (13:26); (4) "the angels" (τοὺς ἀγγέλους) appear in both accounts of the Son of Man's coming (8:38 and 13:27); (5) both accounts follow instruction on discipleship that must endure suffering (8:34–38 and 13:9–13);[133] and (6) Jesus denounces the "adulterous and sinful generation" (γενεά) in 8:38, and in 13:30 he speaks of the generation (γενεά) that is under judgment. The connection between these two passages is strong indeed, which suggests that the reader of Mark is to regard them as speaking of the same event.

Moreover, both accounts include that same temporal limit: the life span of that generation. In 9:1 Jesus promises, "There are some standing here who will not taste death before they see the kingdom of God come with power." "So also, when you see these things taking place, know that he is near, at the very gates" (13:29). The next verse also gives a definite time limit for the coming, "Amen, I say to you, this generation will not pass away before all these things have taken place" (13:30). Whether vv. 29–30 give temporal limits to the vision of the Son of Man coming on the clouds (vv. 24–27) is controversial. However, in light of Jesus' declaration the kingdom would come in power while some of his disciples were alive to see it (a coming juxtaposed to the coming of the Son of man in glory just before), means that the logic of Mark's narrative points in one clear direction – the coming of the Son of Man is to take place within a generation. In other words, Mark 8:38–9:1 helps us see through the thicket of controversy about temporal limits and understand that, for Mark, the coming of the Son of Man in judgment is both imminent and directed at the temple.[134] The reason, I believe, is that the coming of the Son of Man – among other things – relates to the judgment upon the temple.

The eschatological language surrounding Mark's account of the Son of Man's coming is primarily negative, reflecting the judgment oracles from

---

[133] "In addition to terms like 'power', 'glory', 'Son of Man' and 'the coming kingdom' which link 8.38–9.1 with 13.24–27, many historical-critics also point to the striking parallel between 8.34–28 and 13.9–13, both of which contain Jesus' call for radical discipleship and the travail it entails" (Hatina, *In Search of a Context*, 351).

[134] "At the level of the narrative, both 8.38–9.1 and 13.30 serve as temporal clues that direct the reader to the destruction of the temple and not to the consummation of history as most historical-critics maintain" (Ibid., 352).

the prophets. Darkness, the shaking of the powers in heaven, as well as the coming on the clouds taken from Daniel 7, all relate to OT texts that concern judgment. The advent of the Son of Man, however, also has positive effects. In 13:27 the Son of Man's coming brings about the "gathering" (ἐπισυνάγω) of the elect from the four winds. The image of "gathering" from the "four winds" also echoes the eschatological language of the prophets, but this time it evokes oracles about Israel's restoration rather than judgment. According to the prophets, God will "gather" (συνάγω) Israel at the end of the time of punishment and suffering that had effectively scattered them.[135] Isaiah takes up this motif of ingathering and expands it by including the Gentiles.[136] Indeed, one of Isaiah's oracles that treats of the gathering of the Gentiles is Isaiah 56, the very oracle that Jesus cited in his critique of the temple: "for my house shall be called a house of prayer for all peoples (πᾶσιν τοῖς ἔθνεσιν, LXX Isa 56:7)." Two verses later Isaiah speaks of the "gathering" of those "scattered" – one that will include Gentiles: εἶπεν κύριος ὁ συνάγων τοὺς διεσπαρμένους Ἰσραηλ, ὅτι συνάξω ἐπ' αὐτὸν συναγωγήν (LXX Isa 56:8). Jesus condemned the temple not only for being a "den of robbers," but also for its failure to be the focal point for the eschatological ingathering of the nations – "a house of prayer for all nations" (Isa 56:7–8). Now the advent of the Son of Man will bring about the universal gathering that was to be the role of the temple. In other words, the Son of Man, by ushering in the eschatological gathering, is taking up the role of the temple that Isaiah had foreseen.

Thus, the coming of the Son of Man brings about both negative and positive consequences. The negative pole is judgment – judgment against the temple both for being both corrupt ("den of robbers") and for failing to be what it was called to be, the focal point of the eschatological ingathering ("house of prayer for all nations"). The Son of Man's coming brings eschatological judgment upon the temple and thus its end, but with its end the Son of Man can take up the role of Isaiah's eschatological temple by gathering in all the nations in the promised restoration of Israel. The two texts that Jesus cited in his temple demonstration evoked two classic prophetic genres.[137] Jeremiah 7 embodied the eschatological

---

[135] E.g., Deut 30:4; Mic 2:12; 4:6; Zech 2:10; Isa 11:12; 40:11; 43:5; 49:5; Jer 23:8. All these texts in LXX describe "gathering" (συνάγω) as part of the eschatological restoration of Israel.

[136] Isa 56:8; 66:18. It is worth noting that the "gathering" of the Gentiles in Isa 66:18 comes from a text that has shown multiple connections with Mark 13, as noted earlier.

[137] Bryan (*Jesus and Israel's*, 217) sees Jesus' citation of Jeremiah 7 and Isaiah 56 as evoking two distinct prophetic genres, "one tradition – of which Jeremiah 7 is a part – is pre-exilic and anticipates coming judgment on the nation. The other tradition – to which

judgment oracles against Jerusalem and the temple, while Isaiah 56 exemplified the oracles of restoration. The vision of the Son of man coming on the clouds (Mark 13:24–27) draws together these two prophetic genres: oracles of judgment (darkness, cosmic disturbance, coming on clouds) and the oracles of restoration ("gathering" of the elect). Both kinds of oracles come from the eschatological oracles of the prophets, typically begin with judgment, and move to restoration. By joining the judgment and restoration oracles, the Markan Jesus points to the end of the old temple that will lead to the fulfillment of the eschatological hope through a new temple.

### 3.5.7 The Lesson of the Fig Tree (vv. 28–31)

The parable of the fig tree introduces a shift in focus for the discourse of Mark 13. Whereas vv. 5–27 spoke primarily of the "signs" that would accompany the end of the temple, vv. 28–37 take up the issue of "when" the temple will come to an end. This matches well with the twofold nature of the disciples' question that spurred the discourse: Tell us *when this will be*, and *what will be the sign* when these things are all to be accomplished?" (13:4). Undoubtedly, vv. 28–37 have a complex and diverse tradition history, but for our pursuit of Mark's literary aims they need to be read in their present context as Mark's creative use and placing of his sources into his story.[138]

The material in vv. 28–37 is united by its thematic focus on the question of knowing when the tribulations described in vv. 5–27 will occur. This is illustrated by the fivefold repetition of "know" (γινώσκω, 13:28,29,32,33, 35) in this brief section (vv. 28–37). By weaving "know" throughout these verses, all in reference to knowing the "time" (καιρός), Mark has united the disparate material under the overall theme of "when" the tribulation will all occur.

### 3.5.7.1 Reading the Eschatological Fig Leaves (vv. 28–30)

Now that Mark has described the tribulation and the end of the temple, he shows in v. 28 the Markan Jesus taking up the image of the fig tree as a sign of the eschatological time. The image of harvest time (θέρος) has

---

Isaiah 56 contributes – looks ahead to a national restoration to be realized after national judgment. Within the Old Testament the two traditions represent distinct, consecutive states in God's dealings with Israel." Bryan does not connect these two prophetic traditions to Mark's account of the temple's destruction in Mark 13, but the same two traditions are found in 13:24–27 and create a striking parallel.

[138] For a survey of the complex tradition history behind these verses, see Beasley-Murray, *Last Days*, 434–75; Evans, *Mark*, 333–34.

eschatological connotations of judgment.[139] Indeed, if the parable is intended to invoke the imagery of eschatological harvest, it is an appropriate follow-up to the image of the Son of Man bringing judgment upon the wicked and "gathering" the elect – events that correspond to the eschatological harvest described in the prophets.

Mark's opening phrase is deliberately provocative: "From the fig tree learn its lesson" (v. 28a). What fig tree? Immediately the reader thinks back to the notorious fig tree that Jesus cursed (11:14). That tree certainly embodied the temple's imminent demise. How then could the reader, in the midst of a discourse concerning the signs of the temple's destruction, not associate this reference to a fig tree with the withered fig tree? The two fig trees mark the beginning and end of Mark's narrative about the temple's end. "The parallel that exists (however awkwardly) between these two sole references to the fig-tree in Mark is heightened considerably when we take into account the symmetry that can be discerned throughout chapter 11 to 13. ... The material in all three chapters, though composite, is held together by the unifying theme of Jesus' first and last visit to Jerusalem and its Temple."[140]

Given my analysis of vv. 24–27 another link may be suggested. Just as Jesus' cursing of the fig tree is followed by his condemnation of the temple through the citation of oracles on condemnation of the temple (Jeremiah 7) as well as the temple's eschatological purpose of gathering the nations (Isaiah 56), so too now Mark alludes to traditions about eschatological judgment and ingathering in his account of the Son of Man (vv. 24–27), which is followed by another account of a fig tree (vv. 28–29). Thus, the account of the temple's demise is framed by the fig tree, a Markan *inclusio* that is set up to make the reader ponder the narrative meaning of the fig tree and the end of the temple.

The approach of summer is signified through the budding leaves of the fig tree. Likewise, the approach of the eschatological harvest (just described as the ingathering of the elect) means that "he is near, at the very gates" ἐγγύς ἐστιν ἐπὶ θύραις (v. 29). Since there is no antecedent

---

[139] E.g., Isa 5:1–7; 34:4; Joel 3:13–18. After surveying the OT texts that relate to harvest, Telford (*Barren Temple*, 212) concludes that it is a common image for eschatological judgment: "The evidence that we have considered, then, suggests that tree, fruit and harvest imagery was employed in the New Testament, as in the Old, almost exclusively in a spiritual and symbolic sense, that it was frequently applied in respect of both the old Israel and the new, and very often with the express notion of an eschatological judgment upon the former. Mark himself has confirmed this view."

[140] Telford, *Barren Temple*, 216–17. He also observes that "in 11.12–14, the fig-tree withers as a sign of an eschatological judgment; in 13.28–29, it blossoms as a sign of an impending Parousia!" (p. 217).

expressed for the subject of ἐστίν, the identification is left to the reader to discern from the context.[141] Given the present context, the most likely subject is the Son of Man.[142] The motif of being "near" (ἐγγύς) is repeated twice in two verses (vv. 28–29) and is reminiscent of the opening proclamation of Jesus, "The time is fulfilled, and the kingdom of God is at hand (ἤγγικεν)" (1:15). Again, it appears that for Mark the coming of the Son of Man is also the coming of the kingdom. Indeed, this is precisely how Luke reads Mark: "So also, when you see these things taking place, you know that the kingdom of God is near" (Luke 21:31). This once again confirms the view that Mark sees the advent of Jesus as the advent of the eschatological kingdom of God.

If the cursing of the fig tree signified the end of the temple, could not the sign of a budding fig tree signify the coming of the new temple? Telford, followed by several scholars, has suggested that the blossoming of the fig tree in v. 28 puts it in contrast to the withered tree in Mark 11:12–14, 20–21.[143] If the withered tree represents Jerusalem's condemned temple, then surely the blossoming fig tree represents the new temple. Although this interpretation is attractive, it simply cannot be borne out of the narrative details. Indeed, Telford's description of the fig tree in v. 28 as "blossoming" is slightly too robust, for the account is simply about the leaves of the tree budding, ὅταν ἤδη ὁ κλάδος αὐτῆς ἀπαλὸς γένηται καὶ ἐκφύῃ τὰ φύλλα, which is a far cry from blossoming and bearing fruit. In other words, the fig tree in 13:28 is only coming into leaf and is thus no closer to bearing fruit than the tree that was cursed by Jesus. Indeed, the time of budding is April, around the time of Passover, which coincides with the time of Jesus' entry to Jerusalem and his encounter with the barren tree.[144]

---

[141] France, *Mark*, 538.

[142] Moloney (*Mark*, 268) makes a strong case for this with his careful narrative reading: "The context determines the point of reference for 'these things.' Coming hard on the heels of the use of Isaianic symbols that will indicate the imminent end of time, 'these things' must link 13:28–31 with 13:24–27. Furthermore, the sight of 'these things' will betray the truth that 'he is near, at the very gates' (ἐγγύς ἐστιν ἐπὶ θύραις). The link between the signs of 13:24b–25 and the subsequent (see v. 26a: καὶ τότε ὄψονται) coming of the Son of Man and gathering of the elect in 13;25–26 is matched by 'seeing these things take place' (v. 29a) and the approach of the Son of Man, at the very gates (v. 29b)."

[143] Telford, *Barren Temple*, 216–17. He is followed by Hooker, *Mark*, 320; Geddert, *Watchwords*, 147.

[144] "This process takes place in April, around Passover (see 11:13). It is a sure sign that winter is over and summer is near" (Donahue and Harrington, *Mark*, 375).

The point of the parable is that harvest (θέρος) is near, so it is a time to be prepared and vigilant.[145] But when Jesus came to the fig tree on his way to the temple, it was the time for Jesus to harvest the fruit of the temple (as retold in the parable of the wicked tenants, 12:1–10), but it was barren. Once the harvest is understood against the eschatological backdrop of judgment, it is clear that the two fig trees share the same motif of coming judgment – and woe to the tree that is without fruit when the Son of Man comes. The juxtaposition of the two fig trees in Mark's narrative may suggest multiple levels of meaning. Jesus' coming to the temple and judging it for its fruitlessness (Mark 11) is the inauguration of the eschatological harvest, with the Son of Man coming in judgment of Jerusalem's temple as the completion of the judgment. The inclusion of all the material about the temple from Mark 11:15 through Mark 13:27 is framed by the image of the fig tree that is without fruit and soon to be judged.

### 3.5.7.2 Heaven and Earth Will Pass Away (v. 31)

In verse 31 Jesus affirms, "Heaven and earth will pass away, but my words will not pass away." The claim that heaven and earth will "pass away" (παρελεύσονται) links this verse to the preceding one, which promised that "this generation will not pass away (παρέλθη) before all these things take place." The affirmation, "heaven and earth will pass away..." is a striking statement in a discourse about endings. For those who would deny any notion of the end of the world in this discourse, the strong assertion here by Jesus seems to make it clear that heaven and earth will have their end, too.[146] The question arises, however, why Jesus bring would up the end of "heaven and earth" in a discourse about the end of the temple.

The end of the temple and the end of the world are not unrelated events, according to Jewish and early Christian thought. The temple, both in the OT and Second Temple Judaism, symbolized the cosmos.[147] Much of the architecture and artistry employed in of the tabernacle and the temple's design point to an embodiment of the cosmos. For example, the molten

---

[145] "While τὸ θέρος can mean simply the season of summer, summer is the time of fruit and other crops, and θέρος may have a particular connotation of harvest-time (ὁ θερισμός)" (France, *Mark*, 537). See also Evans, *Mark*, 334.

[146] Contra France, *Mark*, 540.

[147] See G. K. Beale, "Cosmic Symbolism of Temples in the Old Testament," in his *The Temple and the Church's Mission: A Biblical Theology of the Dwelling Place of God* (NSBT: Downer's Grove: IVP, 2004) 31–80; Jon Levenson, "The Temple and the World," *JR* 64 (1984) 283–98 and his book *Sinai and Zion* (San Francisco: Harper and Row, 1985) 111–84; C. T. R. Hayward, *The Jewish Temple* (New York: Routledge, 1996).

washbasin is called the "sea" and the altar "the bosom of the earth" (1 Kgs 7:23–26). The twelve bulls that supported the washbasin were divided into groups of three, each group faced one direction of the compass (1 Kgs 7:25), thus signifying the four corners of the world. The seven lamps on the menorah are referred to as "lights" (Exod 25:6; 35:8,14,28; 27:20; 39:37; Lev 24:2; Num 4:9) by the Hebrew word מָאוֹר, which besides the sanctuary lights is used only in reference to the "lights" spoken of in the fourth day of creation, where the sun, moon, and stars are also called "lights" (מָאוֹר, Gen 1:14,15,16).[148] The seven lights were also seen as representing the five known planets as well as the sun and moon.[149] Josephus and Philo both saw the temple as a symbolic microcosm of the cosmos.[150] Concerning the architecture and furniture of the temple, Josephus wrote that "every one of these objects is intended to recall and represent the nature of the universe."[151] There is little doubt that the identification of the temple with the cosmos was made in the OT and Judaism, but the question here is whether such identification is made by Mark. The answer is found in Mark's account of the tearing of the temple veil, the most salient symbol of the cosmos in the temple.[152] In the next chapter, I will demonstrate how Mark sees the temple veil as a symbol of the cosmos.

The relationship between the temple and the cosmos may shed light on the debate whether Mark 13:24–27 refers to the end of the temple or to the end of the world. While scholars are divided on this question, the answer may be that for Mark both references are in play. If Mark recognized the temple as a microcosm of the world, then the end of the temple could not be dissociated from the end of the world – at least not symbolically. Indeed, what better symbol for the end of the world than the demolition of its prototypical representation? This would explain the reference, in the midst of a discourse about the temple's destruction, to the end of the world. Although these two events seem unrelated to our modern sensibilities, they may well be closely associated within the milieu of first-century Judaism. Thus, an investigation into the cosmic symbolism of the temple may undo the Gordian knot that has bound the interpretation of Mark 13. I believe this interpretation will be confirmed in the following chapter.

---

[148] J. H. Walton, *Genesis* (NIVAC: Grand Rapids: Zondervan, 2001) 148.

[149] Beale, *Temple*, 34.

[150] Philo, *Mos.* 2.15–28 §§71–144; cf. *Plant.* 12 §§47–50; *Spec.* 1.12 §66; Josephus, *Ant.* 3.3 §123, §§180–87.

[151] Josephus, *Ant.* 3.7 §§180–87.

[152] Josephus, *War* 5.4 §§210–14. See discussion in Beale, *Temple*, 46.

### 3.5.7.3  *"That Day" and "That Hour" (vv. 32–37)*

In v. 32 the Markan Jesus speaks of "that day or that hour" (τῆς ἡμέρας ἐκείνης ἢ τῆς ὥρας) as if the reader were already familiar with these terms. The reference to "that hour" has already been made in the discourse: Jesus' disciples would be put on trial, and what they would say "in that hour" (ἐν ἐκείνῃ τῇ ὥρᾳ) would be given to them by the Holy Spirit (13:11). So "that hour" seems to refer to the tribulation and the consequent suffering it would bring. The "hour" has a further reference: the "hour" of the master's coming, an hour the servants must not be found asleep (vv. 33–37).[153] The Markan Jesus refers again to this "hour" when he is praying in Gethsemane (14:35,37). Judas's betrayal and the arrest of Jesus, which begins Jesus' passion, is met by Jesus' announcement that the "hour" has come (14:41). Thus, "hour" has two referents: the suffering and tribulation of the disciples and Jesus' own suffering and tribulation.

"That day" is also found earlier in Mark's narrative, where Jesus responds to the disciples' failure to practice fasting by saying that, when the bridegroom is taken away from them, they will fast "on that day" (ἐν ἐκείνῃ τῇ ἡμέρᾳ, Mark 2:20). This is the first allusion to Jesus' death in the Gospel and is therefore important to the reader. Throughout the discourse Jesus has spoken of the tribulation as "those days" or simply "days" (13:17,19,20[2x],24). Is "that day" identical to "the days" for Mark? The answer is in the affirmative, since the Markan Jesus places the plural "days" in synonymous parallelism with "that day" in Mark 2:20: "The days (ἡμέραι) will come, when the bridegroom is taken away from them, and then they will fast on that day (ἐν ἐκείνῃ τῇ ἡμέρᾳ)." Therefore, Mark employs the terms "day" and "days" in reference both to Jesus' passion and to the time of suffering that marks the tribulation following the "desolating sacrilege."

Thus, "that day," just as "that hour," refers to the time of tribulation; hence, Mark's combination of the two terms in v. 32. It is noteworthy that for Mark "that day or that hour" refers to the time of the tribulation to be suffered by the disciples as well as the time of tribulation to be suffered by Jesus. This illustrates that the same account of tribulation can have a twofold subject for Mark, which corroborates the previous suggestion that

---

[153] Gaston (*No Stone on Another*, 478) sums up how the parable structures the passion narrative: "The statement that the lord of the house will come at evening (9PM) or at midnight (12PM) or at cockcrow (3AM) or at dawn (6AM), but in any case at night, seems strange until we recall that Mark partitions the last 24 hours of Jesus' life into three hour intervals (corresponding to the Roman watches) and that every one of these times reappears in the passion story: evening (14:17), midnight (14:41), cockcrow (14:72), and morning (15:1)."

the end of the temple and the end of the world may be behind vv. 24–27 and v. 31. It is also worth noting that the "hour" comes upon Jesus at a different moment than the "hour" that comes upon the disciples. However, both moments for Mark are part of the same eschatological tribulation. Likewise, the reference to the end of the temple and the end of the world may also have their different moments. These events for Mark are synchronized not in time but in meaning. The end of the temple points to the end of the world, just as the "hour" of Jesus' passion points to the future suffering of those who follow him. These connections between Jesus and the disciples, the temple and the world, and Jesus and the temple form a complex web that will be further explored in the next chapter.

## 3.6 Conclusion

It is often observed that Mark frames the eschatological discourse with the sacrificial giving of the two women (12:41–44 and 14:3–9). It is significant that the first gift is to the temple while the second is for Jesus. This movement from temple to Jesus reflects the internal movement of the discourse it frames as the Markan Jesus begins by speaking of the temple's demise but concludes the discourse with the parable about vigilant watching for the "hour" – the "hour" of Jesus' passion (13:32–37). Indeed, the four watches given in this parable serve to structure the subsequent passion narrative. This narrative link between Mark 13 and the ensuing narrative of Jesus' passion in Mark 14–15 illustrates the nature of the Mount of Olives discourse as an important bridge between the end of the temple motif (Mark 11–12) and the account of Jesus' death (Mark 14–15). Within Mark 13 itself, the discourse not only gives an account of the tribulation that will usher in the temple's destruction but also speaks of the "day" and "hour" of Jesus' death. Why does Mark work so hard to juxtapose the end of the temple and the end of Jesus?

Mark's purpose of paralleling Jesus and the temple is to highlight their shared identity. Two women give to a temple. The widow gives to the old temple, barren and soon to be cast down (Mark 13:2). The other woman anoints Jesus' body for burial but as the reader knows – this death will not be the end, for the "stone rejected by the builders will become the cornerstone" (12:10). In other words, both the temple and Jesus share the fate of destruction. Both Jesus and the temple will go through the eschatological tribulation, but only one will come out the other side – Jesus, the new temple that will be the source and center of the eschatological restoration.

Although the eschatological discourse begins with the temple at the forefront of the narrative (13:1–4), many scholars hold that the temple falls out of focus within the discourse itself (vv. 5–37). It has been one of the objectives of this chapter to illustrate that the eschatological language employed in the discourse has significant relation to Mark's temple motif. The language of famine, war, earthquakes, false prophets, persecution, and trial all have an eschatological dimension that Mark calls the reader to "discern" (βλέπω). In spite of this, many commentators have neglected the eschatological nature of this language and simply relate these events to the historical events surrounding the destruction of the temple in A.D. 70. Undoubtedly these historical events are very much related to Mark 13; however, the shortcoming with this approach is its failure to appreciate these "birth pangs" as signs of the eschatological tribulation described with language and imagery from Israel's prophetic corpus. In this chapter it was shown that this language is found throughout the prophetic judgment oracles for the condemnation of a city or nation. Furthermore, I traced out how the eschatological language in Mark 13 more often than not borrows from a particular genre of prophetic writing: the oracles against Jerusalem and its temple.

If the judgment oracles alluded to in Mark 13 come from prophetic texts directed against Jerusalem and the temple, the restoration oracles invoked are primarily focused upon the restoration of Israel that climaxes in the ingathering of the nations. This twofold focus matches Jesus' twofold critique of the temple in Mark 11:17: the temple has become a den of thieves (from a judgment oracle against the temple in Jeremiah 7) when it should have been a "house of prayer for all nations" (from a restoration oracle from Isaiah 56). The restoration foretold by the prophets would be fulfilled in the work that the disciples (13:10) and Jesus (13:27) would accomplish. The disciples will bring the gospel to all nations (13:10) and the Son of Man will "gather" the elect from the four corners of the world. The eschatological role of the old temple, therefore, has been transferred to Jesus and the disciples, the embodiments of the new temple.

A symbolic reading of this language (beyond the literal vs. metaphorical debate) allows the reader to see just how much the temple stands at the forefront of this discourse. Again, a literal reading of the language and imagery of Mark 13 leaves us with just the historical sense of when particular events may have happened. It does not explain why Mark invests these historical events with the theological significance that he does in his story. Redaction critics have argued that the expression in v. 14 "Let the reader understand" is an invitation to leave Mark's narrative world and look to contemporary events for understanding. While the historical events surrounding the temple are very much behind what Mark writes and why he focuses on the temple, a narrative reading of this chapter has proposed that "understanding" is a significant motif colored by the intertextual echoes invoked by Mark from Isaiah 6 and Daniel. Thus, Mark takes the historical events of A.D. 70, of which his readers are well aware, and points them to the deeper theological meaning that underscores them. Thus, Mark's call for the reader to "understand" (13:14) in the midst of the eschatological discourse on the end of the temple is a two-pronged imperative. On the one hand it refers the readers to the events surrounding A.D. 70, but it could also call the reader to interpret these events in light of the eschatological language and imagery of the prophets, such as Daniel. Thus, redaction and narrative criticism need not be opposed: the former shows the importance of the temple and its role and fate in the Jewish War, and the latter shows how the historical events surrounding the temple are to be understood from a theological perspective.

Likewise, a purely metaphorical reading of Mark 13 does not do justice to the realism of Jesus' language, for in the end Mark is sure that "not one stone will be left upon another." The historical context for Mark's story matters, because it conditions the milieu in which Mark wrote. Famines, earthquakes, and wars are not simply metaphors but real events that will bring about a horrific tribulation. The strength of my proposed reading is that it fits well within the intertextual contexts of Isaiah and Daniel and, more importantly, is at home within Mark's narrative world. The elements of this tribulation are cast in the mold of eschatological judgment pronounced by the prophets of old. Mark wants the reader to "discern" (βλέπω) and thereby "understand" (νοέω) how God's eschatological plan of judgment and restoration is being fulfilled within the events of the reader's world.

Concerning the historical context of the gospel, it seems that there is general agreement that the gospel of Mark is to be dated within a decade of time, between the mid 60s to the very early 70s. This time corresponds to the Jewish War that lead to the destruction of the temple in A.D. 70, a time of great political tension in which Jerusalem's temple played a pivotal focus. Much debate has raged on whether Mark was written before or after the conflict, and since it seems that Mark is most interested in giving a theological account of what these historical events mean, it is not easy to discern whether it was written during or after the conflict that lead to the temple's destruction. The arguments made that it must be before A.D. 70 because they do not match up clearly with the events as they happened misses the point that Mark is more interested in giving a theological account of these events than relating them simply as prophecy *ex eventu* (if he is writing post A.D. 70). Mark assumes his readership is aware to some degree of the political events surrounding the temple. What he is at pains to show is the theological significance of these events – a meaning that must be discerned in light of Jesus and the prophetic eschatology of Israel's Scriptures.

Where is the location of Mark's readers, in light of this study? Given the temple focus of Mark's story, it is reasonable to assume that Mark's audience must be located somewhere where the fate of the temple would have significant meaning. This has led many to posit the eastern part of the Roman Empire, around the territory of Syria. The other location put forward by early Christian tradition and by some scholars even today is Rome. I am inclined toward the latter, but the question is, how would the temple be relevant to the community in Rome? Much in every way. The temple was the headquarters of those who rebelled against Rome. Josephus's account of the war, written in many ways for a Roman audience, gives the temple a salient role in the war. Indeed, Josephus's narrative of the triumphal victory parade after the destruction of Jerusalem and the temple focused a great deal on the possession of the temple's treasure and its capture by the Romans.[154] These possessions were later paraded up to the pagan temples of Rome. Certainly, the Christian community in Rome needed a theological answer to the meaning of these events – one that explained how the temple of God could have been destroyed by the pagan armies of Rome. Mark's account of Jesus' judgment of the temple and his claim that the temple's demise should be understood as the eschatological tribulation foretold by the prophets (in similar language as the Solomonic temple's demise) would serve this purpose.

The symbolic and contextual approach to the discourse, as well as the careful literary reading of its final form, also serves to shed light on the debate whether vv. 24–27 are about the end of the temple or the end of the world. This debate has been encumbered by whether Mark is written before or after A.D. 70. The evidence within the Gospel is not conclusive, and thus both sides remain entrenched in their positions. However, if the significance of the temple as a microcosm of the cosmos is recognized, this dichotomy disappears. To destroy the temple is to signal doom for the world. Conversely, to speak of a new temple is to speak of a new heavens and a new earth. I would suggest, therefore, that the answer to this debate

---

[154] See Brian J. Incigneri, *The Gospel to the Romans: The Setting and Rhetoric of Mark's Gospel* (Leiden: Brill, 2003) esp. 163–72. This book was brought to my attention after having written this chapter. Incigneri's book reviews the standard arguments for a Roman provenience for Mark's Gospel and also adds the rather new argument that the events surrounding the destruction of the temple and the triumphal parade of Vespasian and Titus illustrate the vital relevance that the temple would have for the city of Rome.

lies in seeing how the demise of both the temple and the world are held together in the Markan worldview. The clue to this, I believe, is the provocative suggestion advanced in Mark's passion narrative: the end of Jesus leads to the end of the temple. If this can be established, as I hope to show in the next chapter, it will further strengthen my assertion that, for Mark, the end of the temple points to the end of the world. That the tribulation, culminating in the end of the temple, is spoken of as the "day" and the "hour" – language employed by Mark to speak of Jesus' passion and death – indicates that Mark's narrative holds these two events together. The eschatological tribulation begun in Jesus' passion and death sets in motion the tribulation that will bring about the end of the temple and eventually of the world.

Chapter 4

# Eschatology and the Death of Christ

## 4.1 Introduction

Beginning with Jesus' arrival in Jerusalem, Mark's story has been sharply focused on the temple. Jesus' demonstration against the temple (Mark 11), his authoritative teaching against the temple (Mark 12), and his prediction of the temple's destruction (Mark 13) all serve to establish the opposition between Jesus and the temple – a conflict that propels the movements of the latter part of Mark's story. As David Seeley notes, "Opposition between Messiah and temple emerges indirectly and slowly, but ineluctably. The temple story [Mark 11:15–17] is, of course, the beginning of this sequence and is thus the key to the last segment of the earliest gospel."[1] I believe that Seeley has touched upon a key insight: the climax of Mark's narrative must be read in light of Jesus' earlier conflict with the temple.[2]

In this chapter, I will examine four key scenes of the passion narrative in light of the temple motif:

(1) the Last Supper, which for Mark serves as an alternative cult to the temple;

(2) the agony in Gethsemane, which takes up much of the eschatological language from the closing parable of Mark 13 and prepares the reader to see the passion as the eschatological tribulation predicted in Mark 13;

(3) the trial narrative, deployed by Mark to contrast the temple "made with hands" and the temple "made without hands" (14:58);

(4) the crucifixion scene, in which Jesus is mocked for claiming to destroy the temple and build another (15:29), a taunt "answered" by the tearing of the temple veil (15:38), which is directly linked to his death.

The temple theme is so central to Mark's understanding of Jesus that he identifies the end of Jesus with the end of the temple (15:37–38). This

---

[1] Seeley, "Jesus' Temple Act," 282.

[2] Seeley fails to see the relevance of the eschatological discourse for the temple theme in Mark, and thus he does not see that the passion narrative takes up the temple themes of Mark 13 as well as Mark 11–12, something I hope to demonstrate in this chapter.

chapter attempts to answer the following question: why does Mark situate the temple at the forefront of his story of Jesus' passion and death?

## 4.2 Last Supper as First Sacrifice of New Temple

In discussions of the theme of the temple in Mark, the account of the Last Supper is usually not treated.[3] However, recent scholarship on the historical Jesus has noted the importance of seeing Jesus' demonstration in the temple and his Last Supper as mutually interpretive.[4] Jacob Neusner observes that the symbolic actions of Jesus in his demonstration against the temple are parallel to his symbolic actions at his celebration of the Passover:

> For the overturning of the moneychangers' tables represents an act of the rejection of the most important rite of the Israelite cult, the daily whole-offering, and, therefore, a statement that there is a means of atonement other than the daily whole-offering, which now is null. Then what was to take the place of the daily whole-offering? It was to be the rite of the Eucharist: table for table, whole offering for whole offering. It therefore seems to me that the correct context in which to read the overturning of the moneychangers' tables is not the destruction of the Temple in general, but the institution of the eucharist, in particular. It further follows that the counterpart of Jesus' negative action in overturning one table must be his affirmative action in establishing or setting up another table, that is to say, I turn to the passion narratives centred upon the Last Supper.[5]

The case for the historical Jesus intentionally making this connection is intriguing. Here, however, I hope to show that there is a compelling case for seeing that this connection is vitally important for Mark's narrative. Of course, the discusion concerning the Last Supper is immense, as evidenced by its significantly large body of secondary literature.[6] My study here will be brief and will examine it only as it relates to the temple motif in Mark.

---

[3] For instance: Donahue, *Are You the Christ?;* Juel, *Messiah and Temple;* Walker, *Holy City;* Seeley, " Jesus' Temple Act "; Schnellbächer, "Temple as Focus."

[4] Annette Merz and Gerd Theissen, *The Historical Jesus: A Comprehensive Guide* (Minneapolis: Fortress, 1998) 431–36; Jacob Neusner, "Money-Changers," 287–90; Bruce Chilton, *The Temple of Jesus: His Sacrificial Program within a Cultural History of Sacrifice* (University Park, PA: Pennsylvania State University Press, 1992) 153–54; Wright, *Victory*, 557–59; Tan, Zion *Traditions*, 197.

[5] Jacob Neusner, "Money-Changers," 290.

[6] Joachim Jeremias, *The Eucharistic Words of Jesus* (NTL; London: SCM, 1966); Barry D. Smith, *Jesus' Last Passover Meal* (Lewiston: Edwin Mellon, 1993); Vincent Taylor, *Jesus and His Sacrifice: A Study of the Passion-Sayings in the Gospels* (New York: St. Martin's, 1955); Eduard Schweizer, *The Lord's Supper According to the New Testament* (FBBS 18; Philadelphia: Fortress, 1967); Rudolf Pesch, *Das Abendmahl und Jesu Todesverständnis* (QD 80; Freiburg/Basel/Vienna: Herder, 1978); I. H. Marshall,

Mark's narrative of the end of the temple (11–13) begins with Jesus performing a symbolic action in prophetic fashion by overturning the money-changers' tables, driving out those who bought and sold, and shutting down the transportation of any vessels through the temple. Likewise, Mark's account of Jesus' passion (14–15) begins with Jesus performing another symbolic action by taking the bread and wine at his celebration of the Passover and identifying them with himself and his imminent death. Both actions, against the temple and at the meal, are accompanied by words that help interpret the actions.[7] Moreover, these two actions of Jesus are linked, not merely by their being the only symbolic actions he performs in Jerusalem, but also in that the first relates to the end of the temple and the second to the death of Jesus.

The juxtaposition between the two scenes may be suggested by more than thematic links, since a literary parallel seems to be suggested by Mark's narrative.[8] As I noted in the outset of Chapter One, there are significant narrative parallels between the preparation made by the two disciples for Jesus' entry into the temple area in Mark 11:2–7 and the preparation of two disciples for the Last Supper in Mark 14:12–16.[9] This parallel is a narrative invitation to the reader to see the two actions as connected in some way.

Given Jesus' demonstration against the temple, it would seem odd for him to celebrate immediately a feast connected with the temple, as the

---

*Last Supper and Lord's Supper* (Grand Rapids: Eerdmans, 1980); W. Barclay, *The Lord's Supper* (Nashville: Abingdom, 1967); John Reumann, *The Supper of the Lord* (Philadelphia: Fortress, 1985) 1–52; A. J. Saldarini, *Jesus and Passover* (New York: Paulist, 1984); X. Leon-Dufour, *Sharing the Eucharistic Bread* (New York: Paulist, 1987); George Ossom-Batsa, *The Institution of the Eucharist in the Gospel of Mark: A Study of the Function of Mark 14:22–25 within the Gospel Narrative* (New York: Peter Lang, 2001).

[7] Wright (*Victory*, 557) believes that the two symbolic actions of Jesus in his temple demonstration and Last Supper are prophetic signs that should be read in light of each other: "To calculate the symbolic and narratival significance of Jesus' action in the upper room, therefore, we must place it alongside the Temple-action. The two interpret one another." I believe the Markan literary parallels help substantiate this connection.

[8] See Taylor, *Mark*, 536; Myers, *Binding*, 291, 360. Taylor carefully notes the many verbal and thematic parallels between the two scenes, highlighting their differences to show that they are not a doublet, but rather each is redacted by Mark from the tradition he inherited. Myers also sees the two actions as related. The question to be tackled now is: why does Mark go to all the trouble of juxtaposing Jesus' actions in the temple to his actions at the Last Supper? In other words, the connections observed by Taylor and Myers must serve the overall purpose of Mark's plot, a purpose I believe that is very much related to Mark's motif of the temple and its relationship to Jesus.

[9] See the chart of verbal parallels in Chapter 1.

Passover was. Although the Passover meal was celebrated in the home, the lamb had to be sacrificed in the temple (Deut 16:5–6), and for the feast of Passover it was required to make a pilgrimage to Jerusalem and the temple, which is exactly the picture Mark paints of Jesus making his way to Jerusalem and the temple. In Mark's account of Jesus' celebration of the Passover, there is no mention of the Passover lamb.[10] This absence, among other things, has led some to question whether Jesus is celebrating a Passover meal at all, but the narrative context makes it clear that for Mark the Last Supper must be read within the context of the Passover (14:1–2, 12–16). Whether the absence of the lamb is significant for Mark or simply assumed, what is certain is that in the meal the focus is on the sacrifice of Jesus – made manifest in his identification of the bread and the cup with his body and his blood.[11] These elements of cultic sacrifice in the Last Supper connect this scene to the temple.

### 4.2.1  Body, Blood, and Sacrifice

Jesus takes bread and wine, key elements of a Passover meal, and gives these traditional parts of the Passover liturgy a new meaning.[12] Jesus offers himself to the disciples: "Take; this is my body" (14:22). The meaning is clear, as Moloney succinctly observes: "The broken bread is the broken body of Jesus given to the disciples. The primary point of reference is Jesus' coming death, but this death is interpreted as *for others*."[13] This meaning is confirmed by Jesus' parallel words about the cup, where he speaks of his blood as being "poured out for all" (14:24).[14] The ὑπέρ

---

[10] "It is hard to imagine Jesus taking a Passover lamb a few days later from the temple which he criticized so sharply, in order to eat it with the disciples" (Merz and Theissen, *Historical Jesus*, 434).

[11] Hooker (*Mark*, 343) suggests, given the Passover context and the fact that no lamb is mentioned, that Mark sees Jesus death in relation to the Passover lamb, which points to Jesus' death as a redemptive act that brings about the new community of God's people in a new Exodus. Given Mark's aim at showing Jesus as the new temple, the notion that Jesus replaces the lamb that would be sacrificed in the temple for the Passover would further strengthen the argument that Mark views the Last Supper as another step toward replacing the temple. Against the view that the lamb's absence is significant, see, e.g., France, *Mark*, 560; M. Casey, *Aramaic Sources of Mark's Gospel* (SNTSM 102; Cambridge: Cambridge University Press, 1998) esp. 222–24.

[12] Wright, *Victory*, 557.

[13] Moloney, *Mark*, 285 (italics original). Nineham (*Mark*, 383) observes, "The very fact that it is *broken* bread to which Jesus likens his body may well have been intended to suggest the idea of sacrifice" (italics original).

[14] Eduard Schweizer (*Good News According to Mark* [London: SPCK, 1971] 303) sees the close parallel between "body" and "blood" as highlighting the sacrificial nature of the action: "But now 'body,' placed so closely parallel to 'blood,' designates with

πολλῶν gives notice that Jesus' death is more than a martyrdom; it is a sacrifice that has saving power for others. The linking of Jesus' death to the notion of some kind of cultic efficacy was already established in Jesus' explanation of why he must take the up the "cup" in Mark 10:38–45, where he speaks of the Son of Man coming "to give his life as a ransom for all." The identification of Jesus' death as a "ransom" (λύτρον) is explicit cultic terminology, and particularly so given the associations of this meal with the Exodus. Thus, the "for all" (ἀντὶ πολλῶν) of 10:45 is parallel to the "for all" (ὑπὲρ πολλῶν) of 14:24. This link between Jesus' passion as a "ransom" in 10:45 and the sacrifice language of the Last Supper suggests that the two pericopes are mutually interpretive.[15] The overall thrust is the sacrificial nature of Jesus' death.

This is also apparent in the words spoken in association with the cup: "This is my blood of the covenant, poured out for all" (τοῦτό ἐστιν τὸ αἷμά μου τῆς διαθήκης τὸ ἐκχυννόμενον ὑπὲρ πολλῶν, 14:24). The phrase "blood of the covenant" (τὸ αἷμα τῆς διαθήκης) is found in only two texts of the OT, Exod 24:8 and Zech 9:11. Fundamentally echoed here is Exod 24:8, where Moses seals the covenant at the climax of the Exodus, using blood from the sacrificed animals to consummate the covenant. After the blood is poured out upon the altar, the people declare, "This is the blood of the covenant" (Exod 24:8). Since covenants were constituted through blood sacrifices, Jesus' language tying together blood and covenant evokes typical sacrificial imagery as such.[16] The last clause, "which is poured out for all" (τὸ ἐκχυννόμενον ὑπὲρ πολλῶν), is "couched in sacrificial language."[17] It is furthermore reminiscent of the language of Leviticus and its account of the pouring out of the blood of the animal sacrifices. At the Last Supper, however, it is the blood of Jesus that is to be shed.[18]

---

even greater emphasis that it was the person of Jesus which was given for everyone in death. Accordingly, the idea of the 'body' which was sacrificed for the table fellowship becomes predominant."

[15] The link between 10:45 and the Last Supper is commonly seen, e.g., by Evans, *Mark*, 394, Moloney, *Mark*, 286, and France, *Mark*, 570–71.

[16] "That Jesus' blood will be poured out for many (14:24) emphasizes the nature of his death as a covenantal sacrifice for the atonement of sins. As the priest was to pour out (ἐκχεεῖ) the blood of sacrificed animals on the altar to atone for the sins of the people (Lev 4:7,18,25,30,34), so the blood which will be poured out (ἐκχυννόμενον) by the death of Jesus represents a sacrifice for the atonement of sins" (Heil, "Temple Theme," 95).

[17] Hooker, *Mark*, 343. Lagrange (*Saint Marc*, 380) also concludes that since the blood relates to Jesus own body Mark envisions this effusion of blood as a sacrifice.

[18] Evans (*Mark*, 394) sees the echoes to Leviticus as evidence of the sacrificial intent of Jesus' offering: "τὸ ἐκχυννόμενον, 'which is poured out,' recalls the language of sacrificial atonement (cf. Lev 4:7,18,25,30,34; e.g., v 18: καὶ τὸ πᾶν αἷμα ἐκχεεῖ, 'and

By a novel reinterpretation of the Passover meal, Jesus shows that ransom will come no longer from animal sacrifices in the temple but from his sacrifice that will bring about a new exodus that will in some way bring about the kingdom of God.[19] That temple sacrifice would soon be superfluous was hinted at in the dialogue between Jesus and the scribe who was not far from the kingdom – who attested that love is "much more important than all whole burnt offerings and sacrifices" (Mark 12:33). Merz and Theissen recognize the new temple implications contained in this reinterpretation of the Passover: "He simply wanted to replace provisionally the temple cult which had become obsolete: Jesus offers the disciples a replacement for the official cult in which they could either no longer take part, or which would not bring them salvation – until a new temple came."[20] What is the new temple then? Merz and Theissen continue: "This 'substitute' is a simple meal. By a new interpretation, the Last Supper becomes a substitute for the temple cult – a pledge of the eating and drinking in the kingdom of God which is soon to dawn."[21] Read in light of Mark's strong antitemple polemic, the Last Supper is clearly an alternative cultic action that subverts the need for the temple and its sacrifices.[22] Although the overall thrust of Merz's and Theissen's suggestion is correct, it needs to be refined by Mark's narrative. It is not the Last Supper that replaces the temple but rather Jesus.[23] It is Jesus with whom the bread and the cup are identified. It is the shedding of Jesus' blood that will be "for all." The ὑπὲρ πολλῶν, read within the wider context of Mark, must point to the eschatological temple that will be a "house of prayer for all nations."[24] Since Mark can speak of Jesus as the "rejected stone" who will become the "cornerstone" of the new temple, it

---

all the blood he will pour out'; all of these passages employ τὸ αἷμα ἐκχεεῖ, 'he will pour out the blood')."

[19] Hooker, *Mark*, 343.

[20] Merz and Theissen, *Historical Jesus*, 434.

[21] Ibid., 434.

[22] Neusner ("Money-Changers," 90) captures this idea in the image of Jesus' overturning the tables in the temple for the eucharistic table: "one table overturned, another table set up in place, and both for the same purpose of atonement and expiation of sin."

[23] Wright (*Victory*, 558) captures well what Mark sees as the real contrast: "The intended contrast is not so much between the Temple-system and the regular celebration of a meal instituted by Jesus, so much as between the Temple-system *and Jesus himself*, specifically, his own approaching death" (italics original).

[24] "That Jesus' sacrificial blood will be poured out 'on behalf of many' (ὑπὲρ πολλῶν, 14:24; cf. 10:45; a common Semitic way of saying 'for *all* people'), indicates how the 'house' that supplants the temple by the death of Jesus will become a house of prayer for all peoples" (Heil, "Temple Theme," 95, italics original).

would not be difficult for the reader to see that the sacrificial language of the Last Supper account points to Jesus as the new cultic sacrifice for sins.[25]

Jesus' disciples drinking from the cup (ἔπιον ἐξ αὐτοῦ πάντες, 14:23) signifies that they all participate in this new cultic sacrifice that constitutes a restored covenant community.[26] If Jesus is the "cornerstone" of the eschatological temple, the disciples of Jesus must constitute the other "stones."[27] Their participation in the cup (ποτήριον) connotes that they too will participate in the tribulation and suffering that Jesus is about to undergo – a tribulation that will help bring the Gospel to the nations according to Mark 13:10.[28] If Jesus' suffering in some way serves to replace the temple, so too the future suffering of the disciples participates in the temple-replacement motif for Mark. Thus, in Mark the new temple is both Jesus and the community composed of those who follow him. This community, along with Jesus, takes on the role of the temple.

## 4.2.2  Eschatological Fast

After identifying himself with the bread and cup, Jesus is pictured alluding to the eschatological nature of his death, saying, "Amen, I say to you, I shall not drink again of the fruit of the vine until that day when I drink it new in the kingdom of God" (14:25). John Meier observes, "The demonstrative 'that,' if taken with full force, could refer to the *yôm*

---

[25] Daniel J. Antwi ("Did Jesus Consider His Death to Be an Atoning Sacrifice?" *Interpretation*, 45 [1991] 17–28, 27) believes that much of Jesus' public teaching suggests that he identified himself as a substitute for the temple as an institution of atonement. He sees Jesus' demonstration in the temple as pointing to Jesus' intention to be the replacement of the temple: "The process of the self-identification of Jesus with the institution of atonement reaches its climax in the relationship of Jesus to the temple. The manner of Jesus' entry into Jerusalem was symbolic and significant... By entering with such a symbolic gesture, Jesus was laying claim to both the city and the temple and all that they signified. He entered the city with the view to taking over the role of the temple as an institution for atonement... *He was consciously engaged in the process of a functional identification of himself with the cult as an institution for atonement.* From then on he saw himself as destined to be the new institution for atonement" (italics original).

[26] The emphasis on the number 12 for the disciples evokes the prophetic hope of the restored 12 tribes of Israel. See further Sanders, *Jesus and Judaism*, 95–105.

[27] This idea is expressed later in the tradition of the NT in 1 Peter 2:4–8.

[28] The image of "cup" (ποτήριον) recalls the discussion of Jesus' future passion in Mark 10:38–39, which is described in terms of a drinking from the "cup" (ποτήριον). In that passage Jesus affirms that the disciples also will drink from the "cup," which in Mark means that they will participate in the tribulation and suffering of Jesus – a motif unequivocally set forth in Mark 13:9–23.

*yahweh*, that 'day of Yahweh' proclaimed in prophetic and apocalyptic literature, the final day of judgment and salvation for God's people."[29] A strong case can be made for taking the demonstrative with its full force in Mark, for reference to "that day" (τῆς ἡμέρας ἐκείνης) reminds the reader of the eschatological day of tribulation that punctuates the Mount of Olives discourse, also referred to as "that day" (τῆς ἡμέρας ἐκείνης, 13:32).

The combination of "that day" with the coming of the "kingdom" may echo not simply the general prophetic motif of the "day of the Lord" but even more specifically point to the use of the phrase in the prophet Zechariah. In Zech 14:9 "on that day" marks the eschatological coming of God's "kingship," the only other OT text that links these two motifs is Mic 4:6.[30] The phrase ἐν τῇ ἡμέρᾳ ἐκείνῃ is repeated throughout LXX Zechariah 9–14.[31] That Mark's text may be echoing Zechariah is further suggested by the clustering of echoes made to Zechariah in proximity to Mark 14:25. In Mark 14:28 a direct citation of Zech 13:7 is made, and in Mark 14:24 the "blood of the covenant" echoes not only Exodus 24, as mentioned above, but also Zech 9:11. Mention of the Mount of Olives in Mark 14:26 may also echo Zech 14:4, the only OT text besides 2 Sam 15:20 that refers to that mount.[32] The one clear citation, and the many possible allusions that surround it, point to the importance of Zechariah for this portion of Mark's narrative. What is more, references to vv. 4 and 9 of Zechariah 14 may point to the contextual importance of this chapter with Mark's story. Zechariah 14 describes an eschatological tribulation for Jerusalem, "on that day," a motif that coheres well with the eschatological focus of Mark 13, as noted in the previous chapter. This tribulation, according to Zechariah 14, then leads to the eschatological gathering of all the nations to Jerusalem for the worship of God (Zech 14:16–19).[33] This last oracle of LXX Zechariah concludes with the final reference to ἐν τῇ ἡμέρᾳ ἐκείνῃ, which states that "there shall no longer be a trader in the house of the LORD of hosts on that day" (Zech 14:21b). This passage may well be an OT backdrop to Mark's account of Jesus' temple

---

[29] Meier, *Marginal Jew*, 2. 366 n. 56.

[30] Marcus, *The Way of the Lord*, 156.

[31] Zech 9:16; 12:3–4,6,8–9,11; 13:1–2,4; 14:4,6,8,13,20. Marcus (*The Way of the Lord*, 157) notes this repetition, building on the work of M. C. Black, *The Rejected and Slain Messiah Who is Coming with the Angels: The Messianic Exegesis of Zechariah 9–14 in the Passion Narratives* (Ph.D. diss., Emory University, 1990) 48, 53–54.

[32] Evans, *Mark* 399; Marcus, *The Way of the Lord*, 156–57.

[33] Mark's interest in both the tribulation upon Jerusalem and the temple, along with conversion of the Gentiles strengthens this possible intertextuality. The importance of Gentile inclusion will be taken up at the end of this chapter in discussing the confession of the Roman centurion.

demonstration.[34] The story line of Zechariah 14 has many striking connections to Mark's narrative.[35] If Mark intends an eschatological sense to the demonstrative "that day" in speaking about the coming of God's kingdom, it would seem that Zechariah 14 may well stand in the backdrop of Mark's narrative.

The eschatological reference to ἐν τῇ ἡμέρᾳ ἐκείνῃ in Mark 13 and the possible echoes to Zechariah suggest that the demonstrative in Mark 14:25 be taken with its full force; moreover, there is an earlier text in Mark that confirms this reading. In the previous chapter ἐν ἐκείναις ταῖς ἡμέραις was shown to be related to the phrase ἐν ἐκείνῃ τῇ ἡμέρᾳ, which comes from Jesus' first announcement of a day of tribulation, when the bridegroom would be gone and mourning expressed in fasting (2:19–20). Jesus' vow that he will abstain from wine until "that day" when he will drink it in the kingdom is a clear intratextual allusion to the earlier mention of a fast that will come when the bridegroom is taken away from them (Mark 2:20). The mention of "new wine," οἶνον νέον, in 2:22 also resonates well with the idea of drinking wine "new," καινόν, in the kingdom of God (14:25). Thus, the announcement of Jesus' fast in Mark 14:25 was anticipated earlier in 2:20.[36] The fasting that marks the eschatological tribulation of "that day" is begun at the conclusion of Jesus' Last Supper when he vows not to drink of the fruit of the vine until the coming of the kingdom, after which he leaves for Gethsemane, where he will experience the beginning of the tribulation that will mark his passion. It will be the aim of the next section, which focuses on the Gethsemane pericope, to show that Mark sees Jesus' tribulation as the beginning of the eschatological tribulation, a tribulation that will bring about the end of the old temple and the establishment of the new one.

---

[34] Ben F. Meyer, *The Aims of Jesus* (London: SCM, 1979) 198–99.

[35] See Wright, *Victory*, 422, 599. Dale C. Allison (*The End of the Ages Has Come: An Early Interpretation of the Passion and Resurrection* [Philadelphia: Fortress, 1985] 34–35) notes that the key to the story line is the eschatological tribulation: "An examination of the contacts observed between Zechariah 9–14 and Mark 11–16 indicates that Mark recounts the passion of Jesus as though it were the fulfillment of certain eschatological scriptures: the peaceful king enters the holy city (cf. Zech. 9:9), cleanses his temple (cf. Zech. 14:16, 21), establishes the new covenant in blood (cf. Zech. 9:11), experiences a time of trial and affliction (cf. Zech. 13:7–14:3), and is raised from the dead (cf. Zech. 14:4–5)." I believe that Allison's perception that Mark uses Zechariah because of its focus on the eschatological tribulation coheres well with Mark's use of the OT in Mark 13, as observed in Chapter Three. This points to a particular pattern in Mark's use of the OT, with a preference for eschatological texts, especially those that speak of a tribulation – since Mark views the suffering of Jesus as the embodiment of the eschatological tribulation.

[36] Myers, *Binding*, 363.

## 4.3 The Eschatological "Watch" and "Hour" (14:32–42)

The "hour" and the "day" about which no one but the Father knows is eschatological (13:32). This inability to know for certain the eschatological time demands constant vigilance: "Be alert! You do not know when the time will come" (13:33). The time, ὁ καιρός, suggests eschatology.

Since Lightfoot's groundbreaking work on the correlation between the parable of the porter keeping vigil for the coming of his master through the four watches of the night (13:32–37) and the passion, especially the scene at Gethsemane (14:32–42), most scholars have come to recognize the literary relationship between the eschatological parable and the passion narrative in Mark.[37] One of the prominent features of the parable is its mention of the four watches of the night. Lightfoot understood this focus on the watches of the night in light of the careful time references in Mark's account of Jesus' last night:

> Is it possible that there is here a tacit reference to the events of that supreme night before the passion? On that *evening* the LORD *comes* for the last supper with the twelve; the scene in Gethsemane, and still more the arrest, which as we have just seen finally dates the arrival of 'the hour', would take place towards midnight; Peter denies the LORD at cockcrow; and *in the morning* the chief priests with the elders and scribes, and the whole council, held a consultation, and bound Jesus, and carried him away, and *delivered him up* to Pilate.[38]

It is striking that, in Mark's account of the passion, three of the four watches from the parable are explicitly named: "evening" (ὀψίας, 14:17), "cockcrow" (ἀλέκτωρ ἐφώνησεν, 14:72), and "morning" (πρωΐ, 15:1).[39] The one watch that is not named is "midnight" (μεσονύκτιον), but from the narrative this is clearly the time of the Gethsemane events.[40] It is precisely

---

[37] R. H. Lightfoot, *The Gospel Message of St Mark* (London: Oxford University Press, 1950) 48–59; Gaston, *No Stone on Another*, 478–79; Beasley-Murray, *Last Days*, 100, 471–72; Werner H. Kelber, "The Hour of the Son of Man and the Temptation of the Disciples (Mark 14:32–42)," in *The Passion in Mark: Studies on Mark 14–16* (ed. W. H. Kelber; Philadelphia: Fortress, 1976) 41–60; Moloney, *Mark*, 271–72. See most especially Geddert, *Watchwords*, 90–111.

[38] Lightfoot, *Mark*, 53.

[39] Moloney, *Mark*, 271.

[40] From a simple reading of the narrative the reader would assume the scene at Gethsemane takes place in the middle of the night. First, the meal they have is clearly in the evening (14:17), after which they go out to Gethsemane, a scene that is followed by the trial narrative that takes place at cockcrow (14:72). Also, just before they come to Gethsemane Jesus foretells that that "night" (νυκτί) before "cockcrow" (ἀλέκτορα φωνῆσαι) Peter will deny Jesus three times (14:30). Moreover, the three times Jesus prays and then visits the disciples who are sleeping would seem to make up an hour each of the three-hour watch of midnight. See also Lightfoot, *Mark*, 53.

the Gethsemane watch that has the closest thematic and verbal parallels with the parable at the end of Mark 13 where the master is to come in one of the four watches of the night. The keyword in both pericopes is "watch" (γρηγορέω), which is repeated three times in each narrative – the only two pericopes in the Gospel that contain this word. Of course, the warning to "watch" in the eschatological parable "lest he come suddenly and find you asleep" (μὴ ἐλθὼν ἐξαίφνης εὕρῃ ὑμᾶς καθεύδοντας) is poignantly paralleled by Jesus' threefold finding of the disciples asleep (e.g., ἔρχεται καὶ εὑρίσκει αὐτοὺς καθεύδοντας 14:37) despite his call to "watch." Does Mark intend the reader to see the scene at Gethsemane through the lens of the eschatological parable?

It is hard not to affirm this, given the close verbal links and the proximity of these two texts in Mark's narrative. The setting for the eschatological discourse, which closes with the parable of the porter and the four watches of the night, is the Mount of Olives (13:3). The next mention of the Mount of Olives is when Jesus and the disciples leave the upper room after the Passover to return to the mount (14:26). Their destination on the Mount of Olives is Gethsemane (14:32). Thus, the narrative provides subtle clues that nudge the reader to connect Jesus' previous exhortation on the Mount of Olives that concluded with the exhortation to watch and pray, and now Jesus' return to the very mount that is accompanied by the same call to watch and pray. This connection is made in many ancient manuscripts which take the phrase "watch and pray" of 14:38 and add "pray" to the call to "watch" in 13:33 to make the connection even more manifest.[41]

## 4.3.1   The Great Eschatological Trial

In Mark 13, the call to "watch" concerns the "hour" of tribulation that will bring about the suffering of the righteous and the end of the temple. In 14:38, the call to watch and pray has an interesting parallel: "Watch and pray that you may not enter into temptation (πειρασμόν)." The word for "temptation," πειρασμός, can have a wide semantic range – from "solicitation to evil, to temptation, to trial or testing by affliction."[42]

---

[41] There are many textual witnesses that add "and pray" to 13:33, ℵ A C L W Θ Ψ. However, B D 2427 *pc* a c k, all omit the phrase "and pray." Once one sees the parallels of this pericope to the scene at Gethsemane, it becomes evident that the addition was made in order to harmonize 13:33 with Mark 14:38, where "watch and pray" are found together. Obviously, the connection between this parable and the scene at Gethsemane was made early in the textual tradition.

[42] Brown, *Death*, 1. 159.

Raymond Brown notes that most scholars hold that the use of πειρασμός here has a specific eschatological meaning:

> There are a number of times in the NT where *peirasmos* refers to testing in a specific way, namely, the great eschatological trial or struggle involving divine judgment – a context that began with Jesus' proclamation of the kingdom, that continued in the proclamation of the gospel by his followers, and that will culminate soon, as the Son of Man comes in power to destroy the forces of evil. It is in this eschatological sense that, with different nuances, most scholars interpret the *peirasmos* of the Gethsemane scene.[43]

The need for the disciples to "watch and pray" in order not to enter into the "temptation" (πειρασμός) – if "temptation" is to be understood as "the great eschatological trial" as Brown and others have suggested – means that a striking correspondence is made between the imminent eschatological trials in Mark 13 and the "temptation" from which the disciples ought to pray to be spared: both are references to the eschatological tribulation.[44] In other words, Mark, having warned his readers of the tribulation in Mark 13, now calls for immediate "watching" and vigilance because the tribulation has begun in the midnight darkness of Gethsemane.

It is further worth noting that πειρασμός in the LXX can refer to a time of tribulation, especially in reference to the Passover.[45] The plagues and the destruction they wrought upon Egypt are referred to as "the great trials"; for example, LXX Deut 29:2 speaks of the plagues upon Egypt as "the great trials" (τοὺς πειρασμοὺς τοὺς μεγάλους).[46] One may argue that the connection here to the Exodus tradition is not by itself thoroughly persuasive. However, once the context of the Passover night and the other key allusions to the Passover in Gethsemane are illustrated, it becomes

---

[43] Ibid. Brown lists the following scholars who see πειρασμός as eschatological trial here: Beasley-Murray, Dibelius, Dodd, Grundmann, Holleran, Kuhn, Lohmeyer, Nineham, Schniewind, Schweitzer, Taylor, etc. What Meier (*Marginal Jew*, 2. 301) says about πειρασμός in the Our Father fits just as well here: "Hence the πειρασμός of the Greek text refers not to everyday 'temptations' but rather to the final 'test' that God in his sovereign control of history will bring upon the world in its last hour."

[44] Geddert (*Watchwords*, 94) notes the significance that this connection may have for our understanding of Mark's eschatology: "Perhaps it is an eschatological parable passed on by an editor/author with a much more profound view of the relationship between eschatology and the passion than has usually been suspected." I believe that Geddert's observation is correct, although he himself does not see clearly the full significance of what this may mean for Mark's eschatology. I will argue that it points to Mark seeing the passion of Christ as the inauguration of the great tribulation that will bring about a time of suffering and ultimately the destruction of the temple, a tribulation that at the same time will bring forth the birth pangs of a new creation and a new temple.

[45] LXX Deut 4:34; 7:19; 29:2.

[46] See Pitre, *Historical Jesus*, 629.

more compelling that the Markan use of πειρασμός is not only eschatological but also colored primarily by the Exodus tradition.

### 4.3.2 Night of Watching

Thematically, Jesus' call to "watch and pray" on the night of the Passover fits well the tradition of the Passover vigil, which is itself a commemoration of the first Passover night when the Israelites kept vigil against the angel of death:

> It was a night of *watching* by the LORD, to bring them out of the land of Egypt; so this same night is a night of *watching* kept to the LORD by all the people of Israel throughout their generations. (Exod 12:42)

The Passover was to be a night of vigil kept with prayer. The exhortation to watch and be vigilant is the central theme of Mark 13:32–37. Geddert has given a persuasive account of the role of "watching" and "discerning" has in Mark's narrative. He notes Mark's shift from βλέπω (v. 33) to γρηγορέω (vv. 35,37). The former term signifies discernment, right knowing.[47] The latter term signifies faithful vigilance. "Mark 13 is the dividing point. Prior to it, the watchword is βλέπω. They are to discern meaning and truth. Subsequent to it, the watchword is γρηγορέω. They are to follow through in faithful discipleship, taking up their crosses after Jesus."[48] The movement from βλέπω to γρηγορέω signals to the reader that the eschatological time – spoken of in Mark 13 – is near, and vigilant watchfulness is necessary. The eschatological sense of "watch" (γρηγορέω) is strengthened once its connection to the Exodus is seen.[49]

The call of Jesus to the disciples to stay awake, given its context as the Passover night in Mark, is in keeping with the Passover tradition of watching. The first Passover night was spent in prayer and vigil so that the angel of death would pass over their homes. The plague strikes the firstborn in Egypt at "midnight" (μεσούσης τῆς νυκτός, LXX Exod 12:29) – the very hour mentioned in the parable of the master coming in one of the four watches (μεσονύκτιον, 13:35). More importantly, the time of Jesus' prayer in Gethsemane would most likely be midnight.[50] It is interesting

---

[47] See the discussion of this term in Chapter 3.

[48] Geddert, *Watchwords*, 104.

[49] The Exodus background would strengthen Geddert's conclusion about the role of γρηγορέω in Mark's narrative, particularly the eschatological function it has in Exodus 12.

[50] Allison (*End of the Ages*, 37 n. 34) makes the intriguing suggestion that Jesus' three watches make up the three hours of the midnight watch: "If the three prayer watches of Jesus (14:32–42) are calculated to be of one hour's duration (14:37), then Judas's arrival in Gethsemane occurs at midnight (14:42–43)."

that Jesus prays that the hour "pass from him" (παρέλθη ἀπ' αὐτοῦ, 14:35), when the motif of "pass over" (παρέρχομαι) is so central to the Exodus account (παρέρχομαι, LXX Exod 12:23 [2x]). All these echoes to the night of the Exodus reverberate to form a symphony of echoes to the Passover, thereby portraying the scene at Gethsemane in the light of the original Passover. For Mark, the passion of Jesus is a "great trial," the eschatological tribulation marking a new Passover night that brings redemption through tribulation and suffering.

### 4.3.3 Eschatological "Hour"

The linchpin to the eschatological meaning of the Gethsemane scene comes with the motif of the "hour." Jesus' passionate prayer is that the "hour" may pass from him (ἵνα εἰ δυνατόν ἐστιν παρέλθη ἀπ' αὐτοῦ ἡ ὥρα, 14:35). The "hour" is then juxtaposed to the "cup" in the next verse (14:36), which means that the suffering embodied in the image of the "cup" is to be carried over to the "hour" as well.[51] This makes sense since the "hour" referred to in the eschatological discourse is a designation for the tribulation that brings about intense suffering and ultimately the eschatological destruction of the temple (13:11,32). Mark has already created significant tension in his account of the eschatological discourse by Jesus' confession that no one, not even the Son, knows the time of the "hour" but only the Father (13:32). Jesus' prayer in Gethsemane to the Father that "the hour" may pass him reveals why the Son is uncertain as to when the "hour" will come, for the Father may hold back the "hour." By the end of Jesus' prayer in Gethsemane, however, Jesus and the reader learn that the "hour" has come and that it is not the will of the Father to bring about redemption without tribulation. Jesus' words to the disciples, uttered the last time he finds them asleep, are significant: "Are you still sleeping and taking your rest? It is enough; the hour (ἡ ὥρα) has come; the Son of Man is to be handed over into the hands of sinners. Rise, let us be going; see, my betrayer is at hand" (14:41–42). Whereas in Mark 13 the reader is left wondering when the eschatological "hour" will arrive, the conclusion to the Gethsemane scene resolves any curiosity: the betrayal of

---

[51] Brown (*Death*, 1. 170) believes that the "cup" and the "hour" both evoke an eschatological meaning: "As for Mark 14:36, the cup about which Jesus prays would once more be the suffering of a horrendous death as part of the great trial. Some of the connotation of the classical cup of wrath or judgment may be preserved in Mark, not in the sense that Jesus is the object of wrath, but inasmuch as his death will take place in the apocalyptic context of the great struggle of last times when God's kingdom overcomes evil. 'Hour' and 'cup' thus have the same general range of historical and eschatological meaning and can be related to the idea of *peirasmos* discussed above."

Jesus marks the beginning of his passion and also in light of Mark 13, the beginning of the eschatological "hour." The hour known to no one except the Father has now arrived.

In addition to the intratextual link between "hour" and the eschatological discourse in Mark 13:32, "hour" may also allude to Daniel. Brown argues that the use of "hour" in Mark 13:32 informs the meaning of "hour" in Gethsemane, and thus "hour" is clearly eschatological. Brown also sees a similar use of "hour" in an eschatological sense in Rom 13:11 and Rev 9:15. The eschatological background for "hour," Brown suggests, comes from the book of Daniel (e.g., Dan 11:35,40,45; 12:1,4), "where it describes the end time with great battles and tribulation (*thlipsis*) and the intervention of Michael to deliver God's people."[52] Brown is convinced that, in light of Mark's use of "hour" in the eschatological discourse and its parallel to the "cup" in 14:35–36, the eschatological tribulation described in Daniel is precisely what Mark has in mind for the "hour."[53] Thus, the "hour" in Gethsemane must be understood as the eschatological tribulation.

The intertextual connection with the use of "hour" for tribulation with Daniel is supported by the prominent use of Daniel in this section of Mark. In the same passage that speaks of the arrival of the "hour," the Markan Jesus refers to himself as the Son of Man, which features prominently in Daniel 7. What is more, the Son of Man is described as being "handed over to sinners" – a phrase that evokes an important motif in Daniel.[54] In Dan 7:25, the saints are "given into" the hands of a wicked king who blasphemes God. The "handing over" of the saints constitutes their tribulation, but they will eventually be vindicated by the Son of Man when he is presented before the Ancient of Days. This story is a backdrop for Mark, who repeatedly describes Jesus as being "handed over" throughout the passion narrative. Mark also employs this very phrase to describe the

---

[52] Ibid., 168.

[53] Ibid., 1. 167–68. Evans (*Mark*, 411) also sees Daniel as a key backdrop for the eschatological meaning of "hour": "The hour theme derives from Jesus himself, who probably drew upon vocabulary and themes from Daniel (4:17,26; 5:5; 8:17,19; 11:35,40,45), where the idea of "hour" figures prominently, often with eschatological overtones." Evans sees the echo to Daniel as having "eschatological overtones," whereas Brown is more precise in seeing the "hour" as signifying the great tribulation; the latter is much closer to Mark's understanding of the "hour."

[54] "But here in v 21 Jesus links what is written to the 'son of man.' According to Dan 7, the holy ones of God will engage the powers of evil in a fierce struggle. Evil will prevail over the saints for a time and will wear them out (Dan 7:21,25). The handing over of the 'son of man' to those who seek his life coheres with this scenario" (Evans, *Mark*, 377).

suffering of the disciples in the eschatological tribulation (Mark 13) who would be "handed over" to trial. Thus, we have three echoes to Daniel in the Gethsemane scene alone: "Son of Man," "hour," and "handing over" – all of which converge to show that the passion of Jesus is the great eschatological trial spoken of in Mark 13. The "hour" of Jesus' tribulation has now arrived, as he is "handed over" for trial before the Jewish leaders. At this trial, the motif of temple eschatology will once again come to the forefront of Mark's story.

## 4.4 Trial Narrative: Temple Made without Hands (14:58)

At Jesus' trial, false witnesses bring charges against Jesus concerning his statements about the temple, which has held a prominent place in the narrative since Mark 11. Jesus' demonstration against the temple led the chief priests to seek a way to destroy Jesus (11:18), and the growing conflict between the temple authorities and Jesus now reaches its climax at Jesus' trial. Thus, it is not surprising that, in Mark's account of the trial, the opening charges leveled against Jesus concern the temple. As is recognized by many scholars, the temple charge against Jesus is crucial to Mark's story.[55] After informing the reader that "many bore false witness" against Jesus, only one charge is narrated – the temple charge:[56]

ὅτι ἡμεῖς ἠκούσαμεν αὐτοῦ λέγοντος ὅτι ἐγὼ καταλύσω τὸν ναὸν τοῦτον τὸν χειροποίητον καὶ διὰ τριῶν ἡμερῶν ἄλλον ἀχειροποίητον οἰκοδομήσω (Mark 14:58)

This charge is repeated at the crucifixion in Mark 15:29, which reinforces its importance for Mark's narrative.[57]

The Markan reader was warned in the first passion prediction that Jesus would be "rejected" (ἀποδοκιμασθῆναι) by the chief priests (τῶν ἀρχιερέων) and leaders and be killed and "after three days rise" (μετὰ τρεῖς ἡμέρας ἀναστῆναι) (8:31). Now, as Jesus stands on trial before the "chief priests" (οἱ ἀρχιερεῖς), the reader is shown how they "reject" Jesus, fulfilling his prophecy that he would be the "stone rejected by the builders"

---

[55] The primary study on the temple charge and its importance for Mark's story is the classic study by Juel, *Messiah and Temple*. For a more recent and equally thorough treatment of the trial scene in Mark, as well as the rest of the Gospels, see Brown, *Death*, 1. 430–60.

[56] Witherington, *Mark*, 384.

[57] Juel, *Messiah and Temple*, 35.

(12:10) – the only other occurrence of "rejected" in Mark.[58] The reader comes to the trial prepared for the chief priests' rejection of Jesus. It is precisely the reader's preparation from the earlier narrative that Mark uses as he unfolds the trial – a point I will now further explicate.

The specific charge against Jesus in v. 58 refers to two competing sanctuaries (ναός). The contrast between these sanctuaries will be vitally important for Mark's story. Although scholars have long noted that while Mark describes the testimony of the false witnesses (ψευδομαρτυρέω) as inconsonant, there is still a significant truth embedded in the temple charge against Jesus.[59] By employing irony, Mark allows the false testimony to bear witness to an important truth about Jesus. But even if Mark wanted to communicate a truth through the false testimony, why does he go to such pains to preface the charge by claiming the witnesses gave "false" testimony (ἐψευδομαρτύρουν, vv. 56, 57)? Also, why does Mark stress, both before and after the charge, that their testimony did not agree (καὶ ἴσαι αἱ μαρτυρίαι οὐκ ἦσαν in v. 56 and καὶ οὐδὲ οὕτως ἴση ἦν ἡ μαρτυρία αὐτῶν in v. 59)? The reason he highlights these data is to prevent the reader from taking the charge as true, given Jesus' hostile relationship to the temple in preceding episodes.

### 4.4.1　Ironic Truth and False Charges

The charge that Jesus claimed he would "destroy" (καταλύσω) the temple takes up the very term that Jesus used to describe the temple's future "destruction" (καταλυθῇ, 13:2). Given Jesus' demonstration against the temple and his actions and words foretelling its demise, the Markan reader is well prepared to accept the notion that Jesus did in fact threaten to destroy the temple. Mention of building a new temple "in three days" (Mark 14:58) sounds strikingly familiar to Jesus claim in his passion predictions that he would rise "after three days" (μετὰ τρεῖς ἡμέρας, e.g., 8:31). Finally, as illustrated in previous chapters, Jesus has given many hints that a new temple is on the horizon; his teaching about a new cornerstone is just one such example. In summary, since the temple charge is familiar to the reader, Mark feels compelled to emphasize that this testimony is not true.

Why is the charge false? The thrust of the temple charge regarding the destruction of the temple and its replacement with one of a different order – "made without hands" – stands true, as a reading of Mark 11–13 makes clear. Thus, the reader is faced with a problem: many elements in the

---

[58] Juel (ibid., 54) sees the trial as the "rejection" of Jesus that makes him the "rejected stone."

[59] Brown, *Death*, 1. 447.

charge are correct, so why is it characterized as false? By repeating that the testimony is flawed, Mark forces the reader to sort out the details of the charge carefully. In doing so, one prominent flaw emerges: Jesus did speak of the temple's doom, but he never claimed to be the agent of its destruction.[60] The emphasis on Jesus' personal agency, ἐγὼ καταλύσω (since ἐγώ is not necessary), signals that the error is in the claim that Jesus himself would bring about the destruction of the temple.[61] On the contrary, according to the Markan Jesus, the destruction of the temple finds its source in the judgment and the agency of God. Jesus' statement that the temple stones would be "cast down" (καταλυθῇ) is given in the passive (the so-called divine passive) to show that the agency belongs to God. Again, in the vineyard of the wicked tenants, it is not the son but the owner of the vineyard who takes vengeance upon the wicked tenants. What is more, the vindication of the rejected stone (ἐγενήθη εἰς κεφαλὴν γωνίας) is stated in the passive to highlight God's agency (12:10–11). Mark wants the reader to see that Jesus is innocent of the charge that he will destroy the temple. Rather, he stands as the last one in a line of prophets sent to warn of the temple's judgment. Thus, the charge is correct in that the temple will be destroyed and that another will take its place, but it reflects a fundamental misunderstanding as to how and through whom this will take place.

Mark basically admits much of the truth of the charge when he says after the testimony that "yet not even so did their testimony agree." The "yet not even so" (καὶ οὐδὲ οὕτως) hints that there is substantial truth within the false charge.[62] It has been observed that Mark's narrative often operates on two levels.[63] McKelvey suggested this was particularly true with the temple charge:

> How much weight one should give this secondary and deeper meaning is not clear, but Mark's cryptic way of writing (cf. 15:38) and the interpretative words "made with hands ... not made with hands" and "in three days" rather suggests that he invites his reader to read between the lines.[64]

---

[60] Geddert, *Watchwords*, 131.

[61] Brown (*Death*, 1. 447) observes that Mark alone highlights Jesus' personal agency in saying "I will destroy" and then concludes that: "It might be, then, that the witnesses have falsified Jesus' intention by making him the agent of the destruction."

[62] See Geddert, *Watchwords*, 290 n. 50.

[63] "In fact, there are clear signs that the author utilizes this particular stylistic possibility and that the use of the double-level narrative makes possible the use of the most prominent literary feature of the passion story: irony" (Juel, *Messiah and Temple*, 47).

[64] R. J. McKelvey, *The New Temple* (London: Oxford University Press, 1969) 71; Geddert, *Watchwords*, 286 n. 6.

Mark employs irony throughout the trial and passion narrative by using Jesus' opponents to bear witness to the truth about Jesus consistently in a way beyond their understanding and intentions.[65] For example, the soldiers dress Jesus in a royal robe and give him a crown of thorns, but the reader knows the ironic truth – Jesus is king. Pilate puts the title "the King of the Jews" upon the inscription over the cross, and the reader knows the truth of the inscription, with its writing in different languages signifying how the gospel will go to all nations (13:10).[66] The confession of the centurion, "Truly this man was the Son of God (15:39), is true on a level only the reader can appreciate. Throughout Mark the reader is called to look beyond the surface of events in order to gain "understanding." Thus, it is consistent with Mark's style to show that the testimony regarding Jesus' comments about the temple is false on one level, but nevertheless true in a way that escapes the grasp and the intentions of Jesus' perjurers: the old temple is to be destroyed and replaced by another.

### 4.4.2  "Made with Hands"

The temple charge is unique to Mark's gospel. Although false testimony is mentioned in Matthew, the accusation in that gospel does not mention the unique description of the temple as "made with hands" (χειροποίητον) and building another temple "made without hands" (ἀχειροποίητον) (Mark 14:58). Since this language of "made with hands" and "not made with hands" is superfluous to the nature and the authenticity of the accusation, Mark most likely intended these phrases to add another layer of meaning to the trial.[67] "Made with hands" and "not made with hands" create a sharp contrast between two competing temples. Brown believes this contrast is vital to Mark's plot: "If the Marcan contrast between the two sanctuaries comes from adjectives inserted to interpret Jesus' words, the Christian usage of those two adjectives and of Temple/sanctuary imagery may be an important key to what Mark wants his readers to understand (even if he

---

[65] Juel, *Messiah and Temple*, 84, 124.

[66] Juel, ibid., 47. Morna Hooker (*The Signs of a Prophet: The Prophetic Actions of Jesus* [Harrisburg: Trinity, 1997] 57) notes, "Other actions by Jesus' enemies also have a significance they do not understand. The soldiers mock Jesus, clothing him in purple and hailing him as king: they do not realize that they are proclaiming the truth; the inscription on the cross, written in irony, announces that he is King of the Jews. These actions *function* as prophetic dramas, not because those who do them are prophets, but because God is working through them" (italics original).

[67] "What is decisive for interpreting Mark is the distinction between the two 'temples' in 14:58" (Juel, *Messiah and Temple*, 208).

dubs the pertinent statement false)."[68] Therefore, I will now examine what χειροποίητος and ἀχειροποίητος mean for Mark.

The word "made with hands" (χειροποίητος) is found 14 times in the LXX, and in every case it describes idols.[69] This observation is very consequential, for the description of the Jerusalem temple as "made with hands" is not simply saying that the temple is of this world – man-made – but that it has become an idol. It has been noted that such an association may be in the purview of Mark's narrative, given his polemic against the temple.[70] Could this be the view of the Markan Jesus? Geddert's suggests that this is the case: "If Jesus can call the temple a 'den of robbers' (11.17), he can also call it a pagan idol."[71] It should be noted that Jesus' claim that the temple is a "den of thieves" is due to what the corrupt leadership had made of it. Perhaps the suggestion of "made with hands" is likewise a claim that the corruption surrounding the temple has made it into an idol – using the temple in ways that God did not intend (such as usurping the living of widows, 12:40). Of course, it is not the Markan Jesus who contends that the temple is "made with hands," but Mark allows it to be spoken in order to deepen the contrast between the corruption surrounding the Jerusalem temple and the eschatological temple Jesus will build. The new temple is of an altogether higher order than the old.

After describing the destruction of the "handmade" temple, the charge turns to "another" (ἄλλον) temple. The usage of ἄλλον suggests that this temple is of a different order. The word for "made without hands," ἀχειροποίητος, is never used in the LXX. Did Mark coin the term?[72] Or was the term invented by the early Christian tradition that Mark inherited?[73] After careful examination of this term, Juel concludes that Mark invented it in his struggle to describe the new temple that was embodied in the Christian community.[74] Thus, Mark puts the new wine of temple language into the new wineskin of ἀχειροποίητος.

---

[68] Brown (*Death*, 1. 440) believes that Mark's redaction of v. 58 underscores how important it is for his story.

[69] Taylor, *Mark*, 566.

[70] Geddert, *Watchwords*, 132; Juel, *Messiah and Temple*, 149; Brown, *Death*, 1. 439.

[71] Geddert, *Watchwords*, 132.

[72] This is the suggestion of Taylor, *Mark*, 566.

[73] This suggestion is made by Brown (*Death*, 1. 439): "Indeed, it is possible that Christians were the first to formulate the negative adjective [ἀχειροποίητος]."

[74] "Our study would suggest that the terms, particularly ἀχειροποίητος, reflect a struggle on the part of the interpreter to find language appropriate to describe the Christian community by using temple imagery" (Juel, *Messiah and Temple*, 155). Donahue ("Temple, Trial, and Royal Christology," 61–79) suggests that Mark invented

### 4.4.3   Possible Danielic Background

Whether ἀχειροποίητος originates from Mark's hand or from early Christian tradition, one must ask what led to its creation. Since, as shown above, there is a scriptural background for the term χειροποίητος, it seems reasonable to look for the closest parallel to ἀχειροποίητος in the OT and see if it may have contributed to the concept of ἀχειροποίητος. The closest parallel is the stone "cut out by no human hand" (Dan 2:34) that appears in Nebuchadnezzar's dream and crushes the statue made of iron, bronze, clay, silver, and gold (Dan 2:44–45).[75] After the stone strikes the image, it grows into a great mountain and fills the whole earth (Dan 2:35). The interpretation of the dream by Daniel is significant:

And in the days of those kings the God of heaven will set up a kingdom which shall never be destroyed, nor shall its sovereignty be left to another people. It shall break in pieces all these kingdoms and bring them to an end, and it shall stand for ever; just as you saw that a stone was *cut from a mountain by no human hand*, and that it broke in pieces the iron, the bronze, the clay, the silver, and the gold. A great God has made known to the king what shall be hereafter" (italics mine).

The stone "cut from a mountain by no human hand" is strikingly parallel to the term "made without hands" in the temple charge. The only uncut stones mentioned in the OT are those used for cultic purposes. Thus, according to the book of the covenant, Israel is to use "unhewn stones" for their altars: "And if you make me an altar of stone, you shall not build it of hewn stones; for if you wield your tool upon it you profane it" (Exod 20:25).[76] This backdrop suggests that the "uncut stone" of Daniel 2 is meant to have some kind of cultic association.

What would the cultic connotations mean for Daniel's "unhewn stone"? Beale makes an interesting suggestion:

The Daniel stone may also have represented a sacred antithesis of the image that it smashed. The stone smashes the statue which is repeatedly said to be made of 'gold, silver, bronze, iron, and clay' (Dan 2:31–45) and which symbolized the ungodly nations.

---

this term: "We affirm that in 14:58 Mk creates a Christian exegesis of Temple expectations which function within his overall theological purpose" (p. 68).

[75] Evans (*Mark*, 445) follows J. Ådna's ("Jesu Kritik am Tempel: Eine Untersuchung zum Verlauf und Sinn der sogenannten Tempelreinigung Jesu, Markus 11,15–17 und Parallelen" [Ph.D. diss., University of Oslo, 1993] 507) suggestion that the stone of Daniel 2 is a key backdrop to the "made without hands" reference in the temple charge of Mark 14:58. Evans, however, only makes this as a passing suggestion and does not explain how the context of Daniel 2 strengthens the link.

[76] Beale (*Temple*, 226) sees Daniel 2 as shedding light on the NT use of ἀχειροποίητος, and he sees the "uncut stones" as a crucial clue that illustrates the cultic and temple associations intended by the "uncut stone" that grows into a mountain in Daniel 2.

The only other times the same combination of four metals are listed together are in Daniel 5:4, 23, where they refer to Babylonian idols![77]

Daniel's description of the stone as "unhewn" gives it a cultic connotation that proves to be the antithesis of pagan idols, which it destroys. The cultic meaning of the "unhewn stone" is further suggested by the description that it grows into "a great mountain" and fills the whole world (Dan 2:35). Since every temple associated with Israel in the OT is on a mountain, there is good reason to believe that the mountain reference is to the temple mount. The temple is often referred to simply as 'mountain' or 'holy mountain' through the employment of a synecdoche where the mountain represents the entire temple.[78] Mount Zion is a classic example of a mountain representing the temple, which is quite common throughout the OT. This association of "mountain" with temple is so common that one commentator on Daniel suggests that the "unhewn stone" represents Mount Zion as the temple not built by human hands.[79] The apocryphal 4 Ezra 13 makes the connection between Daniel's uncut stone, mountain, and Mount Zion.[80] Given the strong polemic against pagan idolatry in Daniel, that the "unhewn stone" that crushes the idolatrous image should represent Israel's sacred temple mount is rather compelling. Also in support of this argument, as Beale observes, is the mention of the "threshing floors" in connection with the "unhewn stone" (Dan 2:35), since the threshing floor too has cultic connotations. For instance, according to 2 Chr 3:1, Solomon chose the threshing floor of Ornan the Jebusite as the site on which to build the temple.[81]

---

[77] Ibid., 226.

[78] Ibid., 145–46. Beale makes a strong case for the stone growing into a mountain as a reference to the temple: "For example, repeatedly such phrases occur as 'mountain of the house' (Jer. 26:18; Mic. 4:1), 'holy mountain' (about 16 times), 'holy hill' (Pss. 15:1; 43:3; 99:9; Jer. 31:23) and 'temple hill' (1 Maccabees 13:52; 16:20). Sometimes these references are equated with the temple in the following context: e.g., in Isaiah 66:20 'holy mountain' = 'house of the LORD'; in Psalm 15:1 'holy hill' = 'your tent'; in Psalm 24:3 'hill of the LORD' = 'His holy place' (cf. also Ps. 43:3). Thus, 'mountain', when referring to Zion, often includes reference to the temple."

[79] A. Lacocque, *The Book of Daniel* (London: SPCK, 1979) 49, 124.

[80] "But he shall stand on the top of Mount Zion. And Zion will come and be made manifest to all people, prepared and built, as you saw the mountain carved out without hands" (4 Ezra 13:35–36). Bryan (*Jesus and Israel's Traditions*, 194) argues that 4 Ezra is speaking of how the Messiah will reveal the eschatological temple, which he argues is Daniel's stone pictured as Mount Zion.

[81] Beale, *Temple*, 147–48.

This stone/temple association is further evidenced in that Isaiah and Micah both describe the eschatological restoration of Israel in terms of the temple mount growing in size and stature:

It shall come to pass in the latter days, that the mountain of the house of the LORD shall be established as the highest of the mountains, and shall be raised above the hills; and all the nations shall flow to it and many peoples shall come, and say: 'Come, let us go up the mountain of the LORD, to the house of the God of Jacob; that he may teach us his ways and that we may walk in his paths.' For out of Zion shall go forth the law, and the word of the LORD from Jerusalem. (Isa 2:2–3; cf. Mic 4:1–2)

The similarity between the growing mountain in Isaiah and Micah and the "unhewn stone" of Daniel 2, which grows into a mountain that fills the world, is suggestive. Like the temple mount, the stone too enlarges and brings about the submission of the Gentiles to Yhwh. This coheres well with Mark's focus on the eschatological temple as a "house of prayer for all nations." Daniel's vision of an eschatological temple that would reach the entire world also fits well with Mark's focus on the gospel going to all nations (Mark 13:10).

Given the above cultic and eschatological dynamics of the unhewn stone of Daniel 2, it seems quite possible that the description of the new temple in the temple charge "borrows" from Daniel. The fact that the "unhewn stone" is set against pagan idols in Daniel corresponds to the antithetical relationship between ἀχειροποίητος and χειροποίητος in Mark. The temple "made without hands" (Mark 14:58), then, may evoke the image of the "unhewn stone" from Daniel 2, which represents the victory of the kingdom of God over idols and the establishment of the eschatological temple – themes that resonate with Mark's narrative.[82] Indeed, Jesus' response to the high priest, that he will see the Son of Man sitting at the right hand of God and coming with the clouds of heaven is undoubtedly an allusion to Daniel 7. What is interesting to note is that just as the stone comes to defeat the four metals of the statue that represent Gentile kingdoms, so too the Son of Man appears to vanquish the four beasts that arise from the seas, which also represent four pagan kingdoms. Son of Man and stone are parallel, and the connection between them would fit Mark's context well, since Mark sees Jesus not only as Son of Man but also as the "stone rejected by the builders," which will become the head of the corner of a new temple (12:10).

---

[82] Thus Evans (*Mark*, 445) observes: "Incorporation of Daniel's stone that represents the kingdom of God is consistent with Jesus' use of Daniel and coheres with his proclamation of the kingdom of God."

### 4.4.4   Resurrection as New Temple

In the temple charge, mention of the temple "not made with hands" is prefaced by the claim that it would be built "within three days" (διὰ τριῶν ἡμερῶν). This time frame reminds the reader of Jesus' claim that he would suffer and die and then "after three days rise" (μετὰ τρεῖς ἡμέρας ἀναστῆναι, 8:31; 9:31; 10:34). Given the threefold repetition of "after three days" in the passion predictions, it would be hard for the reader not to associate this time frame with the resurrection.[83] Earlier in the narrative, Mark showed that the death of the Son would be vindicated by the rejected stone becoming the head of the corner – an allusion to the resurrection. Here again, the resurrection is being alluded to in the context of a statement about the new temple. The convergence of these themes – temple and resurrection – suggest that, for Mark, Jesus' resurrection in some way brings about the eschatological temple foretold in the restoration oracles of Israel's Scriptures.[84] It is not easy to flesh out Mark's thought on the matter, as he is showing the reader these ideas through a narrative, rather than giving a straightforward teaching. However, the repetition of the twin ideas of temple and resurrection lead the reader to see the promise of an eschatological new temple as somehow fulfilled in Jesus' resurrection. This means that for Mark the resurrection is an eschatological event that brings about the promise of a new temple made in the restoration oracles of Israel's Scriptures.

The idea of Jesus' resurrection cannot be far from the surface of Mark's trial narrative, given Jesus' response to the high priest's question if he was the Messiah: "I am; and you will see the Son of Man seated at the right hand of the Power and coming with the clouds of heaven" (14:62). The many issues surrounding Jesus' answer need not be addressed here, but the one point I wish to make is how this imagery, which combines Daniel 7 and Psalm 110, points to Jesus' vindication through his resurrection. "Son of Man" has been used throughout Mark's story, and his coming on the clouds is found at the climax of the eschatological discourse, as noted in Chapter Three. It is noteworthy that, in the eschatological discourse, the coming of the Son of Man follows the time of tribulation and suffering as well as the temple's destruction. Thus, a clear pattern of thought arises from Mark's narrative: tribulation and suffering are followed by vindication and glory. This pattern is stamped upon the three passion

---

[83] Brown, *Death*, 1. 444; Juel, *Messiah and Temple*, 144, 205.

[84] "The phrase 'in three days' (διὰ τριῶν ἡμερῶν) was too close to the normal way of referring to Jesus' being raised 'after three days' (μετὰ τρεῖς ἡμέρας) for the connection not to have been made. For Mark, therefore, the resurrection of Jesus brought into existence a new kind of temple" (Walker, *Holy City*, 10).

predictions, the parable of the wicked tenants, the eschatological discourse, and now the trial narrative. At the trial, Jesus experiences the rejection he had foretold, yet in his answer to the high priest he speaks of his approaching vindication by citing Daniel 7, which also upholds the Markan pattern of tribulation and vindication. Psalm 110, the enthronement psalm cited by Jesus when his authority over the temple was questioned, is also about vindication: the king (Messiah) of Israel is seated at God's right hand and his enemies vanquished.[85] This explosive juxtaposition of Daniel 7 and Psalm 110 is important for Mark, who more than once portrays Jesus seated in judgment, particularly over the corrupt temple (12:41; 13:3). Perhaps Mark's narrating was influenced by these scriptural passages.[86]

Mark has brought together in the temple charge and Jesus' response the motifs of old and new temple and resurrection – motifs that have been undercurrents in his narrative since Jesus' entry to Jerusalem. In the trial scene, Mark's account of the temple charge functions to reinforce in the reader's mind that the central conflict of the story is once again made manifest in the conflict between two temples – the old one in Jerusalem and the eschatological temple of which Jesus is the cornerstone.[87] The temple motif and the theme of Jesus' vindication have one last stage of development: the scene of the crucifixion. It will be at the cross that the conflict between the two temples will be resolved and Jesus' vindication set in motion.

## 4.5 The Crucifixion and the Temple

In Mark's account of Jesus' crucifixion, the temple motif resurfaces in two prominent ways. First, the temple charge from Jesus' trial – that he threatened to destroy the temple – is reiterated by passers-by in order to

---

[85] Psalm 110 was a favorite of early Christians, and was particularly associated with Jesus' resurrection and exaltation. See Marcus, *The Way of the Lord*, 130–45.

[86] On the combination of Psalm 110 and Daniel 7, see Darrel L. Bock, *Blasphemy and Exaltation in Judaism: The Charge against Jesus in Mark 14:53–65* (Grand Rapids: Baker, 2000) 220–24.

[87] Myers (*Binding*, 375) believes the temple charge is placed first in the trial because Jesus' demonstration is what most provoked his opponents and that it serves to highlight the nature of the conflict of Mark's story, centered on the temple. Myers's second point is worth quoting: "...the charge in 14:58 posits a fundamental opposition between that 'made with hands' and that 'not made with hands.' In this Jesus' opponents have unwittingly articulated the central ideological struggle between him and the temple state. Mark uses this accusation to narratively prepare the way for Jesus' body to replace the temple as the new symbolic center."

mock Jesus. Second, immediately following Jesus' death, the veil in the temple is torn from top to bottom. The climax of Mark's story – Jesus' death and the concurrent tearing of the veil – once again brings the temple into the forefront. The fate of Jesus and the temple are once again entwined as the death of one betokens the destruction of the other. In this section I will examine these two temple-related events in Mark's crucifixion account and explain why the temple theme follows Jesus to the very end.

### 4.5.1  Temple Charge Repeated (15:29–32)

The mocking of Jesus at the cross takes up the two charges leveled against Jesus at the trial: (1) that Jesus threatened the temple with destruction; and (2) that he claimed to be the Messiah.[88] The first two mockings of Jesus create a doublet with parallelism, illustrating Mark's careful narrating of this scene:[89]

| *First Mocking (vv. 29-30)* | *Second Mocking (vv. 31-32)* |
|---|---|
| bystanders mock | chief priests mock |
| "save yourself" | "he cannot save himself" |
| trial charge concerning temple | trial charge concerning the Messiah |

The double charge of the trial becomes the thrust of the first two instances of mocking. In the third occurrence of mocking – by those who were crucified with Jesus – Mark does not mention what was said (v. 32b), thereby leaving the mockings parallel to the accusations made at the trial. Why does Mark carry the subject of the trial into the crucifixion?

By repeating the charge of 14:58 through the slightly altered wording of the bystanders' mock – "Aha! You who would destroy the temple and build it in three days, save yourself and come down from the cross!" (15:29) – Mark reminds the reader that the heart of the conflict lies in the opposition between Jesus and the temple.[90] Indeed, the trial was overseen by the chief priests (οἱ ἀρχιερεῖς, 14:55), who now stand before Jesus (οἱ ἀρχιερεῖς 15:31), in order to gloat in their victory over him.[91] The trial and

---

[88] Brown, *Death*, 1. 438.

[89] Matera, *Kingship*, 57; Painter, *Mark*, 205.

[90] Evans (*Mark*, 505) sees the repetition of the temple charge in 15:29 as Mark's way of putting the conflict between Jesus and the temple front and center in the story.

[91] Brown (*Death*, 2. 991–92) notes that: "It is appropriate that members of the Sanhedrin, under various designations, appear as the main protagonists in the first Luke mockery and the second Mark/Matt mockery since the scene is meant to remind the readers of the challenge to Jesus in the Sanhedrin trial or interrogation. Mark has set the pattern: Charges against Jesus by the Jewish authorities as they interrogated him are resumed to mock him as he hangs on the cross but will ultimately be the subject of God's vindication of Jesus after he dies."

crucifixion scenes are unified by (1) the question about the destruction of the temple and building of a new one; and (2) the identity of Jesus as the Messiah, which has royal meaning in both scenes.[92] Thus, Mark keeps the temple at the center of Jesus' story.

Bailey makes the intriguing suggestion that Mark has conformed his description of the mocking bystanders to Lamentations 2:15:[93]

All who pass along the way clap their hands at you; they hiss and wag their heads at the daughter of Jerusalem; "Is this the city which was called the perfection of beauty, the joy of all the earth?" All your enemies rail against you; they hiss, they gnash their teeth, they cry: "We have destroyed her! Ah, this is the day we longed for; now we have it; we see it! (Lam 2:15–16)

And as those who passed by derided him, wagging their heads. (Mark 15:29a)

The wider context of Lamentations 2 is the mourning of the destruction not just of the city of Jerusalem but of its temple as well. Such an allusion to Lamentations would accentuate Mark's understanding of Jesus as the true temple and resonate with his use of irony throughout the passion narrative. The classic text of Israel's mourning for the temple is applied to Jesus' death – with the chief priests cast in the role the pagans who gloat over Jerusalem's defeat.

Although the wording of the first mocking is slightly different from the original temple charge in 14:58, the same term for temple is used, ναός. The usual term in the gospels and Mark for the temple area is ἱερόν. Beginning with the temple charge, Mark drops ἱερόν and uses ναός. The shift is telling.[94] The term ἱερόν indicates the temple precincts, including all related buildings and the area of the huge temple complex. On the other hand, ναός is more specific, referring to the sanctuary proper.[95] The specific term for the "sanctuary," ναός, occurs only in the passion narrative, and all three instances of its occurrence are intended to be seen together.[96] Thus far, we have seen the first two: the charge in the temple that Jesus would destroy the "temple" (ναός) made with hands and build another made without hands (14:58), and the repetition of this charge in

---

[92] Juel, *Messiah and Temple*, 50–52.

[93] Kenneth Bailey, "The Fall of Jerusalem and Mark's Account of the Cross," *ExpTim* 102 (1991) 102–5, esp. 105. Brown (*Death*, 2. 989 n. 13) agrees with Bailey that Mark may have had Lam 2:15 in mind, particularly because it would fit in well with Mark's use of irony.

[94] France (*Mark*, 606) notes: "The introduction of a new term, 'sanctuary,' rather than 'temple,' thus indicates that something different is afoot here, and in particular distances this alleged threat from what Jesus had in fact predicted about the fate of the ἱερόν."

[95] On the distinction between ἱερόν and ναός, see Juel, *Messiah and Temple*, 127–28.

[96] Ibid., 127.

the mocking at the cross, where ναός is again used (15:29). The third and final occurrence will come with Jesus' death and the tearing of the veil (15:38) – events Mark wants the reader to link with 14:58 and 15:29.

## 4.5.2  Eschatological Darkness and Blindness

After describing the mocking of Jesus, Mark turns to the last three hours of Jesus' crucifixion, a time that is enveloped in darkness. The darkness begins at the sixth hour and lasts until Jesus' death at the ninth hour.[97] Mark describes the darkness as dominant: "There was darkness over the whole land" (σκότος ἐγένετο ἐφ᾽ ὅλην τὴν γῆν, 15:33). The darkness seems to be a response from heaven to the mocking of Jesus. The reader is most likely invited to revisit the eschatological darkness that Jesus warned would come in the tribulation of the day of the Lord (13:24). Since Gethsemane, the reader has known that "the hour" – the day of the Lord – has begun. Jesus' trial and repeated "handing over" confirms for the reader that the events of the tribulation described in the eschatological discourse are now taking place. Moreover, the reader knows that, if the events of Mark 13 are now being fulfilled, the end of the temple must be near.

Darkness, as I highlighted in the previous chapter, is often associated with the day of Yhwh. The prophetic oracles of judgment use darkness to illustrate how God's judgment brings about an unmaking of creation.[98] Of all the uses of darkness in the prophetic oracles, Amos 8:9 is commonly seen as the closest connection to Mark: "'And on that day,' says the LORD God, 'I will make the sun go down at noon, and darken the earth in broad daylight.'"[99] The context of Amos 8 is, interestingly, a "day of the LORD" that particularly stresses the end of the temple (Amos 8:3, 5, 10). Indeed, the very next oracle begins with Yhwh standing beside the altar, commanding the temple to be destroyed (Amos 9:1). This last oracle ends with the promise to rebuild the "booth" of David (Amos 9:11), which seems to be the temple. In Amos, the judgment and destruction of Israel and the temple is followed by the promise to rebuild another temple.

---

[97] The darkness creates an apocalyptic and eschatological backdrop, according to Moloney (*Mark*, 327), for the rest of the passion narrative. This eschatological backdrop, I believe, is crucial for understanding what follows in the narrative.

[98] Lagrange (*Saint Marc*, 432) says that Mark sees the miraculous darkness as relating to the prophetic motif of judgment, particularly Amos 8:9.

[99] Brown (*Death*, 2. 1035) observes that Amos 8:9–10 "seems particularly pertinent" to Mark's use of darkness. Moloney (*Mark*, 325) believes that the darkness in Mark is linked to Amos: "This detail, introduced as a deliberate allusion to Amos 8:9, focuses upon the eschatological nature of the events reported."

The darkness of Amos 8:9 is preceded by the description of upheaval in the land (8:8), which deploys references to Egypt and the Nile to color the judgment with Exodus imagery. Surely this is intended to evoke the plagues, especially since the next sign of judgment is the darkness – another of the fearsome plagues (Exod 10:22). Mark's description that the darkness "covered all the land" parallels the plague of darkness, which also covered "all the land of Egypt" (Exod 10:22).[100] Both Amos and Mark pick up the Exodus imagery of darkness with its accompanying imagery of judgment and unmaking of creation. Given the prominence of Exodus imagery throughout Mark, especially in relation to the eschatological trial in Gethsemane, it may well be that Mark intends to evoke the darkness from the Exodus story – particularly since the passion takes place during the Passover.[101] The advent of the day of the Lord is unraveling creation, and the reader now appreciates Jesus' statement that "heaven and earth will pass away, but my words will not pass away" (13:31). In light of Mark 13, the reader also knows that the eschatological darkness, which accompanies the day of the Lord and signifies divine judgment, is also the precursor to the glorious vindication and coming of the Son of Man. So as the script of the eschatological discourse is played out in the passion narrative, the expectation of the temple's demise and the vindication of the Son of Man intensifies.

### 4.5.3  Seeing and Hearing but Misunderstanding (15:34–37)

The eschatological darkness is matched by another sign of judgment in v. 38: the rending of the temple veil. These two signs frame vv. 33–37 in a chiastic structure:[102]

A Eschatological Sign: Darkness (v. 33)
    B Jesus utters a "great cry" (φωνῇ μεγάλῃ, v. 34)
        C Bystanders *hear* (ἀκούσαντες) and say "Behold, he is calling Elijah (v. 35)
        C' One says, "Wait, let us *see* (ἴδωμεν) whether Elijah will come (v. 36)
    B' Jesus gives a "great cry" (φωνὴν μεγάλην, v. 37)
A' Eschatological Sign: Tearing of temple veil (v. 38)

---

[100] On this connection see Evans, *Mark*, 506; Myers, *Binding*, 389; Brown, *Death*, 2. 1035.

[101] "The (first) Passover context of that plague makes it a likely parallel for the darkness at the Passover of Jesus' death" (Brown, *Death*, 2. 1035).

[102] I have developed this chiasm based on the work of Myers (*Binding*, 389). However, I have added the "hearing" and "seeing" of the bystanders as I believe that the bystanders' misunderstanding of what is going on is at the center of the chiasm and is part of the Markan motif of hearing/seeing/understanding.

The chiasm here certainly bears the imprint of Mark's familiar use of parallelism. At the center is the misunderstanding of the bystanders, despite their "hearing" and "seeing." The eschatological signs and the cries of Jesus are incomprehensible to them, bringing out once again Mark's theme of "seeing" and "hearing," culminating in a failure to "understand."[103]

The motif of "seeing" is already present in the second mocking: "He saved others; he cannot save himself. Let the Messiah, the King of Israel, come down now from the cross, that we may *see* and believe" (15:32). The failure of those around the cross to "see" confirms how far they are from understanding the kingdom of God, for the reader recalls Jesus' warning from Isaiah about those who "may indeed see but not perceive, and may indeed hear but not understand; lest they should turn again, and be forgiven" (Mark 4:12, quoting Isa 6:9–10).[104] This failure to "see" and "hear" who Jesus really is and what he is really about has been threaded throughout the entire story. However, it reaches its climax here on the cross. Now, the eschatological judgment has begun, and there is no longer any time to "turn and be forgiven."

### 4.5.4   Torn Veil (v. 38)

Through his usual paratactic καί, Mark links Jesus' loud cry and expiration with the tearing of the temple veil: "And the curtain of the temple was torn in two, from top to bottom" (καὶ τὸ καταπέτασμα τοῦ ναοῦ ἐσχίσθη εἰς δύο ἀπ᾽ ἄνωθεν ἕως κάτω, 15:38). For Mark, the death of Jesus and the rending of the temple veil are inseparable. The veil being torn "from top to bottom" (ἀπ᾽ ἄνωθεν ἕως κάτω), coupled with the use of the passive ἐσχίσθη, leaves no doubt as to who causes the tearing – God.[105]

---

[103] Moloney's (*Mark*, 327) reading here keenly picks up the Markan motif of "understanding": "The bystanders and this individual have understood neither the signs that surround Jesus' last moments, nor his use of Ps 22:1. As Jesus cried out ελωι, ελωι, they understood him to be crying out for help from Ἠλίας."

[104] "In Mark the challenge to come down from the cross is placed 'in order that we may see and believe.' But the Marcan readers have already heard Jesus speaking of such outsiders in Isaian language (Mark 4:12 from Isa 6:9): 'They may indeed see but not perceive'" (Brown, *Death*, 2. 995). Brown's insight on the "seeing" motif from Isaiah 6 could be strengthened once the "hearing" and "seeing" combination in 15:35–36 is recognized.

[105] Evans (*Mark*, 509, 512) argues that Jesus' last breath exhales his spirit that tears the temple veil: "Just as the descent of the Holy Spirit upon Jesus at his baptism tore the heavens (1:10, σχιζομένους), so now the loud exhalation of Jesus' spirit has torn (ἐσχίσθη) the veil of the temple." Although I think there is a parallel between the "tearing" of the heavens at Jesus' baptism and the "tearing" of the temple veil, I believe

Throughout his story, Mark has carefully juxtaposed Jesus and the temple by (1) framing the eschatological discourse with sacrificial gifts for Jesus and the temple (12:41–44 and 14:3–9); (2) paralleling predictions that both were soon coming to an end (8:31 and 13:2); and (3) underscoring the giving of Jesus' body at the Last Supper as a substitute for the temple cult.[106] Now, by tying together the death of Jesus and the rending of the temple veil, Mark shows in the starkest terms possible that the fate of Jesus and the temple are intertwined.[107]

Since Jesus has foretold the temple's destruction in his demonstration in the temple (11:15–17), his cursing of the fig tree (11:12–14, 20), and his subsequent teaching (11:21–13:37), there is little doubt for the Markan reader that the torn temple veil signifies the destruction of the temple.[108] The coming destruction of the temple has been a focus of the narrative, and now the reader gets a first glimpse of the fulfillment of Jesus' words against the temple.[109] Like the pervasive darkness, the tearing of the veil is an eschatological judgment upon the temple that has become a den of thieves and whose stewards have falsely condemned Jesus to death. Thus, the tearing signifies the temple's destruction and the unleashing of the dreaded "day of the Lord."[110]

---

that Evans is mistaken. First, it is not clear that the Holy Spirit tears the heavens – Mark only says that the heavens were torn and the Spirit descended. Second, Evans does not address the problem that the "tearing" (ἐσχίσθη) in 15:38 is given in the passive mood, indicating divine causality. Finally, this explanation is incongruent with Mark's belief that the charge that Jesus would destroy the temple was false; for Mark, Jesus only predicted what God would do. France (*Mark*, 657) also argues against Jesus' breath as the cause of the tear.

[106] Bailey ("Fall" 102–5), followed by Beale (*Temple*, 193), suggests that Mark creates a literary parallel between the dividing of Jesus' garments and the temple veil being torn. Although Mark often juxtaposes Jesus and the temple throughout his narrative, and sometimes quite subtly, the evidence for this is not very compelling because there are no clear linguistic parallels. For example, both Bailey and Beale see the double offer of wine (fine wine in v. 23 and vinegar in v. 36) as preceding the dividing of garments (v. 24) and tearing of the veil (v. 38), but there is no clear linguistic parallel.

[107] "It is almost as though the last movements of Mark's story had been charted in terms of the temple's projected demise, for its fate and that of Jesus seem tightly interwoven" (Seeley, "Jesus' Temple Act," 274).

[108] The tearing is widely seen among scholars as a portent of the temple's destruction, e.g., Donahue and Harrington, *Mark*, 452; Evans, *Mark*, 509; Geddert, *Watchwords*, 146.

[109] Donahue and Harrington (*Mark*, 452) note that the Markan reader has long anticipated the temple's demise, and the tearing of the veil gives a sense of fulfillment to the reader.

[110] "As a negative sign after the death, the rending stands parallel to the darkness before Jesus' death. The day of the Lord with its burden of judgment was being heralded" (Brown, *Death*, 2. 1102).

This judgment upon the temple serves as much-needed vindication for Jesus in a passion narrative that has seen Jesus abandoned by everyone – even, seemingly, by God. By linking Jesus' death to the temple's demise, Mark shows that Jesus' death is not simply that of another prophet or martyr but that of the Son (12:6), and now the owner of the vineyard responds as never before by punishing the wicked tenants and vindicating his Son (12:9).[111]

Mark makes it clear that the judgment upon the temple serves to vindicate Jesus by his use of ναός for the temple in v. 38 – the third and last occurrence of the term. The first use of ναός came in the trial with the accusation that Jesus intended to destroy the temple (ναός) that was "made by hands" and replace it with one "made without hands." The reader knows that Jesus predicted the temple would be destroyed, not that he planned to destroy it himself. The accusation is repeated in the first mocking at the cross, when bystanders deride Jesus for failing to destroy the "temple" (ναός) and build another. Now, at Jesus' death, which his opponents and mockers believe to be the final proof that Jesus cannot destroy the temple or build a new one – a dramatic reversal in the story takes place.[112] With the symbolic destruction of the temple, through the dramatic, eschatological sign of the tearing of the "temple" (ναός) veil, the temple charge (14:58) and mockery (15:29) ironically come true.[113] Juel keenly observes Mark's masterful irony here: "Jesus is the destroyer of the temple in a figurative and in an ironic sense: its destruction is a result of his death, brought about by those in charge of the temple worship."[114] Mark's careful wording of "temple" as ναός helps the reader to see dramatic reversal brought about through the tearing of the "temple" (ναός) veil and the vindication it brings to Jesus.

---

[111] Robert H. Smith observes: "Jesus' suffering is not just the suffering of one more martyr in a long line of martyrdom. Mark 13 indicates that His death has universal significance, ultimate power, cosmic sweep. His death is itself precisely that event which ushers in the last times, inaugurating eschatology" (cited by Allison, *End of the Ages*, 38).

[112] Brown (*Death*, 2. 1099–1100) suggests that God rends the temple veil in response to the blasphemies against his Son, in direct contrast to the high priest's rending of his garments at Jesus' "blasphemy."

[113] Brown (ibid., 1135; see also 1100) believes that Mark carefully uses ναός as a tool to link 14:58; 15:29 with 15:38, thereby illustrating Jesus' vindication: "On the microscale of the PN [Passion Narrative], the mockery during the Sanhedrin trial and on the cross (14:58; 15:29) of Jesus' claim that he would destroy this 'sanctuary' has now been answered, showing that Jesus spoke the truth: The veil that marked off the sanctuary as holy space has been rent from top to bottom into two – there is no longer truly a sanctuary in the Jerusalem Temple, for God is no longer present there."

[114] Juel, *Messiah and Temple*, 206.

Mark's strategic employment of ναός for "temple" in 14:58, 15:29, and 15:38 is reinforced by the fact that Mark follows each use of ναός with the title "Son of God" (14:61; 15:32; 15:39). And just as the third use of ναός brings about the fulfillment of the earlier occurrences where it was used in disbelief, so too the third occurrence of "Son of God" brings about a vindication: the centurion professes that Jesus was truly "the Son of God" (15:39).[115] This vindication motif sheds light on why Mark shifts from ἱερόν to ναός.

### 4.5.5  Which Veil?

The tearing of the veil in 15:38 has often been seen as symbolically opening up access to God's presence, since the veil limited access into the Holy of Holies. However, this interpretation is complicated by the fact that the temple had two major veils: the outer veil that covered the entrance to the "sanctuary" (ναός) proper (Num 3:26), and the inner veil that served as the barrier to the Holy of Holies (Exod 26:33), into which only the high priest could go – and that only on the Day of Atonement. And both the inner and outer veils could be meant by Mark's term, καταπέτασμα. Complicating the issue further is the fact that the temple also had many other curtains.[116] So the perennial question again arises: which veil is torn?

Although it has been generally recognized that the issue cannot be definitively resolved, the majority of commentators believe that Mark is referring to the inner veil. I believe this position is the most tenable for the following reasons:

(1) καταπέτασμα is by far the most frequently used word in the LXX for the inner veil. Although it is true that καταπέτασμα can translate either the Hebrew word for outer veil (מָסָךְ) or inner veil (פָּרֹכֶת), the 39 occurrences of καταπέτασμα in the LXX translate פָּרֹכֶת 32 times, all of which refer to the inner veil.[117] The outer veil (מָסָךְ) is translated by words other than

---

[115] Brown, *Death*, 2. 1100.

[116] Both Exodus 26 and 36 list dozens of veils. For a thorough survey of the different veils and the complexity of this issue, see Brown, ibid., 1109–13.

[117] See Beale, *Temple*, 191 n. 43. Beale is drawing on an unpublished paper by D. M. Gurtner. In my count, καταπέτασμα occurs 39 times in the LXX, and only four of these times does καταπέτασμα possibly refer to the outer veil. Thus, 35 times out of 39 καταπέτασμα refers to the inner veil. What is also interesting is that the four times that καταπέτασμα might refer to the outer veil are all in Exodus (LXX Exod 26:37; 37:5,16; 38:18). Every other use of καταπέτασμα in LXX OT refers only to the inner veil (Exod 27:21; 26:34,35; 26:33[3x]; 26:31; 30:6; 35:12; 37:3; 39:4,19,40; 40:3,5,21,22,26; Lev 4:6,17; 16:2,12,15; 21:23; 24:3; Num 3:10,26; 4:5,32; 18:7; 1 Kgs 6:36; 2 Chr 3:14; 1 Macc 1:22; 4:51; Sir 50:5). Given that the LXX typically refers to the inner veil by

καταπέτασμα in LXX Greek.[118] Given Mark's familiarity with the OT, it is safe to say that he is drawing on the more typical use of καταπέτασμα for the inner curtain.

(2) There are examples of authors who are aware of the plurality of veils in the temple, yet they simply refer to the inner veil with the nominative singular form of καταπέτασμα (e.g., 1 Macc 1:22; 2 Chr 3:14; 1 Kgs 6:36).

(3) The inner veil held the most symbolic value and importance.[119] Many priests and Levites had access beyond the outer veil, but only the high priest could go beyond the inner veil into the Holy of Holies. The outer veil marked the boundary into the holy court, the inner veil into the Holy of Holies, and was therefore more fraught with significance and reverence.

(4) The outer veil stood just outside large doors into the sanctuary, and so even with the loss of the outer curtain the door to the sanctuary would still remain. On the other hand, the only barrier between the holy court and the Holy of Holies was the inner curtain, and its loss would leave the inner sanctuary wide open. Thus, the splitting apart of the inner veil would be far more consequential for the fate of the temple.

(5) Outside of the Gospels, all Christian tradition in the NT concerning the "veil" (καταπέτασμα) in relation to Jesus' death refers solely to the inner veil.[120]

In light of these arguments, and since Mark's reference to the "veil" is not a passing comment but a dramatically symbolic action, it seems that the inner veil is the most likely referent.[121]

---

καταπέτασμα, it seems quite reasonable to assume Mark is following the practice of the LXX.

[118] κάλυμμα (19x), κατακάλυμμα (8x), ἱστίον (7x) and ἐπίσπαστρον (1x) are the four Greek words used to translate מָסָךְ in the LXX. None of these terms ever refers to the inner veil, thereby distinguishing these three terms from καταπέτασμα. See also Brown, *Death*, 2. 1111 n. 29.

[119] See C. Schneider, "καταπέτασμα" (*TDNT*, 3. 628–30).

[120] E.g., Heb 6:19; 9:3; 10:20. The only other use in the NT of καταπέτασμα, besides the three Synoptic accounts, is in Hebrews – all of which refer to the inner veil. That Christian tradition early on saw the veil as the inner one may also be hinted at by the use of ἱλαστήριον (for the כַּפֹּרֶת, e.g., Exod 25:17) in Rom 3:25. See Beale, *Temple*, 191; Lagrange, *Saint Marc*, 436; Brown, *Death*, 2. 1106–8.

[121] Gnilka (*Evangelium Markus*, 2. 323–24) observes that since Mark was most likely written after the destruction of the temple, the tearing of the veil should be seen as signifying both the destruction of the temple and the revelation of God through the new access opened up by Jesus' death. "Das Zerreißen des Tempelvorhangs war insbesondere zwei Interpretationen Zugänglich. Die eine begreift es als Ausdruck dafür, daß mit dem Tod Jesu der Tempel und sein Kult seine Bedeutung verloren hat, zu seinem Ende gekommen und der zerstörung preisgegeben ist... Die andere Interpretation geht davon aus, daß der Vorhang vor dem Allerheiligsten – nur dieser kann wegen seiner kultischen

## 4.5.6   Tearing Apart Heaven and Earth

The juxtaposition between the "tearing" (ἐσχίσθη) of the temple veil at the end of Jesus' life with the "tearing" (σχιζομένους) of the heavens at Jesus' baptism is now widely recognized.[122] However, given the importance of this parallel for Mark's story, it deserves further comment. Why does Mark frame his story of Jesus with these "tearings" motif?

Some scholars have noted that the temple veil was adorned with the image of the stars and constellations.[123] The representation of the heavens upon the temple veils (in both the outer and the inner veils) makes for a striking parallel to the heavens that are torn open in the baptism of Christ.[124] According to Josephus, the curtain was made with four colors that represented the four elements of the universe – earth, air, water, and fire: "Nor was this mixture of colours without its mystical interpretation, but was a kind of image of the universe."[125] The veils in the temple comprised "colours seeming so exactly to resemble those that meet the eye in the heavens."[126] Both the inner and the outer curtains were colored and

---

Bedeutung gemeint sein – die Funktion hatte, die Erscheinung des Herrn zu verhüllen und den Anblick der unverhüllten Majestät Gottes zu verhindern. Dieser Vorhang dient 'als Scheidewand zwischen dem Heiligen und dem Allerheiligsten' (Ex 26:33)... Seine Entfernung wird dann als Eröffnung des Zugangs zu Gott für die Nichtpriester und Heiden oder als Offenbarung der Majestät Gottes verstanden. Eröffnung des Zugangs beziehungsweise Offenbarung Gottes geschehen im Tod Jesu. Beide Interpretationen sind zusammenzunehmen und bilden keinen Gegensatz. Weil die Zerstörung des Tempels schon in Vers 29 zu verstehen gegeben war, muß das Zerreißen des Vorhangs etwas Neues einbringen. Dies ist der Gedanke, daß sich Gott im Kreuz seines Sohnes enthüllt und für die Heiden zugänglich wird." I agree with Gnilka; the tearing of the veil, for Mark, embraces both the negative meaning of the temple's destruction and is also a positive sign of the openness to a new intimacy and revelation of God. Similarly Lührmann, *Markusevangelium*, 264; Hooker, *Mark*, 378; and Matera (*Kingship*, 139) who likewise observes, "The tearing of the temple curtain is a rich image with both positive and negative poles."

[122] E.g., Moloney, *Mark*, 328; Evans, *Mark*, 509; Brown, *Death*, 2. 1134–35; Marshall, *Faith as a Theme*, 207; Motyer, "Reading the Veil," 155; Matera, *Kingship*, 139.

[123] "When, however, it is remembered from the Old Testament and early Judaism that on the veil was embroidery of the starry heavens, its tearing would be an apt symbol of the beginning destruction, not only of the temple (which itself even as a whole symbolized the cosmos) but of the very cosmos itself" (Beale, *Temple*, 189).

[124] Edwards, *Mark*, 479.

[125] Josephus, *War* 5.5.4 §§212–13. See also *Ant.* 3.7.7 §§181–83. Philo also saw the Temple and the curtain as a microcosm of the cosmos. "In its whole it is a copy and representation of the world; and the parts are a representation of the separate parts of the world" (*Mos.* 2.24 §117) .

[126] Josephus, *Ant.* 3.132. *Ant.* 3.6.7. §§181–83; *War* 5.5.4 §§212–13.

adorned with the heavens.[127] Indeed, for both Philo and Josephus the temple represented the cosmos.[128]

It is important to ask whether Mark would have been aware of the cosmic significance of the temple and the veil and whether Mark would have thought his audience capable of making such an interpretation. First, what is the likelihood of Mark being aware of the cosmic symbolism of the veil? Brown pointedly asks: "More radically, what assurance do we have that the evangelists knew about the number of veils, or details about them and their symbolism?"[129] Given Mark's extensive use of the OT traditions in his Gospel and his choice of καταπέτασμα rather than the four other Greek terms for the outer veil and various curtains, it seems safe to assume that Mark chose the term used in the LXX for the inner veil. It must be remembered that the inner veil is mentioned in LXX approximately 39 times throughout a wide variety of books. Thus, the reader of the LXX would most likely come away with an association of "veil" (καταπέτασμα) with the inner veil – the most important veil related to the temple.

Therefore, I think Brown is understating the case for the inner veil when he observes that "vocabulary, then, slightly favors interpreting the Synoptic reference to the *katapetasma* as having the inner veil in mind (if specificity was intended)."[130] Could Mark's readers have known this? Brown again puts the question forcefully: "How widely were esoteric interpretations of the veils known? Still more radically, is there any likelihood that the readers of the Gospel would have known about all this?"[131] Mark makes many allusions to the OT, and these questions could be applied to any single use he makes. It is evident that Mark makes many overtures to Israel's Scripture traditions, both overt and subtle, and so from the perspective of Mark's ideal reader, we would have to conclude that they would recognize καταπέτασμα as the inner veil, and that it was of great importance.

It should also be remembered that Mark's Gospel was not "published" for a general audience like modern publications, but rather it would be read

---

[127] Philo, *Mos.* 2.17–18 §§84–88: See the discussion in Brown, *Death*, 2. 1112.

[128] "The highest, and in the truest sense the holy, temple of God is, as we must believe, the whole universe, having for its sanctuary the most sacred part of all existence, even heaven, for its votive ornaments the stars, for its priests the angels" (Philo, *Spec.* 1.12 §66). For two recent accounts of Philo's and Josephus' view of the temple as a microcosm of the cosmos, see Robert A. Briggs, *Jewish Temple Imagery in the Book of Revelation* (SBL 10; New York: Peter Lang, 1999) 202–13; Beale, *Temple*, 29–80, esp. 45–48.

[129] Brown, *Death*, 2.1113.

[130] Ibid., 1111.

[131] Ibid., 1113.

within the Christian community.[132] It may not be too bold to assume that the community could interpret the meaning of the veil, without asserting that every individual would have arrived at this conclusion independently. Moreover, Mark's mention of the veil without explanation points in this direction.

The juxtaposition of the tearing of the veil with the tearing of the heavens at the baptism is a strong clue that Mark knew of these connections. It appears that the heavens and the temple veil are parallel in Mark's narrative. Philo and Josephus both see the temple veil as signifying the heavens, and therefore they may point to a view of the temple veil that would help explain why Mark made this connection in the first place.

The question must still be pressed: how does this parallel serve Mark's story? In other words, what, according to Mark, is the significance of the heavens being torn – first at Jesus' baptism, and then symbolically through the rending of the temple veil? I suggest that, in Mark's view, Jesus' ministry, which begins with his baptism at the Jordan and climaxes with his death on the cross – events designated by the two "tearings" – ushers in the end of the old creation.

This is the key to deciphering why the Mount of Olives discourse (Mark 13) takes up both the end of the temple and the end of Jesus – the eschatological tribulation that will usher in the end of the temple begins with the tribulation that brings about Jesus' death.[133] In other words, Mark is at pains to show that eschatology is centered and unleashed in Jesus' passion, not the destruction of the temple. The thrust of his narrative, I believe, tears down the idea that eschatology is centered on the Jerusalem temple. Rather, the cross, not Jerusalem's temple, is the "ground zero" for eschatology. The tribulation and destruction of the temple is, from Mark's perspective, the inevitable "aftershock" of the real eschatological event –

---

[132] Marcus (*The Way of the Lord*, 45) makes the observation that Mark's community must have had members who were very capable at interpreting the OT: "Mark's community, on the evidence of our findings in this chapter, is one that contains at least some readers who have a deep interest in and knowledge of the Old Testament. Their scriptural study may not be as formalized as that of Qumran, where no assemblage of ten community members at any time of night or day took place unaccompanied by exegesis (1QS 6:6–7), but they still live in an atmosphere steeped in the scriptures, and they can be expected to fill in from those scriptures Mark's bare-bones descriptions of the ministries of John the Baptist and Jesus."

[133] Allison (*End of the Ages*, 36–39) argues that Mark recounts the passion narrative as the fulfillment of the eschatological discourse. According to Allison, the eschatological tribulation holds the death of Jesus and the destruction of the temple together.

the death of Jesus. This is why Mark is careful to show that it is Jesus' death that inaugurates the temple's destruction.

The cosmic symbolism of the temple veil discloses another important insight into the Mount of Olives discourse. The mixture of the end-of-the-world symbolism with the destruction of the temple and Jesus' own tribulation is rather puzzling unless the world, the temple, and Jesus himself are seen as congruent entities. The temple veil and its correspond-dence to the heavens is the Rosetta Stone for deciphering this. As shown earlier, the temple was, in its architecture and biblical as well as later Jewish tradition, seen as a microcosm of the cosmos.[134] The destruction of the temple bodes ill for that which it represented. To destroy the temple is to destroy the world symbolically. The radical twist Mark puts to this is the idea that Jesus is also a temple, indeed the prototype and the microcosm of the temple. Therefore, the death of Jesus signals the end of the temple (Mark 15:38), which in turn signals the end of the age. Although this last point may seem overstated from our modern perspective, is this not what Mark is hinting at with the image of eschatological darkness (15:33)? The point is even clearer in 1:10: the heavens are rent apart and the old creation is moving toward its end.

The thesis that Mark sees Jesus as setting off an eschatological chain of events that ushers out the old creation is strengthened by the new creation imagery of the "temple made without hands" ($\dot{\alpha}\chi\epsilon\iota\rho o\pi o\acute{\iota}\eta\tau o\varsigma$). If Jesus' death signifies the end of the temple and thus of the world, then the idea that Jesus is the cornerstone of a new temple likewise points to the renewal of creation.[135] Since the new creation is a familiar theme in the restoration oracles of the prophetic tradition and a common motif in NT writings and early Christianity, such an idea would not be foreign to Mark and his audience. The use of "made without hands" in the rest of the NT carries the sense (sometimes explicitly) of a new creation. For example, in the later

---

[134] Thus Ben Meyer (*Christus Faber: The Master-Builder and the House of God* [Allison Park, PA: Pickwick, 1992] 246) believes that all the Jewish temple symbolism made manifest that the earthly temple represented both the heavens and the earth: "In sum, temple symbols suggest that the temple itself is not only an anitype modeled on the heavenly temple (1 Chron 18:11f. ), but represents the world itself in essence."

[135] "Furthermore, in the light of the eschatological context projected by Jesus' whole career, we should accent the symbolism of the temple as the epitome of the universe, the navel and sanctuary not of Israel alone but of the whole world. Jesus' action accordingly said: 'I have come to purify and renew not only the temple but Israel, not only Israel but the world'" (Ben Meyer, *The Early Christians: Their World Mission and Self-Discovery* [GNS 16; Wilmington: Michael Glazier, 1986] 64). For Meyer, since the temple represents the world, its renewal must point to the renewal of the world and thus a new creation.

tradition found in the letter to the Hebrews, the temple that is made with hands "is a symbol of the present age" (Heb 9:9), whereas the heavenly sanctuary, "not made with hands, that is, not of this creation" refers to a new creation (Heb 9:11). Mark has described the end of the temple with eschatological language, and Jesus' death is likewise colored by eschatological imagery, such as the "darkness" over the land (Mark 15:33). If it were true that the Jerusalem temple represented the present age and the cosmos, then its destruction would foreshadow the eschatological end of the age and the cosmos. Along similar lines, Mark has portrayed the new temple Jesus is to build "within three days" as "made without hands," signifying a new creation.[136] Therefore, Jesus' death and resurrection constitute the turn of the ages – the end of one age (old creation) and the beginning of another (new creation).

### 4.5.7   The Centurion's Confession (v. 39)

Following the description of the tearing of the temple veil, Mark informs the reader that the centurion "saw" (ἰδών) Jesus breathe his last, and responded with a confession that serves as the climax of Mark's Gospel (v. 39). The structure of the sentence accentuates the "seeing" (ἰδών) of the centurion: ἰδὼν δὲ ὁ κεντυρίων ὁ παρεστηκὼς ἐξ ἐναντίας αὐτοῦ ὅτι οὕτως ἐξέπνευσεν εἶπεν· ἀληθῶς οὗτος ὁ ἄνθρωπος υἱὸς θεοῦ ἦν. The prominence Mark gives to "seeing" in the account of the centurion's confession is designed to contrast that of (1) Jesus' mockers, who demanded that they "see" (ἴδωμεν) him come down from the cross so that they may believe (15:32);[137] and (2) those who were mistaken in thinking that Jesus was crying out for Elijah and waited to "see" (ἴδωμεν) if Elijah would save him (15:36).[138] The "seeing" in vv. 32 and 36 triggers Mark's motif of "understanding" – they fail to understand who Jesus is. In stark contrast to those mocking Jesus, the centurion "sees" (ἰδών) and understands who Jesus is – "the Son of God," υἱὸς θεοῦ.[139]

Mark's "seeing"/"understanding" theme was initiated by Jesus' teaching in parables, interpreted through Isa 6:9–10, where the reader was told that many "may look and see but not perceive, and may indeed hear but not understand" (Mark 4:12). The irony, of course, is that the chief priests and those who mock Jesus see and hear him but fail to understand, whereas a

---

[136] Walker, *Holy City*, 10.

[137] See Howard M. Jackson, "The Death of Jesus in Mark and the Miracle from the Cross," *NTS* 33 (1987) 16–37, here 20.

[138] Moloney, *Mark*, 329.

[139] John Paul Heil, "The Progressive Narrative Pattern of Mark 14:53–16:8," *Bib* 73 (1992) 331–58, 349.

Gentile centurion sees and understands. In a narrative where even the disciples often fail to understand Jesus, the profession of faith from this Gentile soldier indeed stands out.

This theme of "seeing"/"hearing"/"understanding" also played a key part in Mark's eschatological discourse (Mark 13:7,14), where it borrows from the Danielic theme of "understanding" the "end." The eschatological vindication of the Son of Man comes with "seeing" (ὄψονται, Mark 13:26), later emphasized in Jesus' dramatic answer to the high priest at the trial (ὄψεσθε, 14:62).[140] This Markan "seeing" is eschatologlical.[141] The important text of Isaiah 56, which called the temple a "house of prayer for all nations," is now seen in light of the centurion's confession as a text that is vital to Mark's story. Jesus judged the temple for failing to be "a house of prayer for all nations" (Isa 56:7; Mark 11:17), thus not realizing its eschatological goal – the inclusion of the Gentiles. Now, after the symbolic destruction of the Jerusalem temple in 15:38 through the tearing of the veil, the first of the Gentiles makes a profession of faith in Jesus, thereby inaugurating the eschatological ingathering of the nations.[142] The gospel going out to the nations was part of Mark's account of the eschatological end of the temple in Mark 13. Given the prominence of the Gentile inclusion in Israel's worship, evident in the restoration oracles of the prophets (notably Isaiah 66), the centurion's acclamation must be seen as much as an eschatological event as the darkness (15:33) and the tearing of the veil (15:38).[143]

In the eschatological discourse it was foretold that, when the Son of Man was "seen," the ingathering of the elect would begin (Mark 13:26–27). Through the centurion's discerning sight, Mark puts forward Jesus' death as the focal point for ingathering of the nations. The centurion is symbolic; he represents the "nations."[144] Thus, for Mark, Jesus fulfills the

---

[140] Donahue (*Are You the Christ?* 204) explains the eschatological nature of "seeing" in Mark by noting the intratextuality of this key word, "recalling that the forms of the verb 'to see' in Mark are used in primary reference to the 'seeing' of Jesus at the parousia, we would suggest that Mark introduces the verb *idōn* at this point precisely to make of the centurion's confession a symbolic presentation of the parousia confession."

[141] Harry Chronis ("The Torn Veil: Cultus and Christology in Mark 15:37–39," *JBL* 101 [1982] 97–114, here 109) notes the eschatological import of this passage, "The use in 15:39 of ἰδεῖν, is a distinctively Marcan term for eschatological insight" (p. 109). See also Donahue, *Are You the Christ?* 204.

[142] See, e.g., Swartley, *Israel's Scripture Traditions*, 168; Beale, *Temple*, 191.

[143] For a discussion on how the centurion manifests the Markan notion of faith, see Marshall, *Faith as a Theme*, 206–7.

[144] "Whatever the centurion might have meant, for Mark this is the climax of the recognition of Jesus. At the depth of his passion a centurion made what for Mark was the most perceptive confession (see 1.1,11; 9.7; [14.61] 15.39). The centurion then represents

eschatological purpose of the temple through his death (and ensuing resurrection) thereby gathering the nations in faith.[145] Hence, Jesus becomes the new eschatological temple that sets in motion the restoration of Israel that includes the ingathering of the Gentiles. On the cross, Jesus becomes the cornerstone of the new temple, which is "marvelous in our eyes" (ἔστιν θαυμαστὴ ἐν ὀφθαλμοῖς ἡμῶν, 12:11).

The centurion's confession of Jesus' sonship matches the proclamation of Jesus' sonship by the Father from heaven at the beginning of the Gospel.[146] The tearing of the heavens at Jesus baptism allowed the reader to view the revelation from heaven about the truth of who Jesus is. Now, at the end of the story the tearing of the temple veil allows the centurion to grasp what the reader was privileged to know at the outset, that Jesus is God's Son. This confession serves to confirm the announcement of Jesus' sonship made by the Father; even despite – or rather in – his death Jesus still is the Son of God.[147] Thus, the tearing motif is vital to Mark's narrative since it frames the story of Jesus and points to the revelation of who Jesus is. The tearing of the veil, however inherently destructive such an act may seem, serves to confirm Mark's portrait of Jesus.

## 4.6 Conclusion

The temple theme in Mark is deeply eschatological. Jesus condemned the Jerusalem temple for failing in its vocation to be a house of prayer for all nations (Mark 11:17). The actions and teaching of Jesus against the temple

---

the mission to the nations (13.10), where the true confession of faith first finds expression in association with the mystery of the crucified Messiah" (Painter, *Mark*, 207).

[145] "If we return to Mark 14:58, the positive image of Jesus' *building* another sanctuary not made by hand would not make us think of a heavenly sanctuary, for surely that has existed timelessly. Mark is more likely depicting replacement by a sanctuary consisting of believers, as in other NT passages that imagine a Temple of living stones. In that interpretation Mark 15:39 would be showing the first new believer after the death of Jesus and thus the commencement of the building of another sanctuary" (Brown, *Death*, 2. 1109).

[146] Matera, *Kingship*, 139; Painter, *Mark*, 207; Nineham, *Mark*, 431.

[147] Kent E. Brower ("Temple and Eschatology in Mark," in *Eschatology in Bible and Theology* [ed. Kent E. Brower and Mark Elliott; Downers Grove, IL: Inter Varsity, 1999] 133) notes that the centurion's confession functions in the narrative as a confirmation of Jesus' identity and mission: "This time, however, the confession is not the prospective announcement by God stating Jesus' being and mission, but the retrospective confirmation that Jesus has been precisely the Son of God in the whole gospel story and supremely so in the death scene."

(Mark 11–12) provoke questions regarding the time of its destruction and the signs that would accompany the time of its doom (13:1–4). Much of the language and imagery applied to the end of the temple in Mark 13 is interwoven throughout the account of Jesus' passion and death. The four watches in the parable of the master's sudden return structures Mark's telling of Jesus' last night, thus designating it as the fateful eschatological night. The handing over of Jesus, with its echoes to Daniel and the eschatological discourse, ushers in the "hour" of the eschaton – an unknown time in Mark 13. With the arrival of the "hour" in Gethsemane, the reader is led into Jesus' passion, knowing that this is the tribulation that will usher in the end of the temple.

Both the Last Supper and the trial narrative take up the theme of temple replacement. By paralleling the preparations for Jesus' entry into the temple and the preparations for the Last Supper, Mark puts forward Jesus' offering of his body and blood – the elements of the Passover meal – as an alternative to the temple cult. This conflict between Jesus and the established cult fuels the initial charge against Jesus at his trial. The subtle description of the Jerusalem temple as one "made with hands" – albeit from the mouth of one of Jesus' accusers – suggests that the Jerusalem temple has degenerated not only into a "den of robbers" but a kind of pagan idol as well. With possible echoes to Daniel 2, Mark suggests that Jesus will usher in a new temple, the eschatological temple identified with the kingdom of God and Mount Zion.

The conflict between Jesus and the temple, further heightened through the ironic charge of the false witnesses, comes to a final head at the cross. Jesus is mocked for prophesying the imminent end of the Jerusalem temple. The failure of his ridiculers to truly "see" and "understand" the eschatological fulfillment revealed through Jesus' death stands in contrast to the Gentile soldier who "sees" Jesus for who he really is – the Son of God. Together with the eschatological darkness and the tearing of the temple veil, the centurion's confession points to Jesus' death as the inauguration of the new eschatological temple. The old creation comes to an end, and – as Mark has hinted – within three days, the new creation "made without hands" (14:58) will arise, vindicating the Son of Man.

Chapter 5

# Final Conclusion

The temple plays a vital role in the plot of Mark's gospel and is deeply connected to the story of Jesus. It serves as the stage for the Markan Jesus' conflict with the Jewish authorities, and moreover it is the vital reference point for the narrative portrait of Jesus' identity, mission, and eschatological message. From the moment of Jesus' entry into Jerusalem (Mark 11), the temple is almost always present in the story, whether as the location of Jesus' teaching (Mark 12), the subject of his eschatological discourse (Mark 13), or the basis of the charge at his trial (14:58) and the point of mockery on the cross, and even in the account of Jesus' death the temple seems to be ever present in Mark's story of Jesus.

In the first chapter, I illustrated Mark's careful anticipation of Jesus entry. The significant Markan motif of the "way," drawn from Isaiah's picture of the Lord's return to Zion, leads not to the cross but rather into the temple area. Thus, the Markan "way" follows Isaiah and perhaps Malachi as well in their story of God's return to the temple. Therefore, Mark's account of Jesus making his way to the temple area is seen as the Lord's eschatological return to the temple. Jesus' arrival brings judgment (as his citation of Jer 7:11 illustrates) and points to the eschatological purpose of the temple (demonstrated by the citation from Isa 56:7). The temple demonstration points to the eschatological nature of Jesus' mission: to usher in judgment for the temple's failure to fulfill its eschtolgoical mission to restore Israel and gather the nations. In the second chapter the theme of a new eschatological temple was examined. The call for Jesus' community to be and to do what the temple was called to be – through faith, prayer, and forgiveness – points to the community gathered around Jesus as a new temple. The questions surrounding Jesus' authority and teaching concerning the temple lead to the parable of the wicked tenants. This story again points, albeit cryptically, to Jesus as the cornerstone of the new temple, the "building" of which is in some way related to his rejection and resurrection. The mention of the rejected cornerstone of Psalm 118 evokes the initial rejection of the second temple in the time of Ezra. By his use of this text, Mark may be suggesting that the establishment of a new temple is met with rejection, but God will again vindicate the cornerstone. The challenge of Jesus' authority becomes a teaching moment that leads to deeper insight into Jesus' identity: heir of the vineyard (temple). This identity, as the owner's son, justifies his authority over the temple in Jerusalem and points forward to his inauguration of a new eschatological temple.

The third chapter focused on Jesus' departure from the temple and subsequent discourse on the Mount of Olives where he speaks of the temple's imminent end. Saturated with echoes and allusions to the OT as well as to the political turmoil surrounding the destruction of the temple, Mark 13 is often viewed as a diverse and loose collection of eschatological sayings. Teasing out the various OT texts and contexts employed in this chapter, however, pointed to a deeper unity behind this chapter than first appears. An examination of these OT texts suggests that a striking pattern stands behind their use by Mark. The vast majority of the texts are drawn from the traditions of prophetic eschatology and, moreover, from oracles specifically aimed at the judgment of Jerusalem and the temple, as well as texts that point to the eschatological restoration of Israel and the gathering of the nations. This pattern sheds light on Mark's purpose behind this discourse and his heavy reliance on OT texts in putting forth the eschatological message of the Markan Jesus. In short, Mark is recounting the life and passion of Jesus in a way that aims to show how Jesus ushered in the beginning of the eschatological end time. A pivotal moment in the plot line of this prophetic eschatology is the great tribulation, the turning point between judgment and restoration. It is precisely this tribulation that becomes the focal point of Mark's eschatological portrait. Why the sharp focus on the tribulation? The answer is found in Mark's account of Jesus' passion and death.

The final chapter traced the eschatological nature of Mark's narrative portrait of Jesus' passion. The connection between the tribulation announced in Mark 13 and Jesus' tribulation and death is carefully made by the way Mark tells the story of Jesus. The scene at Gethsemane, as well as the Passover meal, illustrate that the eschatological "hour" of "testing" (πειρασμός), that is, the great tribulation, has finally arrived and is come upon Jesus. The trial of Jesus brings up the temple motif that is taken up by those who mock Jesus as he suffers on the cross. The eschatological signs accompanying Jesus death remind the reader that the suffering of Jesus is the long-dreaded tribulation. The reader is reminded not only of Jesus' passion predictions that all point toward resurrection but also of the many narrative hints that a new temple would soon arise. Following the plot of prophetic eschatology, the tribulation must lead to restoration, and the confession of the centurion manifests that Jesus' death immediately ushers in the eschatological restoration, as a representative of the Gentiles gives the climactic confession that Jesus is God's Son. The tearing of the veil ties Jesus' fate to that of the temple and shows that the death of Jesus leads to its end. This old temple will be replaced by a new one consisting of those who, like the centurion, put their faith in the rejected-yet-vindicated cornerstone of God's new eschatological temple, Jesus.

This study may point to several significant implications. The first is methodological. Mark's use of intertextuality, particularly in relation to a key theme such as the "way," is often carefully interwoven into his narrative, giving play to many intratextual allusions. Granted the many examples of this particular style, it is well worth pursuing the relationship between Mark's intratextuality and his intertextuality. Second, Mark's predilection for OT texts that embody prophetic eschatology sheds much light on the meaning and purpose of Mark's eschatology. This has many implications for understanding Mark 13 and NT eschatology. Moreover, since the eschatological hope for restoration seems to be a controlling idea for Mark's story, a further study into the restoration motif in the rest of the Gospel of Mark is certainly worth pursuing. Although speculative, the suggested connection between the temple and cosmology may be worth further exploration and may shed light on the apparent link between Mark's language for the end of the temple and the end of the age. Third, the connections between the eschatological discourse and the account of Jesus' passion may have important implications for interpreting the evangelist's understanding of Jesus' death and resurrection. Finally, given the prominent role the temple plays in Mark's narrative, the temple's possible importance for a Roman audience merits further investigation in discussions of the *Sitz im Leben* of Mark's Gospel.

# Bibliography

Ådna, J. "Jesu Kritik am Tempel: Eine Untersuchung zum Verlauf und Sinn der sogenannten Tempelreinigung Jesu, Markus 11,15–17 und Parallelen." Ph.D. diss., University of Oslo, 1993.

Allison, Dale C. *The End of the Ages Has Come: An Early Interpretation of the Passion and Resurrection.* Philadelphia: Fortress, 1985.

–. *Jesus of Nazareth: Millenarian Prophet.* Philadelphia: Fortress, 1998.

–. "Jesus and the Victory of Apocalyptic." In *Jesus and the Restoration of Israel: A Critical Assessment of N. T. Wright's Jesus and the Victory of God.* Ed. Carey C. Newman. Downers Grove, IL: IVP, 1999. Pp. 126–41.

Anderson, H. "The Old Testament in Mark's Gospel." In *The Use of the Old Testament in the New and Other Essays: Studies in Honor of William Franklin Stinespring.* E.d., J. M. Efird. Durham: Duke University Press, 1972.

Antwi, Daniel J. "Did Jesus Consider His Death to Be an Atoning Sacrifice?" *Interpretation,* 45 (1991) 17–28.

Aune, David E. "Early Christian Eschatology." *ABD.* Ed. David Noel Freedman. New York: Doubleday, 1992) 2. 597–605.

Aus, R.D. *The Wicked Tenants and Gethsemane: Isaiah in the Wicked Tenants' Vineyard, and Moses and the High Priest in Gethsemane: Judaic Traditions in Mark 12:1–9 and 14:32–42.* University of South Florida International Studies in Formative Christianity and Judaism 4. Atlanta: Scholars Press, 1996.

Bailey, Kenneth. "The Fall of Jerusalem and Mark's Account of the Cross." *ExpTim* 102 (1991) 102–5.

Balabanski, Vicky. *Eschatology in the Making: Mark, Matthew, and the Didache.* SNTS 97. New York: Cambridge University Press, 1997.

Barclay, W. *The Lord's Supper.* Nashville: Abingdon, 1967.

Bauckham, Richard. *The Gospels for All Christians: Rethinking the Gospel Audiences.* Grand Rapids: Eerdmans, 1998.

Baumgarten, J. M. "4Q500 and the Ancient Conception of the Lord's Vineyard." *JJS* 40 (1989) 1–6.

Beale, G. K. *The Temple and the Church's Mission: A Biblical Theology of the Dwelling Place of God.* NSBT. Downer's Grove, IL: IVP, 2004.

Beasley-Murray, George R. *Jesus and the Last Days.* Peabody, MA: Hendrickson, 1993.

Best, Ernest. "Discipleship in Mark: Mark 8:22–10:52." *SJT* 23 (1970) 223–37.

–. *Following Jesus: Discipleship in the Gospel of Mark.* JSNTSup 4. Sheffield: JSOT, 1981.

Black, M. C. "The Rejected and Slain Messiah Who is Coming with the Angels: The Messianic Exegesis of Zechariah 9–14 in the Passion Narratives." Ph.D. diss., Emory University, 1990.

Bock, Darrel L. *Blasphemy and Exaltation in Judaism: The Charge against Jesus in Mark 14:53–65.* Grand Rapids: Baker, 2000.

Borg, Marcus J. *Conflict, Holiness, and Politics in the Teachings of Jesus.* Harrisburg, PA: Trinity, 1984.

Breytenbach, C. *Nachfolge und Zukunftserwartung nach Markus: eine methoden-kritische Studie.* Zürich: Theologischer Verlag, 1984.

Briggs, Robert A. *Jewish Temple Imagery in the Book of Revelation.* SBL 10. New York: Peter Lang, 1999.

Broadhead, Edwin K. *Naming Jesus: Titular Christology in the Gospel of Mark.* JSNTSup 175. Sheffield: Sheffield Academic Press, 1999.

–. "Which Mountain Is 'This Mountain?'" *Paradigms* 2:1 (1986) 33–38.

Brower, Kent E. "Temple and Eschatology in Mark." In *Eschatology in Bible and Theology.* Ed. Kent E. Brower and Mark Elliott. Downers Grove, IL: IVP, 1999. Pp. 119–43.

Brown, Raymond E. *The Death of the Messiah.* New York: Doubleday, 1994.

–. *An Introduction to the New Testament.* New York: Doubleday, 1997.

Bryan, Steven M. *Jesus and Israel's Traditions of Judgment and Restoration.* SNTS 117. Cambridge: Cambridge University Press, 2002.

Buchanan, G. W. "Mark 11:15–19: Brigands in the Temple," *HUCA* 30 (1959) 169–77.

–. "Symbolic Money-Changers in the Temple?" *NTS* 37 (1991) 280–90.

Carrol, John T. "Eschatology," In *Eerdmans Dictionary of the Bible.* Ed. David Noel Freedman. Grand Rapids: Eerdmans, 2000. Pp. 420–22.

Casey, M. *Aramaic Sources of Mark's Gospel.* SNTSM 102. Cambridge: Cambridge University Press, 1998.

Charlesworth, James H. *The Old Testament Pseudepigrapha.* New York: Doubleday, 1983.

–. "The Son of David: Solomon and Jesus." In *The New Testament and Hellenistic Judaism.* Eds. P. Borgen and S. Giversen. Peabody, MA: Hendrickson, 1997. Pp. 72–87.

Childs, Brevard. *Isaiah.* OTL. Louisville, KY: Westminster John Knox, 2001.

Chilton, Bruce. "Jesus *ben David*: Reflections on the *Davidssohnfrage*." *JSNT* 14 (1982) 88–112.

–. *The Temple of Jesus: His Sacrificial Program within a Cultural History of Sacrifice.* University Park, PA: Pennsylvania State University Press, 1992.

Chronis, Harry L. "The Torn Veil: Cultus and Christology in Mark 15:37–39." *JBL* 101 (1982) 97–114.

Cousar, C. B. "Eschatology and Mark's *Theologia Crucis*: A Critical Analysis of Mark 13." *Int* 24 (1970) 321–35.

Cranfield, C. E. B. "The Baptism of Our Lord: A Study of St. Mark 1:9–12." *SJT* 7 (1955) 53–63.

Cross, F. M. *Canaanite Myth and Hebrew Epic: Essays in the History of the Religion of Israel.* Cambridge: Harvard University Press, 1973.

Davies, W. D. and Dale C. Allison, *Matthew.* 3 vols. ICC. Edinburgh: T & T Clark, 1988, 1991, 1997.

Derrett, J. D. M. "The Stone That the Builders Rejected." *Studies in the New Testament.* Leiden: Brill, 1977. Pp. 112–17.

–. "The Zeal of the House and the Cleansing of the Temple." *Downside Review* 95 (1977) 79–94.

Dewey, Joanna. *Markan Public Debate: Literary Technique, Concentric Structure, and Theology in Mark 2:1–3:6.* SBLDS 48. Chico: Scholars, 1980.

–. "Mark as Interwoven Tapestry: Forecasts and Echoes for a Listening Audience." *CBQ* 53 (1991) 221–36.

Dodd, C. H. *According to the Scriptures.* London: Nisbet, 1952.

Donahue, John R. *Are You the Christ?* SBLDS 10. New York, 1973.

–. "Temple, Trial, and Royal Christology," In *The Passion in Mark: Studies on Mark 14–16.* Ed. W. Kelber. Philadelphia: Fortress, 1976. Pp. 61–79.

–. *The Gospel in Parable: Metaphor, Narrative, and Theology in the Synoptic Gospels.* Philadelphia: Fortress, 1990.

–. "The Quest for the Community of Mark's Gospel." In *The Four Gospels.* Ed. Frans van Segbroeck et al. Leuven: Leuven University Press, 1992.

Donahue, John R. and Daniel J. Harrington. *The Gospel of Mark.* SacPag. Collegeville, MN: Liturgical Press, 2002.

Dowd, Sharyn E. *Prayer, Power, and the Problem of Suffering: Mark 11:22–25 in the context of Markan Theology.* SBLDS 105. Atlanta: Scholars, 1988.

–. *Reading Mark: A Literary and Theological Commentary on the Second Gospel.* Macon, GA: Smyth and Helwys, 2000.

Dowda, R.E. "The Cleansing of the Temple in the Synoptic Gospels." Ph.D. diss., Duke University, 1972.

Dubis, Mark. "Messianic Woes." *Eerdmans Dictionary of the Bible.* Grand Rapids: Eerdmans, 2000. 890–91.

Dyer, Keith D. *The Prophecy on the Mount: Mark 13 and the Gathering of the New Community.* New York: Peter Lang, 1998.

Edwards, James. *The Gospel According to Mark.* Grand Rapids: Eerdmans, 2002.

Evans, Craig. "On the Vineyard Parables of Isaiah 5 and Mark 12." *BZ* 28 (1984) 82–86.

–. "Jesus' Action in the Temple: Cleansing or Portent of Destruction?" *CBQ* 51 (1989) 237–70.

–. *Jesus and His Contemporaries.* Boston: Brill, 2001.

–. *Mark 8:27–16:20.* WBC 34B. Nashville: Thomas Nelson, 2001.

Ford, D. *The Abomination of Desolation in Biblical Eschatology.* Washington, DC., 1979.

Ford, M. J. "Money Bags in the Temple (Mk. 11, 16)." *Bib* 57 (1976) 249–53.

Fowler, Robert M. *Let the Reader Understand: Reader-Response Criticism and the Gospel of Mark.* Minneapolis: Fortress, 1991.

France, R. T. *Jesus and the Old Testament.* London: Tyndale, 1971.

–. *The Gospel of Mark.* NIGTC. Grand Rapids: Eerdmans, 2002.

Fredriksen, Paula. "Jesus and the Temple, Mark and the War." *SBL 1990 Seminar Papers.* SBLSP 29. Ed. David J. Lull. Atlanta: Scholars Press (1990) 293–310.

Gaston, Lloyd. *No Stone on Another: Studies in the Significance of the Fall of Jerusalem in the Synopic Gospels.* NovTSup 23. Leiden: Brill, 1970.

Geddert, Timothy J. *Watchwords: Mark 13 in Markan Eschatology.* JSNTSup. Sheffield: JSOT, 1989.

–. *Mark.* Scottdale, PA: Herald, 2001.

Glazier-McDonald, Beth. *Malachi: The Divine Messenger.* Atlanta: Scholars Press, 1987.

Gnilka, Joachim. *Das Evangelium nach Markus* 2. EKK 2. Zürich: Benzinger/ Neukirchen-Vluyn: Neukirchener Verlag, 1979.

Gray, A. "The Parable of the Wicked Husbandmen (Matthew xxi. 33–41; Mark xii. 1–9; Luke xx. 9–16)." *HibJ* 19 (1920–21) 42–52.

Gray, John. *The Biblical Doctrine of the Reign of God.* Dulles, VA: T & T Clark, 2000.

Guelich, Robert A. *Mark 1–8:26.* WBC 34a. Dallas: Word Books, 1989.

Gundry, Robert H. *Mark: A Commentary on His Apology for the Cross.* Grand Rapids: Eerdmans, 1993.

Hartman, Lars. *Prophecy Interpreted: The Formation of Some Jewish Apocalytic Texts and of the Eschatological Discourse Mark 13 Par.* ConBNT 1. Lund: Gleerup, 1966.

Harvey, A. E. *Jesus and the Constraints of History.* London: Duckworth, 1982.

Hatina, Thomas R. *In Search of a Context: The Function of Scripture in Mark's Narrative.* JSNTS 232. New York: Sheffield Academic Press, 2002.

Hay, David M. *Glory at the Right Hand: Psalm 110 in Early Christianity.* New York: Abingdon, 1973.

Hays, Richard B. *Echoes of Scripture in the Letters of Paul.* New Haven: Yale University, 1989.
–. *The Conversion of the Imagination: Paul as Interpreter of Israel's Scripture.* Grand Rapids: Eerdmans, 2005.
Hayward, C. T. R. *The Jewish Temple.* New York: Routledge, 1996.
Hayward, Robert. *The Targum of Jeremiah.* The Aramaic Bible 12. Wilmington: Glazier, 1987.
Heil, John Paul. "The Narrative Strategy and Pragmatics of the Temple Theme in Mark." *CBQ* 59 (1997) 76–100.
–. "The Progressive Narrative Pattern of Mark 14:53–16:8." *Bib* 73 (1992) 331–58.
Hengel, Martin. *Studies in the Gospel of Mark.* London: SCM, 1985.
Hiers, Richard H. "Eschatology." In *Harper Collins Bible Dictionary.* Ed. Paul J. Actemeier. San Francisco: Harper Collins, 1996. Pp. 275–77.
Holmén, Tom. *Jesus and Jewish Covenant Thinking.* Boston: Brill, 2001.
Hooker, Morna. "Trial and Tribulation in Mark XIII." *BJRL* 65: n. 1 (1982) 78–99.
–. "Traditions about the Temple in the Sayings of Jesus." *BJRL* 70 (1988) 7–19.
–. *The Gospel According to Saint Mark.* Peabody, MA: Hendrickson, 1991.
–. *The Signs of a Prophet: The Prophetic Actions of Jesus.* Harrisburg, PA: Trinity, 1997.
Horne, Edward H. "The Parable of the Tenants as Indictment." *JSNT* 71 (1998) 111–16.
Horsley, Richard A. *Hearing the Whole Story: The Politics of Plot in Mark's Gospel.* Louisville: Westminster John Knox, 2001.
Iersel, B. M. F. van. *Reading Mark.* Collegeville: Liturgical Press, 1988.
Incigneri, Brian J. *The Gospel to the Romans: The Setting and Rhetoric of Mark's Gospel.* Leiden: Brill, 2003.
Jackson, Howard M. "The Death of Jesus in Mark and the Miracle from the Cross." *NTS* 33 (1987) 16–37.
Jeremias, Joachim. *The Eucharistic Words of Jesus.* New Testament Library. London: SCM, 1966.
Juel, Donald. *Messiah and Temple: the Trial of Jesus in the Gospel of Mark.* SBL 31. Missoula, MT: Scholars, 1977.
–. *A Master of Surprise: Mark Interpreted.* Minneapolis: Fortress, 1994.
–. *Messianic Exegesis: Christological Interpretation of the Old Testament in Early Christianity.* Philadelphia: Fortress, 1992.
Kelber, Werner H. "Kingdom and Parousia in the Gospel of Mark." Ph.D. diss., University of Chicago, 1970.
–. *The Kingdom in Mark.* Philadelphia: Fortress Press, 1974.
–. (ed.) *The Passion in Mark: Studies on Mark 14–16.* Philadelphia: Fortress, 1976.
–. *Mark's Story of Jesus.* Philadelphia: Fortress Press, 1979.
–. *The Oral and Written Gospel: The Hermeneutics of Speaking and Writing in the Synoptic Tradition, Mark, Paul, and Q.* Philadelphia: Fortress, 1983.
Kee, Howard Clark. "The Function of Scriptural Quotations and Allusions in Mark 11–16." In *Jesus und Paulus.* Ed. E. Earle Ellis and E. Grasser. Gottingen: Vandenhoeck and Ruprecht, 1975. Pp. 165–88.
–. *Community of the New Age: Studies in Mark's Gospel.* Philadelphia: Westminster, 1977.
–. "Christology in Mark's Gospel." In *Judaisms and Their Messiahs at the turn of the Christian era.* Ed. Jacob Neusner, William Scott Green, and Ernest S. Frerichs Cambridge: Cambridge University Press, 1987. Pp. 187–208.
Keel, O. *The Symbolism of the Biblical World: Ancient Near Eastern Iconography and the Book of Psalms.* New York: Seabury, 1978.
Kittel, G., and Friedrich, G. (ed.) *Theological Dictionary of the New Testament.* 10 vols. Grand Rapids: Eerdmans, 1964–76.

Lagrange, M.-J. *Evangile selon Saint Marc*. Paris: Gabalda, 1966.

Lambrecht. *Die Redaktion der Markus-Apokalypse: Literarische Analyse und Struktur-untersuchung*. AnBib 28. Rome, 1967.

Lane, William L. *The Gospel of Mark*. NICNT. Grand Rapids: Eerdmans, 1974.

Lacocque, A. *The Book of Daniel*. London: SPCK, 1979.

Leon-Dufour, X. *Sharing the Eucharistic Bread*. New York: Paulist, 1987.

Levenson, Jon. "The Temple and the World." *JR* 64 (1984) 283–98.

—. *Sinai and Zion*. San Francisco: Harper and Row, 1985.

Lightfoot, R.H. *The Gospel Message of St. Mark*. London: Oxford University Press, 1950.

Lohmeyer, Ernst. *The Lord of the Temple: A Study of the Relation between Cult and Gospel*. London: Oliver and Boyd, 1961.

Luhrmann, D. *Das Markusevangelium*. HNT 3. Tübingen: Mohr-Siebeck, 1987.

Malbon, Elizabeth Struthers. "OIKIA AYTOY: Mark 2:15 in Context." *NTS* 31 (1985) 282–92.

—. *Narrative Space and Mythic Meaning in Mark*. San Francisco: Harper & Row, 1986.

—. "Echoes and Foreshadowings in Mark 4–8: Reading and Rereading." *JBL* 112/2 (1993) 211–30.

—. *In the Company of Jesus: Characters in Mark's Gospel*. Louisville: Westminster John Knox, 2000.

Mann, C. S. *Mark*. AB 27. Garden City, New York: Doubleday, 1986.

Manson, T.W. *The Teaching of Jesus*. Cambridge: Cambridge University Press, 1963.

Marcus, Joel. *The Way of the Lord: Christological Exegesis of the Old Testament in the Gospel of Mark*. Louisville, KY: Westminster John Knox, 1992.

—. *Mark 1–8*. New York: Doubleday, 2000.

Marshall, Christopher D. *Faith as a Theme in Mark's Narrative*. SNTSMS 64. Cambridge: Cambridge University Press, 1989.

Marshall, I.H. *Last Supper and Lord's Supper*. Grand Rapids: Eerdmans, 1980.

Marxsen, W. *Mark the Evangelist: Studies on the Redaction History of the Gospel*. Translated by R. A. Harrisville. Nashville: Abingdon, 1969.

Matera, Frank J. *The Kingship of Jesus: Composition and Theology in Mark 15*. SBLDS 66. Chico: Scholars, 1982.

Matthew, Sam P. *Temple-Criticism in Mark's Gospel: The Economic Role of the Jerusalem Temple during the First Century CE*. Delhi: ISPCK, 1999.

McKelvey, R. J. *The New Temple*. London: Oxford University Press, 1969.

Meier, John. *A Marginal Jew: Rethinking the Historical Jesus*. 3 vols. Anchor Bible Reference Library. New York: Doubleday, 1994.

Mell, U. *Die "anderen" Winzer: Eine exegetische Studie zur Vollmacht Jesu Christi nach Markus 11,27–12:34*. WUNT 77. Tübingen: Mohr-Siebeck, 1995.

Merrill, Eugene H. "Pilgrimage and Procession: Motifs of Israel's Return." In *Israel's Apostasy and Restoration*. Ed. Avraham Gileadi. Grand Rapids: Baker, 1988.

Meyer, Ben F. *The Aims of Jesus*. London: SCM, 1979.

—. *The Early Christians: Their World Mission and Self-Discovery*. GNS 16. Wilmington: Michael Glazier, 1986.

—. *Christus Faber: The Master-Builder and the House of God*. Allison Park, PA: Pickwick, 1992.

Meyers, Carol. "Temple, Jerusalem." *ABD* 6. 364–65.

Moloney, Francis J. *The Gospel of Mark*. Peabody, MA: Hendrickson, 2002.

Moor, Johannes C. de. "The Targumic Background of Mark 12:1–12: The Parable of the Wicked Tenants." *JSJ* 19 (1998) 63–80.

Myers, Ched. *Binding the Strong Man: A Political Reading of Mark's Story of Jesus*. New York: Orbis, 1988.

Neusner, Jacob. "Money-Changers in the Temple: The Mishnah's Explanation." *NTS* 35 (1989) 287–90.

Nineham, D. E. *The Gospel of St Mark.* Baltimore: Penguin Books, 1963.

Ossom-Batsa, George. *The Institution of the Eucharist in the Gospel of Mark: A Study of the Function of Mark 14:22–25 within the Gospel Narrative.* New York: Peter Lang, 2001.

Painter, J. *Mark's Gospel.* New Testament Readings. London: Routledge, 1997.

Perrin, N. *What is Redaction Criticism?* London: SPCK, 1970.

–. "The Christology of Mark: A Study in Methodology." In *The Interpretation of Mark.* Ed. William Telford. Philadelphia: Fortress, 1985. P. 99.

Pesch, Rudolf. *Das Markusevangelium.* HTKNT 2. Frieburg: Herder, 1977.

–. *Das Abendmahl und Jesu Todesverständnis.* QD 80. Freiburg/Basel/Vienna: Herder, 1978.

Pitre, Brant James. "The Historical Jesus, the Great Tribulation and the End of the Exile: Restoration Eschatology and the Origin of the Atonement." Ph.D. diss., Notre Dame University, 2004.

Reumann, John. *The Supper of the Lord.* Philadelphia: Fortress, 1985.

Rhoads, David, and Donald Michie. *Mark as Story: An Introduction to the Narrative of a Gospel.* Philadelphia: Fortress, 1982.

Richardson, Peter. "Why Turn the Tables? Jesus' Protest in the Temple Precincts." In *Society of Biblical Literature 1992 Seminar Papers.* Ed. E. H. Lovering. SBLSP 31. Atlanta: Scholars, 1992.

Robbins, Vernon. *Jesus the Teacher.* Philadelphia: Fortress, 1984.

Rowe, Robert D. *God's Kingdom and God's Son: The Background to Mark's Christology from Concepts of Kingship in the Psalms.* Boston: Brill, 2002.

Saldarini, A. J. *Jesus and Passover.* New York: Paulist, 1984.

Sanders, E. P. *Jesus and Judaism.* Philadelphia: Fortress, 1985.

Schneck, R. *Isaiah in the Gospel of Mark 1–8.* BIBALDS 1. Vallejo, CA: BIBAL, 1994.

Schnellbächer, Ernst L. "The Temple as Focus of Mark's Theology." *HBT* 5:2 (1983) 95–112.

Schweitzer, Albert. *The Quest of the Historical Jesus.* New York: Macmillan, 1961.

Schweizer, Eduard. *Good News According to Mark.* London: SPCK, 1971.

–. *The Lord's Supper According to the New Testament.* FBBS 18. Philadelphia: Fortress, 1967.

Scott, B. B. *Hear Then the Parable: A Commentary on the Parables of Jesus.* Minneapolis: Fortress, 1989.

Seeley, David. "Jesus' Temple Act." *CBQ* 55 (1993) 263–83.

Sheppard, G. T. "More on Isaiah 5:1–7 as a Juridical Parable." *CBQ* 44 (1982) 45–47.

Smith, Barry D. *Jesus' Last Passover Meal.* Lewiston: Edwin Mellon, 1993.

Smith, Stephen H. "The Literary Structure of Mark 11:1–12:40." *NovT* 31:2 (1989) 104–24.

–. "The Role of Jesus' Opponents in the Markan Drama." *NTS* 35 (1989) 161–82.

Snodgrass, Klyne R. "Streams of Tradition Emerging from Isaiah 40:1–5 and Their Adaptation in the New Testament." *JSNT* 8 (1980) 24–45.

–. *The Parable of the Wicked Tenants: An Inquiry into Parable Interpretation.* WUND 27. Tübingen: Mohr-Siebeck, 1983.

–. "Recent Research on the Parable of the Wicked Tenants: An Assessment." *BR* 8 (1998) 187–215.

Soskice, Janet. *Metaphor and Religious Language.* Oxford: Carendon Press, 1985.

Stern, David. "Jesus' Parables from the Perspective of Rabbinic Literature: The Example of the Wicked Husbandmen." In *Parable and Story in Judaism and Christianity.* Ed. C. Thomas and M. Wyschogrod. New York: Paulist, 1989. Pp. 42–80.

Sternberg, Meir. *The Poetics of Biblical Narrative: Ideological Literature and the Drama of Reading*. Bloomington: Indiana University, 1987.

Such, W. A. *The Abomination of Desolation in the Gospel of Mark: Its Historical Reference in Mark 13:14 and Its Impact in the Gospel*. Lanham: University Press of America, 1999.

Swartley, Willard M. "The Structural Function of the Term 'Way' (ὁδός) in Mark's Gospel." In *The New Way of Jesus*. Ed. W. Klassen. Newton, KS: Faith and Life, 1980.

—. *Israel's Scripture Traditions and the Synoptic Gospels: Story Shaping Story*. Peabody, MA: Hendrickson, 1994.

Tan, Kim. *The Zion Traditions and the Aims of Jesus*. SNTS 91. Cambridge: Cambridge University Press, 1997.

Taylor, Vincent. *Jesus and His Sacrifice: A Study of the Passion-Sayings in the Gospels*. New York: St. Martin's, 1955.

—. *The Gospel According to St Mark*. London: Macmillan & Co., 1963.

Telford, William R. *The Barren Temple and the Withered Tree*. JSNTSup 1. Sheffield: JSOT, 1980.

—. *The Theology of the Gospel of Mark*. New York: Cambridge University Press, 1999.

Theissen, Gerd. *The Historical Jesus: A Comprehensive Guide*. Minneapolis: Fortress, 1998.

—. *The Gospels in Context: Social and Political History in the Synoptic Tradition*. Minneapolis: Fortress, 1991.

Tolbert, Mary Ann. *Sowing the Gospel: Mark's World in Literary-Historical Perspective*. Minneapolis: Fortress, 1996.

Tuckett, C. M. "Redaction Criticism." In *A Dictionary of Biblical Interpretation*. Ed. R. J. Coggins and J. L. Houlden. London: SCM, 1990. Pp. 580–82.

Vorster, W. S. "The Function of the Use of the Old Testament in Mark." *Neot* 14 (1981) 62–72.

—. "Literary Reflections on Mark 13:5–37: A Narrated Speech of Jesus." In *The Interpretation of Mark*. Ed. William Telford. Edinburgh: T & T Clark, 1995. Pp. 269–88.

Waetjen, H. C. *A Reordering of Power: A Socio-Politcal Reading of Mark's Gospel*. Minneapolis: Fortress, 1989.

Walker, P. W. L. *Jesus and the Holy City: New Testament Perspectives on Jerusalem*. Grand Rapids: Eerdmans, 1996.

Walton, J. H. *Genesis*. NIVAC. Grand Rapids: Zondervan, 2001.

Watts, Rikki. *Isaiah's New Exodus in Mark*. Grand Rapids: Baker, 1997.

Watty, William W. "Jesus and the Temple — Cleansing or Cursing." *ExpTim* 93/8 (1982) 235–39.

Weihs, A. "Die Eifersucht der Winzer zur Anspielung auf LXX Gen 37,20 in der Parabel von der Tötung des Sohnes (Mk 12,1–12)." *ETL* 76 (2000) 5–29.

Weren, W. J. C. "The Use of Isaiah 5,1–7 in the Parable of the Tenants (Mark 12,1–12; Matthew 21,33–46)." *Bib* 79 (1998) 1–26.

Willis, J.T. "The Genre of Isaiah 5:1–7." *JBL* 96 (1977) 337–62.

Witherington, Ben. *The Gospel of Mark: A Socio-Rhetorical Commentary*. Grand Rapids: Eerdmans, 2001.

Wright, Addison G. "The Widow's Mites: Praise or Lament? — A Matter of Context," *CBQ* 44 (1982) 256–65.

Wright, N. T. *Jesus and the Victory of God*. Minneapolis: Fortress, 1996.

Yee, G. A. "The Form-Critical Study of Isaiah 5:1–7 as a Song and a Juridical Parable." *CBQ* 43 (1981) 30–40.

# Index of Ancient Sources

## 1. Old Testament

# 2. New Testament

# 3. Old Testament Pseudepigrapha

# 4. Philo

# 5. Josephus

# Index of Modern Authors

# Index of Subjects and Key Terms